Reading and Writing Acquisition

Reading and Writing Acquisition

A Developmental Neuropsychological Perspective

Virginia Wise Berninger
University of Washington

WestviewPress
A Division of HarperCollins*Publishers*

Developmental Psychology Series
Wendell Jeffrey, Series Editor

Peer Prejudice and Discrimination, -
Harold D. Fishbein

Communication Development During Infancy,
Lauren B. Adamson

Reading and Writing Acquisition: A Developmental Neuropsychological Perspective,
Virginia Wise Berninger

Children's Numbers, Catherine Sophian

How Divorce Affects Offspring: A Research Approach,
Michael R. Stevenson and Kathryn N. Black

Human Auditory Development, Lynne A. Werner and G. Cameron Marean

Copyright © 1994, 1996 by Westview Press, Inc., A Division of HarperCollins Publishers, Inc.

Published in 1996 in the United States of America by Westview Press, Inc., 5500 Central Avenue, Boulder, Colorado 80301-2877, and in the United Kingdom by Westview Press, 12 Hid's Copse Road, Cumnor Hill, Oxford OX2 9JJ

Library of Congress Cataloging-in-Publication Data
Berninger, Virginia Wise.
  Reading and writing acquisition : a developmental
neuropsychological perspective / Virginia Wise Berninger.
    p. cm.
  Originally published: Madison, Wis. : Brown & Benchmark
Publishers, c1994.
  Includes bibliographical references and index.
  ISBN 0-8133-3000-9 (pbk.)
  1. Reading, Psychology of. 2. Writing—Psychological aspects.
3. Neuropsychology. 4. Learning, Psychology of. I. Title.
BF456.R2B38 1996
418'.4'019—dc20   96-1280
                                                              CIP

The paper used in this publication meets the requirements of the American National Standard for Permanence of Paper for Printed Library Materials Z39.48-1984.

10   9   8   7   6   5   4   3   2

This book is dedicated to children who struggle to learn to read and write or who underachieve in reading and writing relative to their intellectual ability. The developmental neuropsychological perspective, with its focus on *individual differences* in brain systems related to reading and writing and on *prevention during critical developmental periods,* holds promise for helping these children achieve their literacy potential.

CONTENTS

5   Levels of Language and Intraindividual Differences in Levels of Language in Reading Comprehension and Composition   110

PREFACE

Only relatively recently in the history of the human race has there been a great deal of interest in how children learn to read and write. The prior lack of interest is not surprising because until the advent of education of the masses only a small fraction of the population acquired literacy skills—in general, religious leaders, scribes who made written records of business transactions, and children of the wealthy and ruling classes.

Interest in how children learn to read and write has been motivated by changes in the literacy requirements for employment as societies have moved from agricultural and industrial to technological economies. Even when public education became free to all, students with reading and writing problems were likely to drop out of school long before their peers who were skilled readers and writers, but these dropouts were still able to get jobs that required minimal or no reading and writing skills in agriculture or industry. In the United States, for instance, completion of elementary school was common at the time of World War I, but completion of high school did not become common until the World War II era. Increasingly, jobs in the post-Cold War era require education beyond the high school level. Thus, schools are under greater pressure than ever before to teach all children from diverse socioeconomic and cultural backgrounds to read and write so that they can complete the necessary education to compete in the work force. Those who do not become competent readers and writers can no longer quit school and be as likely to find meaningful, stable employment as was the case in the past.

Over the years, the question of primary interest about literacy acquisition has been about the best *method* for teaching reading and writing. The controversy over whether reading should be taught with a *whole word, phonics,* or *word family method* has a long history. The controversy over the best method of writing instruction is more recent and concerns whether the focus should be on the *product* (conventional spellings or well-formed prose) or the *process* of generating that product (invented spellings and multiple drafts).

Since the 1970s, however, interest has begun to move beyond questions of method to questions of the *normal process* of reading and writing acquisition and of *individual differences* among children that affect the process of learning to read and write. Three developments have promoted this trend. First, cognitive psychologists initially focused on adult skilled reading and writing but later turned attention to the developmental process of learning to read and write. Second, the 1975 Education of All Handicapped Children Act (United States Public Law 94–142) and similar laws enacted in Canada and England stimulated a great deal of research on the characteristics of learning disabled students with written language disorders. Third, the federal government and private foundations provided greater financial support than had previously been available for research on the process of literacy acquisition and individual differences among beginning and developing readers and writers.

The purpose of this book is to show how questions about the best methods of teaching literacy skills need to be informed by current research findings on the process of literacy acquisition and individual differences among children in literacy acquisition. These research findings on the normal process of literacy acquisition and individual differences in literacy acquisition are organized within a conceptual framework that draws upon cognitive, developmental, and neural psychology and has implications for understanding both normal and disabled reading and writing acquisition.

This *developmental neuropsychological perspective,* which is timely given the declaration of the United States Congress that the 1990s are the decade of the brain, is introduced in chapter 1. The key to this perspective is that both *biological constraints* (explored in chapter 2) and *educational constraints* (explored in chapter 3) exert influences on reading and writing acquisition. This perspective has motivated research on theoretical models of how *multiple brain systems* contribute to learning to read and spell written words (discussed in chapter 4), to comprehending and composing connected text (discussed in chapter 5), and to producing written text automatically, grammatically, and coherently (discussed in chapter 6). One of the unique aspects of this book is that in chapter 7 it bridges the communication gap between *basic, theory-driven research on learning processes,* of which many teachers and clinicians are unaware, and the *practical considerations in assessing, preventing, and remediating reading and writing disabilities,* of which many researchers are unaware.

Thus, this book is directed primarily toward an audience of undergraduate students in psychology interested in becoming researchers, for example, in developmental psychology, or practitioners, for example, in child clinical psychology, school psychology, or education. In addition, it should be of interest to (a) parents who want to ensure that their children optimize their reading and writing skills and/or want to understand why their children may have difficulty in learning to read and write, (b) basic researchers open to the issues facing practitioners who work with learning-disabled children, (c) and teachers and clinicians open to the contribution of research to improving educational practice.

Acknowledgments

The author thanks her husband, Ronald Berninger, for his extraordinary support, without which the research program featured in this volume would not have been started or completed. He contributed the term "peapod psychology." Also, this research would not have been possible without the participation of over one thousand students in the public schools of Bellevue, WA; Mukilteo, WA; Northshore, WA; Norwood, MA; Seattle, WA; Shoreline, WA; and in the Lakeside Academy, WA. The author is grateful to them and to the teachers, principals, school psychologists, and research administrators in those schools who took the time from their busy schedules to help make this research possible.

The author also acknowledges the contribution of colleagues and graduate students at the University of Washington to this research program. Robert Abbott gave generously of his time in providing statistical assistance for applying multivariate techniques such as structural equation modeling and for grappling with the unit of analysis issue. Donald Mizokawa created the computer programs for the initial experiment on levels of written language in developing writing and lent his expertise in psycholinguistics to developing coding schemes. James Morishima was instrumental in finding funding sources to initiate the research. Graduate students who contributed to data collection and/or analyses include Barbara Alsdorf, Russell Bragg, Ana Cartwright, Yuen Feng, Frances Fuller, Teresa Hart, James Johnston, Elizabeth Remy, Judith Rutberg, Hillary Shurtleff, Dean Traweek, Dianne Whitaker, and Cheryl Yates.

In addition, the author is grateful to colleagues at other institutions. Lee Swanson (University of California, Riverside) made a valuable contribution to the project by contributing his expertise and measures on working memory. David Gray (National Institute of Child Health and Human Development), George Hynd (University of Georgia), Reid Lyon (National Institute of Child Health and Human Development), Dennis Molfese (University of Southern Illinois), and Merlin Wittrock (University of California, Los Angeles) provided encouragement for integrating biological and educational approaches to literacy acquisition. David Andrews and Bruce Dunn (Past Presidents of the Brain and Education Special Interest Group of the American Educational Research Association) were instrumental in providing a forum to discuss this research as it evolved. The author is grateful to Melvin Levine for the opportunity to observe normal variation in children with school problems in his clinics at Boston's Children's Hospital, to Peter Wolff at Boston's Children's Hospital for introducing her to the concept of alternative pathways to the same developmental outcome, to Catherine Garvey at Johns Hopkins University for introducing her to the concept of levels of language, and to Marvin Minsky at the Massachusetts Institute of Technology for discussing with her the implications of society of mind theory for reading acquisition. The developmental neuropsychological perspective was originally inspired by the psychobiology, quantitative, and cognitive area seminars for doctoral students in psychology at Johns Hopkins University.

A grant from the Graduate School of the University of Washington supported the initial research on writing reported in chapter 5. A grant from the Institute for Ethnic Studies in the United States supported research reported in chapters 4 and 7. A grant from the National Institute of Child Health and Human Development (Grant Nos. 255858–01, 255858–02, and 255858–03) supported the research reported in chapters 4 through 7.

Preparation of this book was supported in part by a Shannon Award from the National Institutes of Health. The author thanks Suzanne Hidi (Ontario Institute for the Study of Education), Christiana Leonard (University of Florida College of Medicine and Visiting Scientist, National Science Foundation), Reid Lyon (National Institute of Child Health and Human Development), and Merlin Wittrock (University of California, Los Angeles) for thoughtful comments on an earlier draft of the book. The author also thanks Allen Glenn, Dean of the College of Education, and Ellis Evans, Chair of Educational Psychology, University of Washington, for the sabbatical that made preparation of this book possible.

Theoretical Foundations

1

Defining the Developmental Neuropsychological Perspective

. . . top-down strategies (as characteristic of philosophy, cognitive psychology, and artificial intelligence research) and bottom-up strategies (as characteristic of the neurosciences) for solving mysteries of mind-brain function should not be pursued in icy isolation from one another.

–Patricia Churchland (1986, p. 3)

Outline

Introduction to Part I (Chapters 1 Through 3)

Part I discusses the theoretical rationale for the research on reading and writing from a developmental neuropsychological perspective. Chapter 1 explains the rationale for basing developmental neuropsychology on the functional as well as the structural level of analysis. Chapter 2 reviews current research on the structural and functional development of the brain with respect to reading and writing acquisition. Chapter 3 explores educational issues relevant to reading and writing acquisition. The developmental neuropsychological perspective is based on an integration of biological and educational approaches. To assist the reader, the glossary contains definitions of the technical terms in neuropsychology and other disciplines that are used throughout this book. For readers who may have a background in education, cognitive psychology, and/or developmental psychology but not neuropsychology, the following provide excellent introductions to the human brain: *Fundamentals of Human Neuropsychology* (Kolb & Whishaw, 1990), *The Human Brain Coloring Book* (Diamond, Scheibel, & Elson, 1985), and *Left Brain, Right Brain: Revised Edition* (Springer & Deutsch, 1985, see appendix titled *Functional Neuroanatomy: A Brief Review*).

Differentiating Developmental and Adult Neuropsychology

Neuropsychology is a field that attempts to relate what is known about the functioning of the brain to what is understood about human behavior and development. Developmental neuropsychology is a relatively young discipline, which has become established, at least in the United States, in response to the federal mandate in 1975 to identify all handicapped children for the purpose of providing them with an appropriate education (Obrzut & Hynd, 1986). In contrast, adult neuropsychology is more established; it emerged at the end of the nineteenth century and was firmly established as a discipline in the decade following World War II to treat veterans whose nervous systems had been injured in the war.

Developmental neuropsychology deals primarily with the struggle to acquire function, whereas adult neuropsychology deals primarily with loss of previously acquired function. There has been considerable controversy over whether knowledge of brain-behavior mechanisms gleaned from studies of loss of function can be generalized to principles of acquiring function. A reasonable resolution of this controversy is that developmental neuropsychologists should be knowledgeable about research in adult neuropsychology because there are probably some parallels between brain mechanisms in developing and mature organisms. However, they should also recognize that unique brain processes may be involved in learning a skill that are not involved in losing a skill, and that the brain changes across development.

Given the relatively shorter history of developmental versus adult neuropsychology, relatively less research has been done in developmental neuropsychology. However, the research that has been done with children, like that done with adults, has tended to focus on brain *pathology,* that is, analyzing behavior and behavioral changes in individuals with diagnosed damage to the central nervous system. It is difficult to generalize across these traditions because children and adults differ in the kind of damage they are likely to sustain, with children more likely to have *diffuse* damage, and adults more likely to have *focal* lesions (Obrzut & Hynd, 1986).

Although some developing children may have sustained localized lesions through injury or disease, which can cause loss of function, many more are likely to face a struggle to acquire function rather than a loss of function. The focus on pathology may not be appropriate for learning-disabled children who struggle to acquire function but have not sustained brain damage. Rather, they are likely to have minor structural anomalies of the brain, such as misplaced or misformed neurons, or they may lack the normal right-left asymmetries of brain structures (e.g., Galaburda, 1986; Semrud-Clikeman, Hynd, Novey, & Eliopulos, 1991). Despite these minor *structural anomalies,* learning-disabled students may use alternative neural pathways or compensatory mechanisms to develop *functional* or *working brain systems* (see Luria, 1973). These structural anomalies may make it more difficult to learn but do not necessarily make it impossible to learn.

Differentiating Educational and Clinical Approaches Within Developmental Neuropsychology

Compared with adult clinical neuropsychology, child clinical neuropsychology is a recent specialty but, like adult clinical neuropsychology, has tended to focus on pathology. For example, children and adolescents who have sustained damage to the nervous system because of head injury, seizure disorder, spinal cord injury, brain tumor, sequelae of radiation/chemotherapy treatment for cancer, or congenital disorders such as cerebral palsy or spina bifida are likely to be evaluated by a child clinical neuropsychologist. Several issues are fundamental in such an evaluation: whether the right or left cerebral cortex sustained damage, whether tone is abnormally high or low on the right or left side of the body, and whether and to what degree the child may reacquire (in case of loss of function) selected functions that may influence the struggle to acquire other functions in the course of development. In addition to these issues of laterality and plasticity, the locus in the brain of any dysfunctions is considered.

Because children with problems in learning to read and write are more likely to have structural anomalies than brain damage, right-left involvement, plasticity of function, and locus of dysfunction are probably not the most important issues to consider. It may be surprising to many readers that a book on neuropsychology will not focus primarily on right-left brain differences or plasticity issues. The reasons are threefold. First, both the right and left brain are involved in reading, as shown by Posner, Petersen, Fox, and Raichle (1988) for word recognition and by Huettner, Rosenthal, and Hynd (1989) for reading comprehension. Second, most of what is known concerning differences between the right and left brain are based on (a) studies of split-brain adults with severe seizure disorders, the results of which may not generalize to developing children without brain damage; (b) tachistoscopic studies of normal children and adults that can lateralize stimuli for only a fraction of a second (Springer & Deutsch, 1985), after which both hemispheres have access to the information, as is also the case in classroom learning; or (c) studies of normal children and adults with dichotic listening, which is fraught with test-retest reliability problems for individuals (Segalowitz, 1986). Third, plasticity or recovery of function is relevant when function is lost, but not when function has not yet been acquired.

Given the large number of children without brain damage who struggle to learn to read and write, we need a second specialty within developmental neuropsychology—educational neuropsychology—to supplement the first specialty—child clinical neuropsychology. In contrast to child clinical neuropsychology that is a medical specialty, with its own unique issues, educational neuropsychology is an educational specialty with its own unique issues. Of course, some of the principles of educational neuropsychology, which focuses on learning in children without brain damage, may also be useful in facilitating learning in children with brain damage.

We have learned much about the brain by studying how its function breaks down when diseased or damaged. We can also learn a great deal about it by studying it when it functions normally. In fact, knowledge of normal brain mechanisms may be more helpful than knowledge of abnormal brain mechanisms in understanding children without brain damage who struggle to read and write. In the case of those without brain damage, what is relevant is the profile of skills across different developmental domains that each child brings to the task of learning or performing specific academic tasks. Which of these skills are developed adequately for the child to learn or perform a particular academic task? Which of these skills are not developed sufficiently and need to be remediated if the child is to learn or perform a particular academic task? That is, what is the *nature* of the dysfunction rather than the *locus* of dysfunction? How do the brain systems supporting these skills function in concert to support learning? In other words, educational neuropsychology emphasizes the interconnected brain systems of the learner rather than the locus of discrete dysfunctions.

The focus of child clinical neuropsychology has traditionally been on diagnosis and what is wrong with the brain of a child with diagnosable damage or disease. In contrast, the focus of educational neuropsychology is on what is right as well as what is wrong with the function of the brain of a child without diagnosable damage or disease. Educational neuropsychology then uses that profile of strengths and weaknesses to plan and implement an optimal educational program for the child and thus links diagnosis with intervention. Both approaches are needed within developmental neuropsychology to serve different populations and sometimes the same populations; they supplement one another and are not mutually exclusive approaches within developmental neuropsychology. However, this book reflects an educational neuropsychological approach rather than a child clinical approach because (a) the child clinical approach has received far more attention than the educational neuropsychological approach and (b) the educational neuropsychological approach underlies the line of research described in chapters 4 through 7.

Levels of Analysis in Brain-Behavior Equations

Neuropsychology is often defined as the study of brain-behavior relationships. This definition, however, is deceptively simple because both the brain and behavior can be analyzed at multiple levels; therefore, relationships between the brain and behavior depend greatly on the levels of analysis employed. This levels-of-analysis framework is fundamental to both contemporary neuroscience (e.g., Galaburda, 1988; Squire, 1986; Wolpaw, Schmidt, & Vaughan, 1991) and contemporary cognitive psychology (e.g., Lachman, Lachman, & Butterfield, 1979). Table 1.1 on page 8 illustrates the variety of levels of brain structure and function at which any given mental or behavioral act might be analyzed.

Not much is known about how the different levels are interrelated within the structural architecture or within the functional architecture or between the structural and functional architectures. It is unlikely that these relationships exhibit simple one-to-one correspondence with a particular structure having a single function associated with it. Different patterns of underlying structural deficits may result in the same functional symptoms, and different functional symptoms may be related to a common structural deficit, depending on what other structures are also affected (Luria, 1973). All the levels of the architecture, ranging from the molecular (Skinner, 1991) and cellular (Beery & Spector, 1986) properties of the neuron to the positioning of neurons that determines potential synaptic connections with other neurons (Barnes, 1986; Beery & Spector, 1986), place constraints on functional systems. Considering that there are an estimated 10^{14} synapses (Barnes, 1986), the number of potential combinations is infinite, and functional systems may be more complex than their neural architecture.

In a similar but somewhat different vein, cognitive psychology allows for different levels of processing incoming stimulus information. For example, routines may operate at different levels of a partially hierarchical system (Stanovich, 1984), which codes and then processes information. Also, stimulus information can be described

TABLE 1.1 Levels of Analysis of the Brain

I. Brain architecture (structural level)
  A. Microstructure
    1. Molecules
    2. Cells (neurons)
    3. Neural pathways (axon-dendrite connections between neurons; synaptic transmission)
  B. Macrostructure (brain geography—labeling large collections of neurons)
    1. Bottom-up axis (lower brain to midbrain to forebrain)
    2. Right-left axis (right hemisphere to left hemisphere of cerebral cortex)
    3. Back-front axis (occipital to temporal and parietal to frontal lobes of cerebral cortex)
    4. Convolutions or folds (fissures—deep valleys between folds, sulci—shallow valleys between folds, and gyri—peaks in folds)
II. Brain function (functional level)
  A. Microfunction—activity of individual neurons
  B. Macrofunction
    1. Electrophysiology—activity of collections of neurons
    2. Representations in short-term, working, and long-term memory
    3. Operations (computations, procedures, algorithms)
    4. Systems of temporally and/or spatially connected representations and operations

at different levels of abstraction, ranging from the physical attributes to the abstract informational structure of the stimulus (Lachman et al., 1979). Furthermore, learning occurs in a social context and social interaction can be analyzed at different levels.

When one combines the levels of analysis within the brain and the brain interacting with the environment, the potential complexity is mind boggling. *Generalizations about structure-function relationships will depend upon the level of structure and level of function involved.* The importance of multilevel analysis (Cacioppo & Bernston, 1992) will be emphasized throughout this book.

Systems Models: Reconciling Localized and Distributed Function

One of the most heated controversies during the early history of neuropsychology was between the localization and mass-action views of brain function. According to the localization view, specific functions are tied to specific brain sites. According to the mass-action view, the amount of brain tissue involved is more important than the specific site and brain structures are flexible in that they can support a variety of functions. (See Kolb & Whishaw, 1990, for further discussion of this controversy.)

Clinicians who deal with patients who clearly have brain damage through disease or injury often adopt a localization view and seek the locus of dysfunction. Cognitive scientists have recently introduced a new version of mass action—connectionism—in which specific functions emerge from the connections between large numbers of simple processing units that send excitatory and inhibitory signals to other units in massively parallel, distributed systems (McClelland, Rumelhart, & Hinton, 1986). However, many neuroscientists and psychologists have tended toward a hybrid view that combines elements of localization and mass action.

Posner's Orchestration of Mind

One example of the hybrid view is orchestration of mind (Posner et al., 1988). In this model, which is supported by the results of positron emission tomography (PET) scan studies for reading single words, component processes of a function occur at local brain sites in various parts of the brain (the localization view). However, for these component processes to function in a unified manner, the local sites must be coordinated throughout the brain (similar to the mass action view). To capture this notion of localized and distributed processes, Posner and colleagues use the metaphor of the orchestra, in which each musician plays a specific instrument, but the conductor orchestrates the individual musicians to play in concert. Figure 1.1 illustrates how different brain sites are activated by passive detection of visual words than of auditory words. In both cases multiple sites are activated that vary with stimulus characteristics. Figure 1.2 shows yet another pattern of activation when the input modalities are the same as in figure 1.1 but the added requirement of motor output is added. Again, multiple local sites are activated that vary with the task characteristics. Note that (a) when motor demands are the same, and sensory-specific responses are subtracted (fig. 1.2), the locus of activity is closer across visual and auditory presentation than when there are no common task requirements (fig. 1.1); and (b) different locations are activated for input (fig. 1.1) and output (fig. 1.2) tasks.

The unresolved question is how the orchestration is achieved, considering that there probably is not a conductor or homunculus in the head directing the process. To answer this question requires consideration of how the brain may be *organized* to accomplish the large number of functions that it does.

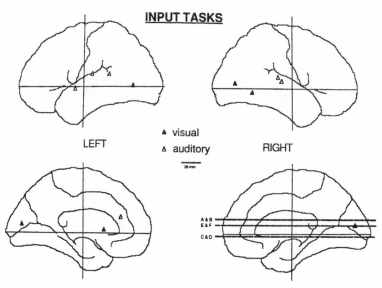

INPUT TASKS

▲ visual
△ auditory

LEFT   RIGHT

20 mm

FIGURE 1.1

Locations of significant activations for passive word input tasks on the lateral (upper row) or medial (lower row) surfaces of the brain. Note the nonoverlapping distributions of areas related to visual (filled triangles) and auditory (open triangles) word presentation.

Reprinted from *Journal of Cognitive Neuroscience,* vol. 1, no. 2, Petersen, et al., "Positron Emission Tomographic Studies of the Processing of Single Words," by permission of The MIT Press, Cambridge, Massachusetts, Copyright © 1989.

Luria's Working Brain

Perhaps the first scientist to deal with the organization issue was an English neurologist, Jackson, who in the nineteenth century proposed the novel idea that mental processes should be studied from the perspective of their *level of construction in the nervous system* rather than from the perspective of their *location in the brain* (e.g., Jackson, 1887). According to Luria (1973), Jackson was ahead of his time, and it was not until fifty years later that neurologists grasped the fact that, although simple sensory and motor functions can be studied in terms of localization, more complex cognitive functions cannot. Kolb and Whishaw (1990) concur that Jackson was ahead of his time and point out that his ideas are being considered more seriously now than in his own time.

Luria (1973) expanded upon this notion of level by introducing the concepts of cortical zones and functional units of the working brain. The cerebral cortex has three zones. The first includes the *primary projection areas* that receive impulses from and send impulses

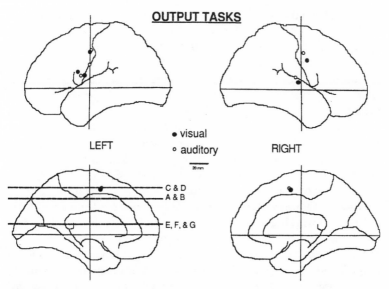

OUTPUT TASKS

• visual
○ auditory

LEFT RIGHT

C & D
A & B

E, F, & G

20 mm

FIGURE 1.2
Locations of significant activations on the lateral (upper row) or medial (lower row) surfaces of the brain when words were presented visually (filled circles) or auditorially (open circles), as in figure 1.1, but the task required vocal repetition and added a motor requirement.

Reprinted from *Journal of Cognitive Neuroscience,* vol. 1, no. 2, Petersen, et al., "Positron Emission Tomographic Studies of the Processing of Single Words," by permission of The MIT Press, Cambridge, Massachusetts, Copyright © 1989.

to the external world; they are modality-specific (e.g., visual or auditory) but do not reflect the contralateral principle, in which one side of the brain controls the opposite side of the body. The second includes the *secondary association areas,* where information from the primary zones is processed and synthesized; they are less modality-specific than the primary projection areas but retain some modality-specificity and show some signs of the contralateral principle. The third includes the *tertiary association areas,* where input from the overlapping secondary zones is integrated; they are abstract rather than modality-specific and reflect the contralateral principle.

The working brain has three functional units. The *arousal unit,* which is a subcortical unit connected to the frontal lobes of the cerebral cortex, regulates arousal and responsiveness to the environment. The *information processing unit,* which includes the occipital, temporal, and parietal lobes of cerebral cortex, obtains, stores, and processes information from the external world. The functional organization of these lobes is complex, but in general, the occipital lobe is associated with visual processing, the temporal lobe with auditory/ language processing, and the parietal lobe with somatic-sensory processing (see Kolb & Whishaw, 1990). The *programming/regulating unit,* which includes the frontal lobes (especially the motor areas), makes and carries out plans of action directed to the future and performs executive functions such as monitoring and modulating mental activity.

Hooper and Boyd (1986) provided an overview of the interrelationship of cortical zones and functional units in neurodevelopmental stages, which partially overlap but differ as to when zones become functionally mature. Table 1.2 summarizes the relationships among the working units, their neuroanatomical correlates, and these neurodevelopmental stages, which overlap to some degree but differ as to which working unit matures. In Stage 1 (birth to 1 year) the first functional unit matures. Infants learn to regulate their sleep-awake cycle and thus attention to and responsiveness to the environment. In Stage 2 (birth to 2 years) the primary zone of the second functional unit matures. Infants and toddlers develop their perceptual and motor skills and thus their sensorimotor intelligence. In Stage 3 (2 to 5 years) the secondary zone of the second functional unit matures. Preschoolers develop their perceptual-motor integration skills. In Stage 4 (5 to 12 years) the tertiary zone of the second functional unit matures. School-aged children learn to perform abstract, integrative functions that are needed to learn academic subjects. In Stage 5 (6 to adult years) the tertiary zone of the third functional unit matures. Children, adolescents, and adults achieve increasing skill in planning and regulating behavior. (Hooper and Boyd did not discuss the secondary and tertiary zones of the first functional unit or the primary and secondary zones of the third functional unit.) The mechanisms that cause a zone to become functional are not fully understood, but they may be due in part to myelination of nerve fibers in which myelin, a fatty sheaf, forms and permits more rapid and efficient neural conduction.

Luria's neurodevelopmental stages are educationally relevant for two reasons. First, Hooper and Boyd (1986) hypothesized that Stage 4 may be a prerequisite for learning academic skills, which is why children in all cultures begin formal schooling about the time that the tertiary zones of the second functional unit develop. Shurtleff, Abbott, Townes, and Berninger (1993) used structural equation modeling to test this hypothesis by comparing the structural relationships among a factor underlying measures of Stage 3 neurodevelopment, a factor underlying measures of Stage 4 neurodevelopment, a factor

TABLE 1.2 Luria's Model of the Development of the
Working Brain

Functional Unit	Neuroanatomical Correlates	Neurodevelopmental Stage
Arousal unit	Reticular activating system with connections to frontal lobe	Stage 1 (birth to 1 year)
Information processing unit		
Primary zone	Sensory or motor areas	Stage 2 (birth to 2 years)
Secondary zone	Association areas for modality-specific integration in the occipital, temporal, and parietal lobes	Stage 3 (2 to 5 years)
Tertiary zone	Association areas for abstract integration in the occipital, temporal, and parietal lobes	Stage 4 (5 to 12 years)
Programming/ regulating unit	Frontal lobes	Stage 5 (6 to adult years)

underlying IQ, and a factor underlying academic achievement in reading and spelling. Results were consistent with the prediction that Stage 4 is associated with early academic learning.

In kindergarten the model treating the Stage 3 and Stage 4 factors as independent provided a better fit, suggesting that children varied considerably in whether they had achieved Stage 4 neurodevelopment, but in first grade the model treating Stages 3 and 4 as a single factor provided the best fit, suggesting that most children had achieved Stage 4 neurodevelopment. However, Stage 4, which contributed to the fit of the model, contributed indirectly to academic achievement via the IQ factor. Because items on IQ tests tend to measure abstract thinking rather than modality-specific functions, this finding points to the importance of tertiary zones in early academic learning. Indeed, Thompson (1916) showed that the pattern of test intercorrelations used to support the concept of *factor g* intelligence could also be accounted for by sampling theory, in which different tasks sample broadly from a large number of neural connections in the cerebral cortex. Not only may Thompson have anticipated connectionism, but also the fact that IQ tests tap general functioning of tertiary zones rather than a quantitative index of a homogeneous construct called intelligence.

Second, the widespread idea that some students are visual learners and some are auditory learners, which has not been supported by research (Arter & Jenkins, 1979), is inconsistent with Luria's model of brain development. Pure visual learning and pure auditory learning is mediated by the primary zones during Stage 2 neurodevelopment long before children achieve Stage 4, which is associated with academic learning. Indeed, academic learning most likely requires some visual-auditory integration (Stage 3, where some modality-specificity is retained) but mostly abstract processing (Stage 4, which is modality-free).

Minsky's Society of Mind

To fully understand the organization of the brain, one must go beyond the levels in a hierarchy. The cerebral cortex consists of not only layers (horizontal levels) but also columns (vertical organization). Cells within each column are well connected to each other but poorly connected to cells in other columns with which they communicate via higher-order structures (Mountcastle, 1957). The brain is probably a heterarchy, with organization within and across levels within a hierarchy and between coexisting hierarchical systems. Figure 1.3 shows a schema of what heterarchical organization might entail. Minsky's society of mind theory (1986) is based on *heterarchical organization.*

According to Minsky, the human brain contains a vast number of agents organized into agencies and connections between agents and agencies. It resembles a great society composed of smaller cities and towns linked by a communication network of roads; in fact, at this stage of evolution it consists mainly of the connections, which Minsky refers to as cables or wires. He speculated that the reason the human brain has so many convolutions, folding upon itself five or six times, is to make it possible for a given agent to become connected to a million other agents via a few indirect connections. The typical agent is highly specialized and has few direct connections to other agents but can influence many other agents through a few indirect steps. The mind is built from many small agents or processes, each mindless, but when they are joined together in a society or system, they function intelligently. Over the course of development, communication among the societies increases but is always indirect—only in terms of the models they construct of one another.

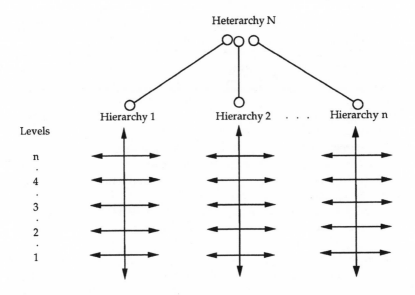

Heterarchy N

Hierarchy 1   Hierarchy 2 . . . Hierarchy n

Levels

n
.
4
.
3
.
2
.
1

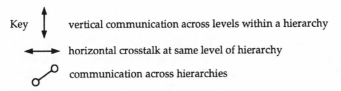

Key — vertical communication across levels within a hierarchy

↔ horizontal crosstalk at same level of hierarchy

communication across hierarchies

FIGURE 1.3
Heterarchical organization of the mind.

The power of the mind stems from the messy way these agents cross-connect, not from neatly ordered, simple principles. An agent does not know anything—it is a simple process that switches other agents on and off, but the agency of which an agent is a member knows its job. Each agent in a society is at any moment in either a quiet or an active state. A total state of mind represents all agents and specifies which agents are active and which are quiet at a particular moment in time. A partial mental state specifies that certain agents are active, but does not specify which agents are quiet. Mental processes are thus not only the result of neural transmission across synapses of interconnected neurons but also the result of the *constellation* of neural networks that happens to be firing at a particular moment in time.

None of this neural activity is orchestrated by a homunculus or little man in the head, but rather by complex managerial systems in the heterarchy. Conflicts may arise when two different mental states are imposed on the same agency, or when two competing agencies are activated simultaneously. One such managerial mechanism is Papert's principle, which sends conflict to higher levels in the organization. Mental growth can stem not just from acquiring new skills but also by creating new, higher level administrative systems for managing already existing abilities. Another managerial system is the cross-exclusion principle, whereby each agent in a group is wired to send inhibitory signals to other agents in the group to prevent uncontrollable spreading activation.

In another kind of managerial system, which is sensitive to the developmental history of the learner, new layers are created based on previous layers. A-brains are wired to detect world-caused *stimulus* events; B-brains are wired to detect brain-created *simulus* events. The A-brain's inputs and outputs are connected to the real world, but the B-brain's inputs and outputs are connected to the A-brain (and not the external world) in order to influence, supervise, and keep track of what is happening in the A-brain. In the course of development, a C-brain can become connected to watch a B-brain, and so on infinitely, until each new brain layer or society learns to exploit the capabilities of agencies in previous layers. Thus, minds develop from infancy as a sequence of many layers of interconnected societies. Expert knowledge in the most recently formed layers may be easier to explain than common sense that evolved slowly in the earlier layers of childhood. If so, the mind is far more complex than contrasts between right and left brain suggest. Thus, beginning and developing reading (see chapter 4) and writing (see chapter 6) are best explained from the perspective of the developing child's mind and not from the perspective of the adult, skilled reader or writer.

Learning is a process of changing connections and creating connections to other structures in the mind. In one kind of learning, K-lines (knowledge lines or wirelike structures) attach to partial mental states to represent an experience. To recreate that experience, that is, to remember, the K-line reactivates that partial mental state, that is, those agents that were active when the experience was represented. To avoid too many memories at one time, K-lines weaken attachment above and below a certain level of detail, thus conforming to the level band principle. Too strong a connection below the lower band will lead to remembering of too much detail and confusion of the present and past. Too strong a connection above the upper band will interfere with accurate perception of the present (not enough detail will be perceived).

Society theory is not based on real time, which is linear, but rather on momentary time: Each agent lives in a slightly different world of time with a different sense of what happened in the past and what is happening now; no agent can know everything that is happening at the same time in all other agencies. Because different agencies are on different time scales, what may be a moment to one agency may be like an era to another agency, and memories are only indirectly linked to linear, real time in the physical world. Agents may be sensitive only to time changes. Time blinking, which is finding the difference between two mental states by activating them in rapid succession and noticing which agents change their states, may be the fundamental mechanism of synchronizing the brain's activity, which gives rise to brain waves.

Minsky's theory is not the kind of theory that integrates empirical findings based on years of research. Rather it is the kind of theory that provides a framework for generating research questions in the initial stages of research. The society of mind theory is meant to stimulate thinking about how brain machinery might be organized to accomplish the vast number of functions that it does. Although the research reported in Part II of this book does not directly test any claims of the society of mind theory, this research was influenced by that theory in two ways. First, reading and writing acquisition were investigated from the perspective of the developing child rather than the perspective of the adult, skilled reader or writer. Second, the focus was not on a single process but rather on multiple processes and how these processes might learn to communicate and be orchestrated to accomplish reading and writing activities within functional systems of the working brain.

Thus, in keeping with the systems models of the brain proposed by Posner, Luria, and Minsky, the research reported here was concerned with the functional organization of the brain during reading and writing acquisition. However, even though this research concerns brain *function* rather than *structure,* it does not fit neatly within the cognitive tradition for two reasons. First, it is not narrowly focused on a single construct (see Vellutino, Scanlon, & Tanzman, 1991, for discussion of the tendency of cognitive researchers to take a univariate approach). Second, unlike cognitive approaches, which often seek *one* variable that accounts for the most variance, it takes into account the various systems that may be contributing in both major and minor ways to a particular reading or writing function. It is grounded in a functional organizational approach (Fletcher & Taylor, 1984) that focuses on relationships between central nervous functioning and behavioral variables and how these relationships change over development.

However, the research also does not fit neatly into the traditional neuropsychological approach, which often makes inferences about structure from functional data. For example, when a child has problems with simultaneous processing of visual information, the conclusion may be drawn that there is a right hemisphere deficit. A key principle of the developmental neuropsychological perspective is that inferences must be restricted to the level of the data collected. That is, inferences about structure require data at the structural level of analysis. Inferences about function require data at the functional or behavioral level of analysis. The research discussed in chapters 4 through 7 is based on behavioral data, and inferences are restricted to the functional/behavioral level of analysis.

To summarize, the developmental neuropsychological perspective draws upon cognitive psychology and neuropsychology but does not represent the traditional views of either of these disciplines. It also draws on theories of brain organization that recognize principles of *hierarchical organization* (with cross-talk within and across levels within the hierarchy) and of *heterarchical organization* (with cross-talk between hierarchies).

The Individual as the Unit of Analysis and Normal Variation at All Levels of Analysis

Most quantitative research on reading and writing has used inferential statistics in which the unit of analysis is the group. Inferential statistics were developed by Sir Ronald Fisher when he was employed at an agricultural station in England (Fisher, 1951). In his application of inferential statistics it made sense to use the group as the unit of analysis. He evaluated the effects of treatments (for example, particular kinds of fertilizer) on particular fields or plots where certain seed varieties were planted. He analyzed whether the variance between groups due to the treatments exceeded the variance within the group or field due to factors such as variations in the fertility of soil or the weather conditions. Using the variance within the plot or field (that is, the group) as the error term was justifiable for three reasons. First, seeds of the same variety share a common genetic constitution and should respond to the treatment in the same way. Second, seeds do not have the ability to think about the treatment and decide how to respond to it. Third, the treatment effects are unidirectional rather than bidirectional—the fertilizer affects growth of seeds, but the seeds do not affect the treatment in a reciprocal fashion. Thus, individual differences among the seeds are minimal.

However, educational "treatment" is never applied to a group of children or class in the same sense that agricultural treatment is applied to seeds in a plot of land. Learners, unlike peas in a pod, do not share the same genetic constitution and do not respond as a unit to treatment. Children may sit together in the same instructional group, yet their brain mechanisms are statistically independent in that children can use instructional cues in varying ways. Treatment effects are bidirectional rather than unidirectional, with children's responses affecting instructional content and teachers' strategies, and conversely, with instructional content and teachers' strategies affecting children's learning. Thus, individual differences among children in their genetic constitution and response to treatment may be significant compared with the insignificant individual differences among peas in a pod. Although treatment effects between groups may be larger than individual differences within groups, individual children may have responded differently to the treatment than other children in the group; the findings for the treatment groups will not apply to all children in a sample, let alone in the population. Thus, developmental neuropsychology needs alternatives to "peapod psychology" for conceptualizing research and analyzing data.

Even when reading and writing researchers investigate individual differences, they still tend to use the group rather than the individual as the unit of analysis. For example, they compare good and poor or skilled and less skilled readers or writers in analysis of variance designs. They treat all the individuals at a certain level of achievement in a domain as a homogeneous unit and ignore the individual differences that may occur among children in (a) component skills within that domain, (b) developmental skills related to that domain, and (c) the processes leading to that achievement outcome. Moreover, they usually consider only the extremes of the distribution and not the entire continuous distribution of skill, and they consider only interindividual differences within a domain and not intraindividual differences across domains. In contrast, research from a developmental neuropsychological perspective takes into account *interindividual differences* among learners along the entire continuum within a domain (see chapters 4, 6, and 7) and *intraindividual differences* across domains within the same learner (see chapter 5). Multivariate techniques such as multiple regression, structural equation modeling, and profile analysis are most appropriate for studying these individual differences.

Reading-level matched designs in which older, poor readers are compared with younger, good readers matched on reading achievement are widely used despite methodological problems (Jackson & Butterfield, 1989). These designs are not consistent with the developmental neuropsychological perspective for two reasons. First, the goal of research from a developmental neuropsychological perspective is not to find the single causal mechanism for reading disability based on the one variable on which matched groups differ; rather it is to discover the multiple constraints affecting the reading and writing acquisition process of individuals across the entire continuum of reading achievement. Second, the reading-level match design masks the normal variation in learner characteristics or learner strategies among children at the same level of achievement.

To evaluate whether group comparisons may miss important individual differences, Berninger and Abbott (1992a) applied four data analysis approaches to the same set of reading-related processing measures in a first grade sample. In the first approach, variation among children within achievement-level groups (high, middle, and low) was treated as error, as is typically done in studies in which the group is the unit of analysis for individual difference variables. On the reading-related process variables (measures of lexical decision, naming, and written reproduction for phonically regular real words conforming to phonics rules, phonically irregular real words not conforming to phonics rules, and pronounceable nonwords), performance of the low group at the end of first grade was comparable to that of the middle group at the middle of first grade; performance of the middle group at the end of first grade was comparable to that of the high group at the middle of first grade. These results were consistent with the view that there is one process of learning, but individuals vary in the rate of mastering that process.

In the second, third, and fourth approaches, instructional groups (high, middle, and low) were compared at the beginning, middle, and end of first grade. Within an instructional group, the instructional program (materials, lessons, assignments) was as constant as an instructional treatment can be outside the laboratory. Of interest was whether individual differences would be found within the same group in response to the same instructional program.

In the second approach, like the first, variation among children within an instructional group was treated as error. The results were essentially the same as for the first approach. Thus, when the unit of analysis was the group, regardless of whether the groups were defined on the basis of achievement on standardized tests or achievement within the instructional program, there was evidence for one process in learning to read and variation in rate of mastering that process.

In the third approach, variation among children in an instructional group was treated as systematic variance; that is, the effect due to individual differences within the groups was evaluated statistically by aggregating data over individual stimulus items rather than over individual subjects, and by using individual response over stimulus trials to estimate error. The main effect for individuals was statistically significant, and all the two- and three-way interactions involving individuals were statistically significant. These results were at odds with the previous results and indicated that more than one process might be operating in learning to read and write single words. Individual differences in the process variables became apparent only when they were considered as an explanatory variable in their own right.

In the fourth approach, a separate analysis of variance was performed on the stimulus trials for each subject at the beginning, middle, and end of first grade. Of interest was whether the same pattern of results would occur for each child in the same instructional group. Children within the same instructional group varied considerably as to which main effects or interactions were significant. Even when the same main effects or interactions were significant, the pattern of the levels of a variable was often not the same across children. Sometimes individual children differed from the significant main effects or interactions found in the group analyses. These results are consistent with the notion of alternative pathways or mechanisms in the developing nervous system for dealing with the same stimulus and task requirements. Berninger and Abbott (1992a) attributed these alternative mechanisms partly to the constructive processes of the learner (Bartlett, 1932; Wittrock, 1974) for using the same instructional cues in varying ways. That is, children are not programmed externally, as computers are, and may vary in how they use external cues to construct their own mental programs. Berninger and Abbott concluded that researchers should analyze data at the individual unit of analysis, as well as the group unit of analysis, or important information about the brain mechanisms in learning may be missed.

The observation that results based on data for individuals and on data aggregated across individuals do not necessarily correspond is not new and is known as the *ecological fallacy* (e.g., Burstein, 1980; Robinson, 1950). Engel (1960) showed that psychophysiological data can be analyzed simultaneously from the perspective of both similarities across individuals in a group and differences among individuals in a group. Evidence has been found for both *stimulus response specificity,* in which a stimulus situation elicits a consistent pattern of physiological response in everyone, and *individual response specificity,* in which individuals differ in their characteristic physiological response (Sternbach, 1966).

Considering the enormous amount of normal variation in brain neuroanatomy (Churchland, 1986), it would be surprising not to find sizable normal variation at other levels of brain structure and function (table 1.1) as well. Specifying structure-function relationships will depend not only on keeping levels of analysis distinct but also on taking into account normal variation—diversity not related to pathology—at all levels of analysis (Berninger, 1986).

The concept of normal variation may seem foreign to some experimentalists. The unexamined presupposition of much scientific inquiry has been that an either/or answer exists that can be discovered by ruling between two alternative explanations for the same phenomenon. Variability is considered a nuisance that well-designed experiments will minimize (Kantowitz & Roediger, 1978). A more realistic presupposition in the case of learning, however, is that the process is open to modification and refinement and thus variability. In fact, learning processes may vary (a) *within the same individual over a short period of time,* as a result of random variation in signal detection (Swets, 1964) or of systematic variation in on-line processing (Rayner, 1984); (b) *within the same individual over a long time period,* as a result of normal variation in neural maturation (Wolff, 1981); or (c) *among individuals at a given point in time,* as a result of interactions between inherited processing capabilities and qualitatively different procedural operations constructed by the learner for processing instructional information (Berninger, 1986). Moreover, monitoring moment-to-moment variation may be a fundamental mechanism of the nervous system, as in Minsky's time-blinking mechanism discussed earlier.

On the one hand, we can assume individual differences are error variance and look for group effects based on aggregations of individuals to infer generalizations about the commonalities in nature. On the other hand, we can assume that individual differences are fundamental to understanding the learning process and look for person effects based on aggregations of stimulus trials, intraindividual profiles, or individual growth curves (see chapters 5 and 7) to make generalizations about normal variation in nature. By focusing on either approach exclusively we may miss important and interesting aspects of the learning process, which can be described in terms of both its relative uniformity and its relative variability. The uniformity results because genetic inheritance is similar, if not identical (Minsky, 1986), and instructional experiences are similar, if not identical. The variability results because of (a) the individual differences in developmental skills, stemming from genetic and experiential factors, that children bring to the task of learning to read and write, and (b) the constructive processes of the learner in using instructional cues to represent declarative knowledge and to create procedural knowledge in varying ways.

In sum, given the potential variation in the developmental skills children bring to the task of learning to read and write, and in their constructive processes, there is probably more than one way to learn to read and write. Instead of seeking one process for learning to read and write, we should investigate multidimensional models of the various processes involved, any one of which might break down, excel, or be used in a variant fashion by an individual child. That is the heart of the developmental neuropsychological perspective.

Developmental Dissociations as Technique for Disconnecting Interconnected Functions

A dissociation, a concept that originated in neuropsychology (Luria, 1973), occurs when one process is disturbed but a related process is left intact. In a developmental dissociation not all component processes are developed to comparable levels. Analyzing data at the individual unit permits examination of developmental dissociations. Berninger and Hart (1992) proposed that this technique can be used to study component processes of brain systems related to reading and writing in children who are not brain damaged. Because component processes usually function in concert, it is difficult to identify component processes of normally functioning brain systems, but nature teases these apart when a dissociation occurs.

Berninger and Hart (1992) examined a data set based on an unreferred sample (in schools rather than a clinic) of 300 primary grade children and 20 measures of developmental skills related to reading or writing and of reading or writing skills for evidence of developmental dissociations. They tested the null hypothesis that all developmental and achievement skills were developed to comparable levels, but found support for the alternative hypothesis that in some children specific skills were overdeveloped or underdeveloped relative to the individual's skills in general. More than a third of the first and second graders and more than half of the third graders fell in the bottom 5 percent of the normal distribution on at least one skill. More than a third of the first, second, and third graders fell in top 5 percent of the normal distribution on at least one skill. More importantly, developmental dissociations—extremely high skill (top 5 percent) in one domain and extremely low skill (bottom 5 percent) in another domain—occurred in about 10 percent of the primary grade sample.

This heterogeneity in profiles of developmental and reading/writing achievement skills may be the result of *noncontingent, normal variation.* Low functioning did not tend to co-occur across a set of developmental or achievement skills, as happens in syndromes in which symptoms cluster and do not develop independently. Rather, low functioning in one developmental domain tended to occur independently of low functioning in another developmental domain, suggesting that the various domains develop independently and are not contingent upon one another. Consequently, the profiles of relative development of the twenty developmental and achievement skills varied considerably across individuals.

Thus, normal variation occurs not only in the level to which a particular skill is developed (Berninger, 1986) but also in the combination of relative strengths and weaknesses in developmental skills related to particular academic skills (Berninger & Hart, 1993). This noncontingent, normal variation is fundamental to the developmental neuropsychological perspective, which views each learner as an individual with a unique profile of learning capabilities and possibly learning disabilities.

Constraints Versus Causality in Modeling Brain-Behavior Relationships

Science has made much progress in understanding the physical world by adopting a view of causality known as determinism. This view assumes that causal mechanisms are linear, unidimensional, and unidirectional. Determinism is less likely to be a fruitful view of causality for the biological world for three reasons. First, biological systems operate at multiple levels (table 1.1), and causal relationships across levels are probably multidimensional, reflecting the net effect of the contribution of all these levels. Second, biological systems interact with their environment, which exerts reciprocal influences on the biological system, resulting in bidirectional rather than unidirectional causal mechanisms. Third, the combination of multidimensional and reciprocal influences results in *constraints* rather than simple causal mechanisms (Berninger, 1991; Berninger & Thalberg, 1988). Constraints are probabilistic and predictive but are associated with some degree of freedom, whereas determinism has no degrees of freedom. The degrees of freedom result because constraints at one level cannot determine behavioral outcomes independent of constraints at other levels.

This view of multiple constraints differs from a view of multiple causality in two ways. First, not only are multiple variables influencing behavior, but these variables are operating at different levels within a system, and the different levels may have indirect or no links to one another. Second, stochastic developmental mechanisms may be operating that lead to *probabilistic* rather than certain outcomes. For example, stochastic developmental mechanisms can produce distinct phenotypes in genetically identical animals (Nowakowski, 1990).

In the next chapter, research pertinent to biological constraints at the genetic, neuroanatomical, and electrophysiological levels is reviewed. It is unlikely that any of these levels determines learning independent of some contribution from the other levels. Indeed, the challenge for genetics is to understand how internal or external *extragenetic* factors modify brain circuitry as coded in the genome (Barnes, 1986). Also, it is unlikely that learning is determined by brain structure and organization independent of the learner's interaction with the environment. According to the developmental neuropsychological perspective, each level of analysis adds constraints to the system. Learning is "caused" by the net effect of these various constraints, the influence of which may vary depending upon what is happening at the other levels of constraint.

Brain as a Dynamic System: Responsiveness to Educational Intervention

Many educators and cognitive psychologists have resisted a neuropsychological approach, but for different reasons. Educators favor applied research with direct applications to practice, and neuropsychology often advances conceptual understanding of learning and performance without producing direct educational applications (Wittrock, 1991). Cognitive psychologists are more interested in immediate (psychological) than ultimate (neurological) causality (Vellutino, 1979a). Indeed, constraints on school learning or performance often are at the behavioral or psychological level, amenable to educational interventions, rather than at the neurological level (Berninger & Thalberg, 1988).

This resistance to neuropsychology, however, is often based on two misconceptions. The first misconception is that the brain is the independent variable that causes learning or behavior in a unidirectional manner without consideration of reciprocal influences from the environment. In reality, the brain is often the dependent variable (Wilson, 1986), and its structure and/or functional organization is changed as a result of representing and operating upon instructional input. The second misconception is that calling attention to the genetic basis of learning is synonymous with claiming that learning processes are nonalterable (Wittrock, 1991). Genetic factors exert constraints on learning, but so do instructional factors. Except when brain systems are diseased or severely damaged, they may continually reorganize as a function of experience (Luria, 1973). Children with problems in learning to read and write often respond positively to appropriate remedial instruction (see chapters 3 and 7).

Critical Developmental Periods

Reading and writing may have critical developmental periods in which they are most easily acquired, but after which it is less probable, but not impossible, for them to be acquired with a reasonable degree of proficiency. For example, in a large-scale study of reading disabilities (sample of 10,000 children), 82 percent of those diagnosed in grades 1 or 2, 46 percent of those diagnosed in grade 3, 42 percent of those diagnosed in grade 4, and 10 to 15 percent of those diagnosed in grades 5 to 7 were brought up to grade level (cited in Keeney & Keeney, 1968, p. 92). Early intervention directed toward prevention of severe reading or writing disabilities may also be more effective because the emotional consequences of learning problems do not interfere as much after short-term failure as they do after chronic failure.

Multidisciplinary Mandate

Churchland's quotation at the beginning of this chapter illustrates the necessity of studying both brain structures (the bottom-up approach) and brain functions (the top-down approach) within integrated, multidisciplinary research programs in order to discover the structure-function relationships. Although multidisciplinary collaboration makes sense in principle, it is often difficult to achieve in practice. As Dennett (1991, p. 254) has pointed out, multidisciplinary efforts can result in conflict between peers in the same field and between scientists in different fields: "Such unabashed eclecticism is often viewed askance by the researchers in the fields from with it borrows. . . . I have grown accustomed to the disrespect expressed by some of the participants for their colleagues in the other disciplines.'' Nevertheless, given the complexity of the levels of analysis involved in the brain itself and its interactions with the environment, multidisciplinary efforts are mandatory because no one discipline has sufficient tools to deal with all the relevant levels. Furthermore, research directed toward understanding the functional level is just as important in this endeavor as research directed toward understanding the structural level; and developmental, cognitive, and educational psychologists with tools for studying function have an important role to play in solving the mysteries of mind-brain function.

Summary

The developmental neuropsychological perspective differs from other approaches to neuropsychology (the study of brain-behavior relationships) in that it focuses on the struggle to acquire function rather than on the loss or locus of function. Key concepts of the developmental neuropsychological perspective include levels of analysis, systems models of brain function, the individual as the unit of analysis, normal variation at all levels of analysis, developmental dissociations, the brain as a source of constraints on learning rather than a simple cause of learning, the brain as a dynamic biological system whose structure and function can change in response to educational intervention, and critical developmental periods. Developmental neuropsychology requires multidisciplinary team efforts, with participation from developmental and educational psychologists, cognitive scientists, neuroscientists, and physicians.

Biological Constraints on Reading and Writing Acquisition

The human brain probably contains more than 10^{14} synapses, and there are simply not enough genes to account for this complexity.

–Jean-Pierre Changeux, cited by Barnes (1986)

So within genetic constraints, extragenetic factors can influence the number and details of synaptic contacts in the cortex.

–Pasco Rakic, cited by Barnes (1986)

Outline

Definitional Issues

Most of the developmental research from a biological perspective has focused on reading rather than on writing and on disabled reading rather than on normal or exceptionally good reading. This almost exclusive focus on disability is unfortunate for basic developmental research, because neuropsychological mechanisms underlie average and talented performance as well as impaired performance; but it is understandable that our limited resources have been directed to the applied problem of understanding disabled performance and of ultimately remediating it.

Thus, the literature discussed in this chapter deals primarily with reading disability, which is often referred to as dyslexia, especially in the medical and neuropsychological literature. In selecting subjects for these studies, investigators have for the most part selected children who meet operational criteria for dyslexia or specific reading disability and have not considered whether these children may also have writing problems. In fact, many children with reading problems have problems with written language in general, but some have problems just with reading or just with writing (e.g., Berninger & Hart, 1993; Berninger, Mizokawa, & Bragg, 1991). Thus, findings are discussed in terms of dyslexia or reading/writing disabilities, but it is not clear whether they are specific to reading or to written language disabilities in general.

A perennial problem complicating interpretation of findings across studies is that researchers have not reached a consensus on how to define learning disability in general or reading and writing disability in particular. One cannot assume that children selected by different investigators meet the same inclusion criteria or operational definitions of reading disabilities (Gray, 1991). For example, one of the unresolved controversies is whether reading disability must be defined on the basis of a discrepancy between IQ (an estimate of expected level of achievement) and actual level of reading achievement, or can be defined on the basis of extremely low reading achievement, regardless of IQ. (For further discussion of this issue, see Berninger, Hart, Abbott, & Karovsky, 1992.)

Another problem is that dyslexia is not a categorical variable like a disease that one either has or does not have; rather it is a disorder that lies at the lower end of a continuous distribution of reading ability (Shaywitz, Escobar, Shaywitz, Fletcher, & Makuch, 1992). The cut-off point between normal reading and disabled reading along that continuum is always arbitrary.

Yet another problem is that most researchers have not ascertained whether reading disabled subjects in their studies may also have attentional deficit disorder, which Dykman and Ackerman (1991) have shown co-occurs in some but not all reading disabled individuals. However, there is some evidence that the cognitive deficits in reading disability do not depend on whether or not attentional deficit disorder is present (Felton, Wood, Brown, Campbell, & Harter, 1987).

Thus, reading disability has been defined in different ways by various investigators, and reading disability may be confounded with writing disability and/or attentional deficit in many studies. Conclusions should therefore be based on converging evidence across laboratories and definitional variations.

One final definitional issue is the sheer number of technical terms used in the research literature on the biology of dyslexia. Readers who do not have a background in neuropsychology are encouraged to make ample use of the glossary when reading this chapter.

Genetic Constraints

Family Studies

Thomas (1905) was probably the first to speculate that severe reading disability, which at that time was referred to as "congenital word blindness," had a hereditary basis because it ran in families. Beginning in the 1930s a number of researchers carefully documented that reading and writing disorders tend to occur across generations in some families, with probabilities higher for first-degree relatives (parents and siblings) than for second-degree relatives (grandparents, aunts, and uncles). For review of early family studies, see Finucci, Guthrie, Childs, Abbey, and Childs (1976) and Owen (1978).

More recent family studies have provided strong evidence for the familial nature of reading disorders. Finucci et al. (1976) used measures that made it difficult for adults who had developed compensatory mechanisms for their reading problems to apply these mechanisms, and showed that over half of the adult siblings and parents of reading disabled children also had residual reading problems. Further, they showed that one third of these reading disabled children had siblings who were reading disabled. Decker and DeFries (1981) conducted a large-scale psychometric study of reading disabled children, their parents and siblings, and members of matched control families. They found that both parents and siblings of reading disabled children obtained significantly lower mean factor scores on reading and coding/speed than did parents and siblings of non-reading disabled children. Hoien, Lundberg, Larsen, and Tonnessen (1989) compared the profiles of dyslexic adolescents and their family members on word recognition, nonword reading, visual processing, lexical decision, sound blending, syllable reversal, and naming tasks. They demonstrated that each family displayed a unique profile pattern but that within families the profiles of fathers and sons were remarkably similar.

Scarborough's prospective study (1989, 1990), in which children in families with a history of reading problems were assessed at age 2, age 5, and grade 2, showed that some of these children became normal readers, whereas others developed reading problems. Thus, a history of dyslexia in the family is a risk factor but does not indicate that a child will necessarily become dyslexic.

Sex Incidence Studies

For years, reports in the literature claimed that the incidence of reading disorders was much higher for males than females, with reported incidence being as high as four to six times greater in males than females (Duane, 1991). Despite this sex difference in the incidence of dyslexia, investigators (e.g., Hallgren, 1950) have not assumed that the gene responsible for dyslexia occurs on a sex chromosome (Finucci et al., 1976; Owen, 1978). Rather, there has been much discussion of how genetic effects may exert sex-related influences on brain development via fetal testosterone levels that vary between the sexes (Galaburda, 1986; McManus & Bryden, 1991). However, the best fitting model in a recent segregation analysis based on families in four samples across the country supported major gene transmission in a dominant or additive fashion with *sex-dependent penetrance* (Pennington, Gilger, Pauls, Smith, Smith, & DeFries, 1991).

Although the preponderance of males may be attributed to genetic factors, there are other explanations. For example, in the 1950s some investigators attributed the higher incidence of identified males to (a) boys being more likely to act out and call their teacher's attention to their reading problems, and (b) parents' greater concern for the school achievement of sons than of daughters (see Owen, 1978).

Recently, Shaywitz, Shaywitz, Fletcher, and Escobar (1990) showed that sex differences are not found when dyslexics are identified on the basis of investigator-defined criteria for reading problems. Referral bias, possibly for the reasons discussed above, may artificially inflate the number of boys among school-identified samples of dyslexics and among clinic samples of dyslexics assessed outside the school system. Subsequently, many other investigators reported about equal incidence of boys and girls with dyslexia in their research cohorts (e.g., DeFries, Olson, Pennington, & Smith, 1991; Lubs, Duara, Levin, Jallad, Lubs, Rabin, Kushch, & Gross-Glenn, 1991; Wood, Felton, Flowers, & Naylor, 1991).

However, further research is needed to test the hypothesis that although dyslexia may occur at about the same rate in both sexes, males with dyslexia may be more severely affected than girls with dyslexia (Lubs et al., 1991). Indeed, in a large-scale study of kindergartners, no mean differences were found between boys and girls in reading achievement, but nearly twice as many boys as girls fell in the bottom 10 percent of the reading achievement distribution (Vellutino, Scanlon, Clark, Small, Fanuele, & Pratt, 1992). Sex differences may be more apparent when absolute criteria (performance in the bottom 5 percent of the distribution) are used instead of relative criteria (discrepancy from IQ), and may affect writing disabilities more than reading disabilities (Berninger & Fuller, 1992).

Twin Studies

A disorder that runs in families is not necessarily genetic (Decker & DeFries, 1981; McClearn, 1978), because families share common environments as well as common genes. Twin studies have provided stronger evidence for the genetic basis of reading disorders than have family studies.

In one approach to twin research, the concordance rate (percent of twin pairs in which both twins have a reading disorder) is compared for monozygotic (MZ or identical) twins and dizygotic (DZ or fraternal) twins. This approach has led some to conclude that reading disability is almost always under genetic control because the concordance rate is much higher for MZ twins than for DZ twins. However, the concordance rate for MZ twins appears to be much higher for younger children than for adolescents (Stevenson, Graham, Fredman, & McLoughlin, 1987), suggesting that genetic influences may be more constraining earlier in development. This possibility is consistent with the notion of critical developmental periods. Genetic constraints may exert their greatest influence on phonological and orthographic coding during the early primary grades, when school instruction focuses heavily on teaching word recognition. These genetic influences may not be as constraining at later developmental levels, when the instructional program tends to place greater emphasis on higher order comprehension skills. However, the instructional program at later developmental levels may not provide sufficient instruction in word attack skills now that the student might be ready to benefit from it. Thus, critical developmental periods result from interactions between instructional and genetic constraints.

In a second approach to twin research introduced by DeFries, Fulker, and LaBuda (1987), probands (index cases) are identified, and then MZ and DZ co-twins for each proband are compared on the amount of their regression to the mean in reading achievement. This approach is more appropriate than comparing concordance rates when the probands are selected for their extreme scores on a continuous variable, as is the case with reading disabilities. The logic of demonstrating that a disorder is heritable is as follows. The scores of both the MZ and DZ co-twins can be expected to regress to the mean, but the scores of the DZ co-twins will regress more toward the mean than will the scores of the MZ co-twins *if* the disorder is under genetic control. In fact, DeFries et al. showed that the DZ co-twins showed more regression to the mean than did the MZ co-twins. The heritability index suggested that about 30 percent of the reading deficit of the probands was related to heritable factors. In a subsequent study Olson, Wise, Conners, Rack, and Fulker (1989) reported a heritability estimate in which about 40 percent of the reading deficit of the probands was related to genetic factors. Thus, 60 to 70 percent of the variance may be related to environmental factors. Genetic factors may *constrain* reading ability, but they do not determine it independently of environmental factors.

A third approach to twin research, in which MZ twins reared apart are compared to disentangle the contribution of heredity and environment, has not been applied to reading disability research. However, comparing the finding of the Minnesota Study of Twins Reared Apart, that about 70 percent of the variance in IQ is associated with genetic variation (Bouchard, Lykken, McGue, Segal, & Tellegen, 1990), with the reported heritabilities above for reading disability suggests the intriguing possibility that reading disabilities may be relatively more amenable to environmental intervention than is general intelligence. Relevant to this speculation is the multivariate genetic analysis of cognitive and achievement measures for MZ and DZ twins aged 6 to 12 in the Case Western Reserve Twin Project (Thompson, Detterman, & Plomin, 1991). Both genes and common environment were significant in the variance of cognitive ability measures and of reading and math achievement measures, and in the covariance between the ability and achievement measures. However, heritabilities tended to be higher for cognitive abilities than for achievement, and common family environment tended to influence achievement more than ability measures. Taken together, these findings provide evidence for the speculation that achievement may be more amenable to intervention than is cognitive ability.

The work by the Case Western Reserve Twin Project is important also for showing that although achievement was influenced by both environmental and genetic factors, *ability-achievement associations* were almost exclusively genetic in origin, and *ability-achievement discrepancies* were due to environmental influences (Thompson et al., 1991). These findings suggest that the same underlying genetic factors may be responsible for both ability and achievement, but the child's environment will affect whether a discrepancy between ability and achievement occurs.

A potentially fruitful approach to investigation of genetic-environmental interactions has not been explored—that is, comparison of MZ twin pairs in which only one is reading disabled. The concordance rate for MZ twins based on the proband or index case in the Colorado Reading Project is 70 percent (DeFries et al., 1991), suggesting that 30 percent of MZ twins would be available for such research. Because identical twins are usually placed in separate classrooms, they could be compared on the nature of the instructional program, amount of practice in specific skills, developmental history, and so on, for clues as to why one twin developed a reading problem but the co-twin with identical genes did not.

The effects of genetic constraints on on-line processing compared with overall level of achievement also have not been adequately addressed. Twin studies usually compare MZ and DZ twins on overall level of performance on psychometric tests of ability or achievement and do not compare their performance on an item-by-item basis. Pilot work based on item analysis suggested that MZ twins taught by different teachers are no more congruent in on-line processing than unrelated children matched on age and ability taught by the same teacher (Berninger, 1986).

Most twin studies have not considered the possibility that different subcomponents of reading may be differentially affected by genetic factors. An important exception is the work of Olson et al. (1989). They investigated the heritability of *phonological coding in word recognition* (which they measured by the accuracy and speed of pronouncing nonwords that are pronounceable but have no meaning) and of *orthographic coding in word recognition* (which they measured by the speed and accuracy of selecting the real word in a pair of differently spelled words, one of which was a nonword, e.g., "sammon," pronounced exactly the same as the real word, e.g., "salmon"). Based on the sample available in the initial study, phonological coding as measured by nonword reading was highly heritable, but orthographic coding as measured by the homophone/pseudohomophone task was not heritable and was more influenced by environmental factors. However, as the sample size and thus power increased in the ongoing work of this research group, orthographic coding turned out to be heritable, although not as heritable as phonological coding (Olson, in press).

Preliminary analyses of Olson et al. (1989) suggested that the heritable aspects of phonological coding in word recognition may be due to the heritability of segmental oral language skills. More recent work has confirmed the significant heritability of phoneme awareness and phoneme deletion and has shown that the bivariate genetic covariation estimates between these phonemic tasks and nonword reading were significant (Olson, in press).

Olson and colleagues (1989) did not include segmental measures of orthographic coding (e.g., a letter or letter cluster in a word), so it is not possible to evaluate whether segmental orthographic coding, which contributes along with segmental phonological coding (e.g., a phoneme or syllable) to nonword reading (see chapter 4), may also be heritable. Stevensen et al. (1987) found that spelling ability and disability are more heritable than are reading ability and disability; so to the extent that segmental orthographic coding skills contribute to spelling (Berninger, Yates, & Lester, 1991), they may be heritable. Clearly, more research is needed like that initiated by Olson and colleagues, in which the heritability of component reading/writing skills and component processes contributing to those skills is examined.

Mechanisms of Genetic Inheritance

Heritability studies provide information on the degree to which genetic factors influence a particular behavior, trait, or disorder in the *population*, but they provide no information about *individuals*

(Childs, Finucci, & Preston, 1978). Research on the mechanism of genetic transmission and the locus of the genes responsible for a particular behavior, trait, or disorder is necessary to apply genetic knowledge to an individual case. The major question that has been addressed is whether genetic transmission is through (a) a single gene with a major focus, (b) a large number of genes with polygenic loci and effects, or (c) a combination, in which a few major genes operate in the context of a multifactorial background (Pennington et al., 1991). Identification of a single locus is much more difficult for polygenetic inheritance than for single gene inheritance as described in classic Mendalian genetics (for explanation, see McClearn, 1978).

Recent advances in molecular genetics have provided a powerful tool—linkage analysis—for investigating modes of transmission and locus of the gene structure(s) responsible for dyslexia (Pennington & Smith, 1988). *Linkage analysis* is a method of testing statistically whether two genes segregate together in a nonrandom way, thus indicating that they are located close together on the same chromosome; it also permits tests of the location of specific genes on specific chromosomes. Linkage analysis is challenging because the human genetic code is contained in perhaps 100,000 loci (McClearn, 1978). Linkage analyses support a mixed model in which the genetic mechanisms are heterogeneous, with evidence for a major gene effect related to Chromosome 15 (Smith, Kimberling, Pennington, & Lubs, 1983; Smith, Pennington, Fain, Kimberling, & Lubs, 1986) in some families; however, linkage to Chromosome 15 has not been replicated in other laboratories (Lubs et al., 1991; Pennington & Smith, 1988). There is also evidence for a major gene effect related to Chromosome 6 (Lubs et al., 1991) and Chromosome 1 (Lubs, 1990), and more families show linkage to Chromosome 6 than to Chromosome 15 (DeFries et al., 1991).

Recent advances in computer programs for performing *segregation analyses* on family pedigree data to determine which cross-generational family members are and are not affected have also provided more rigorous tests of alternative genetic mechanisms (Pennington et al., 1991). Segregation analyses also support a mixed model with evidence for a single major gene and for polygenetic influences (Pennington et al., 1991).

In sum, there is much to be learned yet about the mode of genetic transmission for reading/writing disorders. It appears to be heterogeneous, which is not surprising, because written language disorders are heterogeneous at the phenotypical level of observable behavior, a theme that is emphasized throughout this book. Progress in mapping the underlying genotype will depend on progress in describing and measuring the expressed phenotype (Pennington & Smith, 1988). Evidence to date suggests that different genetic mechanisms may underlie the same phenotype (Pennington & Smith, 1988), but developing more reliable and valid procedures for subtyping the phenotype—procedures that take into account normal variation in multiple variables—may lead to a clearer understanding of the underlying genotypes.

Extragenetic Effects

As reflected in the quotations at the beginning of this chapter, neuroscientists believe that genes determine global aspects of brain architecture and its wiring patterns, but that factors outside the genes—both in the brain and in the environment—modify the details of the overall organization of the individual brain (Barnes, 1986). The primary activity of genes is the production of unique enzymes that regulate biochemical reactions, which influence the structural development and function of the nervous system. However, extragenetic factors such as overall health status of the organism, ingested substances, and interactions with the environment also influence the structural development and function of the nervous system. Progress is being made in understanding how neuronal activity triggered by those interactions with the environment leads to altered function at various levels of the nervous system (Wolpaw et al., 1991). In the current view among neuroscientists, development of synaptic circuitry is controlled by (a) *genes,* which influence the response to specific neural activity patterns, (b) *neural activity,* which turns certain genes off or on and thus influences their function, and (c) the *interaction between genes and neural activity.* Learning involves local molecular events and neural activity causing synaptic changes at multiple sites throughout the central nervous system (Wolpaw et al., 1991).

Extragenetic factors, such as developmental history of interactions with the environment, have important implications for both basic research and educational practice. In the case of basic research, extragenetic factors complicate inferences about causality and thus theory building. Basic researchers have developed a technique in which they "knock out" or inactivate a single gene in a mouse embryo and note the specific behavior that fails to develop in the adult mouse as a consequence of the missing gene. However, one cannot necessarily conclude that the inactivated gene is responsible for the specific missing behavior, because the manipulation also affects every other aspect of development influenced by that gene; the inferential link between gene and behavior is not straightforward (Barinaga, 1992).

In the case of educational practice, results of heritability studies offer reason to be optimistic about the potential effectiveness of instructional interventions for improving reading and writing skills at least to some degree. Although genetic factors play a role in reading and writing acquisition (reading/writing disabilities are 30 to 40 percent heritable), environmental factors play an even greater role. Moreover, the prediction of a behavioral geneticist that in the future teachers will design individual education programs based on students' genetic makeup (Aldhous, 1992) seems premature. Effective individualized educational programs are based on extragenetic factors at a different level of analysis, such as current level of functioning in related developmental domains, current knowledge and skills in academic domains, past learning history, repertoire of characteristic strategies, teacher knowledge, and so on. Genetic factors are most likely to shed light on why a particular child struggles to learn and not on how a lesson plan should be constructed.

Neuroanatomical Constraints

Developmental Anomalies Associated with Reading/Writing Disorders

In chapter 1 the point was made that reading and/or writing disabled children are usually not brain damaged and are more likely to have minor structural anomalies. Current knowledge of these structural anomalies is based on autopsy studies, sometimes referred to as cytoarchitectonic studies, and imaging studies of live individuals, both of which are reviewed below.

Autopsy Studies
Drake (1968) reported anomalies in the parietal lobes, including abnormal cortical folding. Galaburda, Sherman, Rosen, Aboitz, and Geschwind (1985) conducted gross inspections and microscopic analyses of the brains of four adult or adolescent males, all of whom had been diagnosed early in schooling as having severe reading disability and two of whom had a history of late onset of speech. Humphreys, Kaufmann, and Galaburda (1990) did the same for three adult females, all of whom had significant problems in learning to read and

two of whom also had attentional problems. For the most part, gross examination revealed no abnormalities in the male or female brains other than a *symmetrical planum temporale,* a triangular region of the temporal lobe that is the locus for the auditory association area and that shows a left > right asymmetry in 75 percent of the population (Galaburda, 1991). Microscopic examination of stained tissue sections, however, revealed *dysplasias* (disordered cellular architecture in which excessive numbers of large cells distort the normal organization of cerebral cortex into columns and layers) and *ectopias* (presence of neural elements in layer I of cerebral cortex, which usually does not have neurons) in all males and *polymicrogyria* (excessive folding and absence of columnar organization) in two males. Microscopic examination revealed ectopias in all females and neuronal loss and vascular malformations in two females.

Although the microscopic anomalies tended to be in the left hemispheres and in the frontal and temporal lobe regions, distribution of the anomalies varied across both male and female patients. In three males these anomalies occurred bilaterally; of the females, one had ectopias in the left hemisphere, one in the right hemisphere, and one in both hemispheres. This variability across patients within and across studies and the finding of anomalies in brain regions not associated with language should not be surprising because there is ''. . . no a priori reason to predict that a single localization or a unique form of pathology must account for all the witnessed developmental reading disorders.'' (Galaburda, 1988, p. 127)

Although these autopsy studies are based on a small sample, the observed microscopic structural anomalies provide clues to the neuroanatomical constraints on learning to read. These anomalies may result in miswiring of the brain, thus impairing connectivity among neurons, or in abnormal electrical activity, thus creating interference in the function of affected brain systems (Galaburda et al., 1985). The developmental origin of these microscopic anomalies is probably in midgestation during the peak of *neuronal migration* from the germinal zone to the cerebral cortex. Analogous anomalies have been created in experimental animals that are lesioned before neuronal migration is complete. On the other hand, the developmental origin of the symmetry of the planum temporale may be the *postmigration period,* when excess cells are normally pruned through selective cell death but in some cases may not be pruned (Galaburda et al., 1985; Galaburda, 1986, 1988, 1991). Thus, anomalies that occur very early in development may be responsible for problems such as reading and writing disorders much later in development.

TABLE 2.1 Technologies for Direct Brain Measures in Living Subjects[a]

Technology	Invasive	Resolution?	Cost	Concurrent Task
CT or CAT scan[b]: Computer-assisted tomography	Yes (x-rays)	< MRI	< MRI	No
MRI scan[b]: Magnetic resonance imaging	No	> CT	> CT	No
PET scan[c]: Positron emission tomography	Yes[d]	Good	Highest	Yes
rCBF[c]: Regional cerebral blood flow	Yes[e]	< PET	< PET	Yes
EEG[f]: Electro-enceph-alography	No	g	Low	No (at rest or sleeping)
ERPs[g]	No	g	Low	Yes

[a]< = less than, > = greater than
[b]Yields measures of neuroanatomical structures.
[c]Yields measures of metabolic activity.
[d]Inject radioactively labeled glucose.
[e]Depends on whether marker gas inhaled is radioactive.
[f]Yields measures of brain waves that reflect electrophysiological activity.
[g]Components of the brain wave are analyzed; no brain image.

In Vivo Imaging

Advances in imaging technology have made it possible to scan the brains of living people. Table 2.1 provides an overview of the technologies that yield direct measures of the living brain. Both computed tomography (CT) and magnetic resonance imaging (MRI) scans provide *structural* images of the brain. MRI has better resolution (precision of detail) than does CT. MRI is also relatively less invasive—the patient must lie still in a large coil to which a magnetic field is directed—than CT, in which the patient is exposed to X-rays. The advantage of in vivo imaging over postmortem cytoarchitectonic studies is that functional measures can be correlated with the structural indices in a scan. For MRI and CT, the tasks must be given before or after the scan, but for PET and rCBF, the tasks can be given concurrently with the scan (table 2.1). The disadvantage of in vivo imaging is that the resolution is not as good as with the autopsy studies; however, autopsy studies do not have resolution at the level of the single neuron (Galaburda et al., 1985).

Hynd and Semrud-Clikeman (1989) reviewed the early findings based on CT or MRI scans and discussed the methodological issues to consider in evaluating this research and designing future research, especially in regard to criteria for subject selection and use of appropriate control groups. Less than 7 percent of the scans of dyslexics reported in the literature as of 1990 were abnormal (also see Filipek & Kennedy, 1991), reinforcing the point that neuroanatomical constraints for dyslexia involve minor structural anomalies rather than pathology.

Current MRI technology is not yet developed to the stage where it can be used for clinical diagnosis of reading and writing disabilities, but the technology is rapidly changing. Three-dimensional volumetric scans, which can be reformatted in any plane, are replacing two-dimensional scans of length and area. Figures 2.1 and 2.2 show images obtained with state-of-the-art volumetric procedures. Figure 2.1 shows sagittal images representing contiguous 1.1-mm sections through the right sylvian fissure of an 8-year-old child. Note the clear signal intensity differences between gray and white matter. Figure 2.2 shows coronal images from the same child through the midbrain. Again, note the clear differentiation of gray and white matter. New computer algorithms for quantitative analysis of multivariate information in scans are being developed. Shape analysis techniques are being applied to defining boundaries of brain structures that are continuous rather than discrete. Progress in MRI research will depend on investigators reaching a consensus on procedural issues for acquisition of brain images and for interpretation of metric information in the images. (See Filipek & Kennedy, 1991, for a description of the basic principles of MRI technology and a discussion of the above issues.)

Differences in findings across laboratories may be related to differences in how the boundaries of brain structures are defined. Currently there is no single established method for defining boundaries of brain structures such as the planum (Filipek & Kennedy, 1991; Witelson, 1982). For example, based on MRI scans, some investigators (e.g., Larsen, Hoien, Lundberg, & Odegaard, 1990) report a

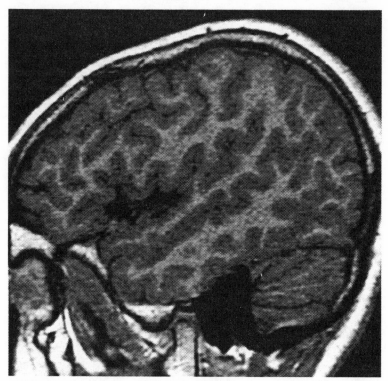

FIGURE 2.1

Magnetic resonance image, sagittal.

Obtained with volumetric acquisition under the direction of Jay Tsuruda, M.D., Chief of Magnetic Resonance Imaging, University of Washington.

greater percentage of symmetry of the planum (right = left) in developmental dyslexics, whereas others (e.g., Hynd, Semrud-Clikeman, Lorys, Novey, & Eliopulos, 1990) report a greater percentage of reversed asymmetries of the planum (right > left) in developmental dyslexics. MRI studies attribute symmetry or reversed asymmetry to a small left planum (e.g., Hynd et al., 1990; Larsen et al., 1990), whereas autopsy studies attribute symmetry to a large right planum (e.g., Galaburda et al., 1985). Progress in research on neuroanatomy in general will depend on reaching a consensus on defining boundaries of brain structures.

Although MRI technology is still evolving, research to date based on computerized measurement of brain metrics sheds light on what neuroanatomical constraints may be associated with developmental dyslexia. Available evidence implicates structures associated

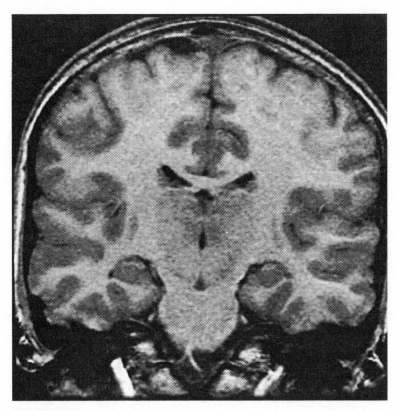

FIGURE 2.2
Magnetic resonance image, coronal.

Obtained with volumetric acquisition under the direction of Jay Tsuruda, M.D., Chief of Magnetic Resonance Imaging, University of Washington.

with language processing, as discussed below. The size of the corpus callosum, which connects the left and right hemispheres of cerebral cortex, does not seem to be a factor (Larsen, Hoien, & Odegaard, 1992); but further research is needed before a final conclusion on this issue is reached.

Hynd et al. (1990) carefully selected their child subjects so that one group had dyslexia but not attention deficit disorder, one group had attention deficit disorder but not dyslexia, and the control group, matched on age and sex, had no reading or attentional problems. Although there were no significant differences in the total brain area among the three groups, width or length of specific brain regions and the patterns of left-right asymmetries in specific brain regions varied across the groups. Normally, the right frontal region is larger than the left, as was the case in the control group; but dyslexics had symmetric frontal regions, and both dyslexic children and those with attention deficit disorder had smaller right frontal regions than did the control group. Dyslexics also had a shorter insular region (which, like the planum temporale, is a language processing area) than did the control group on both the left and right, and a shorter left planum than the control group. In 90 percent of the dyslexics, the length of the planum was shorter on the left than on the right, a reversal of the normal asymmetry.

Semrud-Clikeman, Hynd, Novey, and Eliopulos (1991) administered measures of reading and language to these same subjects to examine the structure-function relationships. For dyslexics only, smaller right frontal width was related to significantly poorer passage comprehension; reversed asymmetry (left > right) or symmetry of this right frontal region was related to significantly poorer word attack skills. For the children in general, regardless of group, reversed asymmetry (right > left) or symmetry of the planum was related to significantly lower scores on the verbal comprehension factor of the Wechsler Intelligence Scale for Children—Revised, indicating that this structure is related to language processing. A shorter insular cortex was associated with poorer naming skills.

Leonard, Voeller, Lombardino, Alexander, Andersen, Morris, Garofalakis, Hynd, Honeyman, Mao, Agee, and Staab (1993) studied children and adults and compared computer-based measurements of MRI scans for dyslexics, nondyslexic relatives of dyslexics, and controls. In contrast to the studies discussed above, they used volumetric acquisition to image the brains, but three-dimensional reconstruction was not necessary because cortical anomalies were well visualized without it. They examined four kinds of anomalies: interhemispheric and intrahemispheric asymmetries of the planum temporale (the cortical structure thought to be associated with phonological processing), anomalous sylvian fissures (in which the planum lies), and multiple Heschl's gyri (structures that receive ascending auditory projections and relay them to the planum).

Most subjects, regardless of group, showed the expected interhemispheric asymmetries, in which the temporal bank of the planum is larger on the left, and the parietal bank of the planum is larger on the right; but many dyslexics showed reversed intrahemispheric asymmetry in the right hemisphere. Compared with the controls, the dyslexics tended to have enlarged parietal banks of the planum on the right. In addition, the dyslexics had extra gyri in the parietal operculum, an area Ojemann (1988) has found contains sites specific to reading and not to other language functions, such as naming. Multiple

Heschl's gyri occurred on the right and left in some dyslexics. None of the controls had multiple Heschl's gyri.

All groups had a few anomalies, but dyslexics had a significantly greater proportion of *bilateral* anomalies than did the controls. Bilateral anomalies were associated with phonemic segmentation problems. Anomalies occurred in nondyslexic family members but not as frequently as in dyslexics. Thus, the investigators concluded that brain anomalies do not cause dyslexia but do present a risk factor for it. In their view, risk increases with increasing *number* of anomalies (also suggested by Semrud-Clikeman et al., 1991) and increasing *bilateral* anomalies.

Clinicopathological Studies

Hynd and Hynd (1984) described the classical model of sequential neural pathways in reading (fig. 2.3 on page 46), which is based on the clinicopathological method of studying acquired reading deficits in adults with known brain lesions. In this method, functional data acquired before death are correlated with neuroanatomical data obtained after death. The *left occipital lobe* processes letter strings as words, whereas the *right occipital lobe* processes imageable words, which as concrete nouns can be visualized. The *angular gyrus,* once thought to be *the* reading center, is now thought to be where cross-modal integration occurs between incoming visual information in printed words and auditory linguistic information in spoken words. A mechanism for *grapheme-phoneme* (letter-sound) *correspondence* may operate here. *Wernicke's area* in the left temporal lobe is where comprehension and whole-word recognition occur. *Broca's area* in the left frontal lobe, which mediates speech, is involved in oral reading.

This model makes predictions about the sequential neural pathways involved in both normal and disabled reading. In normal reading, neural pathways from the primary visual cortex lead to the left and right occipital lobes, then converse in the angular gyrus, from which they proceed to Wernicke's area (a comprehension center for silent reading), and on to Broca's area (a speech center for oral reading). In contrast, in *surface dyslexics,* who can read orally by phonics rules but have trouble with sight words, the neural pathways may lead directly from the primary visual cortex to the angular gyrus and then on to Broca's area. In *phonological dyslexics,* who can read familiar sight words but have difficulty with phonics rules, the neural pathways may lead directly from the left and right primary visual cortex to Wernicke's area. In *deep dyslexics,* who can read familiar

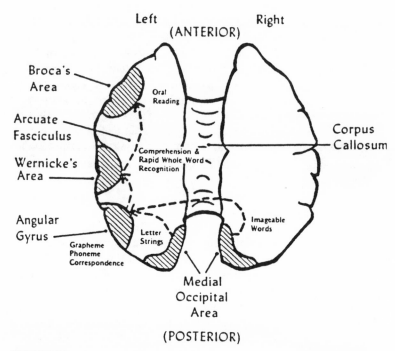

FIGURE 2.3

The brain as viewed in horizontal section. The major pathways and cortical regions thought to be involved in reading, based on the clinicopathological method, are depicted.

From "Dyslexia: Neuroanatomical/neurolinguistic perspectives" by G. Hynd and C. Hynd, 1984, *Reading Research Quarterly, 19,* p. 490. Reprinted with permission of George W. Hynd and the International Reading Association.

sight words (especially nouns, but not more abstract words), make many paralexic errors (semantic confusions, for example, calling duck "bird," or puddle "water"), have trouble with phonics rules, read better silently than orally, and read better in context than in isolation (see Berninger & Hart, 1992), the neural pathways may lead directly from the right primary visual cortex to Wernicke's area.

Less is known about the neural structures underlying writing. Different neural structures probably are involved in the motor planning and motor execution aspects of handwriting (Berninger & Rutberg, 1992) and the motor and linguistic aspects of spelling (Roeltgen & Heilman, 1984). Luria (1973) noted that lesions in the left or right parieto-occipital region resulted in great difficulty in drawing letters, whereas lesions in the left temporal lobe resulted in inability to write words because of sound confusions. Roeltgen and Heilman (1984) identified two dissociable spelling systems—*lexical* (ability to spell phonically irregular real words) and *phonological* (ability to spell phonically regular nonwords). Acquired lexical agraphia was associated with lesions in the angular gyrus, whereas acquired phonological agraphia was associated with lesions in the supramarginal gyrus.

Functional Constraints

PET and Blood-Flow Studies

PET and blood-flow techniques provide functional images of the parts of the brain that are activated as a specific task is performed (table 2.1). PET provides better temporal and spatial resolution (precision), but blood-flow techniques provide better separation of gray and white matter. It is not known whether activation reflects the activity of excitatory or inhibitory neurons. (See Wood, 1990, for a review of the procedural and interpretational issues concerning these techniques.) PET and blood-flow techniques are more invasive than the structural imaging techniques—the patient is injected with or inhales a radioactive substance, that enters the blood stream, travels to the brain, and serves as a marker of the location of neural activity at a given moment in time. Consequently, PET and blood-flow techniques are used in studies of adults, but not of children. Nonetheless, the adult studies yield clues about functional constraints in reading.

Ingvar (1983) reviewed blood-flow studies showing that multiple local sites were activated in both hemispheres during silent reading (frontal regions, including Broca's speech area, visual areas, and paravisual areas) and during oral reading (the same regions as in silent reading plus the mouth and auditory areas). Different patterns of areas were activated by visual discrimination of geometric figures (e.g., the parietal or somatosensory areas) than were activated by reading written words.

Petersen, Fox, Posner, Mintun, and Raichle (1989) used PET to identify brain areas related to single word reading. Visual word processing activated multiple areas bilaterally in occipital regions, but the same occipital areas were not activated by nonlinguistic visual stimuli such as checkerboards. Auditory word processing activated multiple areas in some temporal regions bilaterally and a left temporal region unilaterally, but the same temporal areas were not activated by nonlinguistic auditory stimuli such as clicks, tones, and noise bursts. Visual word forms did not activate temporal areas, and auditory word forms did not activate occipital areas, indicating that orthographic coding and phonological coding are localized in different parts of the brain (fig. 1.1). Semantic word processing activated yet other regions of the brain in the left frontal region. Petersen et al. (1989) interpreted these results to mean that reading a single word involves the orchestration of component computations localized in these various regions distributed throughout the brain.

Brain regions also seem to be specialized for graphemic symbols that are wordlike compared with graphemic symbols that are not wordlike. Both PET (Petersen, Fox, Snyder, & Raichle, 1990) and blood-flow studies (Wise, Chollet, Hadar, Friston, Hoffner, & Frackowiak, 1991) have shown that the same brain areas are activated by real words and pronounceable nonwords. Petersen et al. (1990), however, showed that different brain areas are activated by strings of letterlike symbols or consonants than are activated by real words or nonwords.

Petersen et al. (1989), who found no activation of either Wernicke's area or angular gyrus during single word reading, believe their results are inconsistent with the prevailing model of a single, sequential pathway in normal reading (see section on neural pathways based on clinicopathological studies earlier in this chapter). Instead, they propose a network model based on PET results and behavioral studies of dissociations among component reading skills caused by specific lesions. In their model (fig. 2.4), visual word codes (analogous to orthographic codes) have relatively independent access to receptive phonological codes, semantic codes, and articulatory codes, and there is more than one pathway from visual word codes to the other linguistic codes. This network model is consistent with the functional model of the multiple connections model proposed in chapter 4.

Given that PET and the clinicopathological method tap different levels of analysis, it is not surprising that the two approaches yield different conclusions. As Ojemann (1988) pointed out, some brain structures may normally participate in a function but may not be essential for the function to be achieved. Some methods may be tapping structures that normally participate in a function, whereas others may be tapping essential structures. Also, a structural problem in one region may translate into functional problems in a broader region or different regions as a result of the connectivity of neural systems. Seemingly contradictory findings at different levels of analysis should

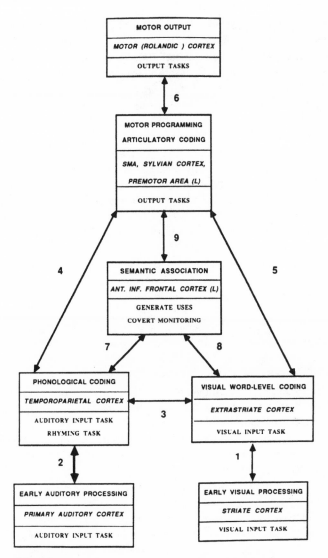

FIGURE 2.4

A general network relating some of the areas of activation to the different levels of lexical processing. There are many alternative networks consistent with the conditions under which the areas are activated, but this arrangement represents a simple design consistent with our results, and some convergent experiments from other types of studies.

Reprinted from *Journal of Cognitive Neuroscience,* vol. 1, no. 2, Petersen et al., "Positron Emission Tomographic Studies of the Processing of Single Words," by permission of The MIT Press, Cambridge, Massachusetts, Copyright © 1989.

not necessarily be treated as conflicting evidence; rather they may be useful in explaining how one level of analysis maps onto another level. For example, the clinicopathological studies may shed light on the *sequential* synaptic transmission along neural pathways, whereas the PET studies may capture the *simultaneous* metabolic activity at multiple local sites. Both sequential and simultaneous processes, at different levels of analysis, may be involved in reading.

Some studies have focused on comprehension of connected text rather than on single word reading. Although blood-flow studies tend to find greater activation in the left hemisphere for single word reading, they tend to find activation in both hemispheres for reading comprehension of connected text (e.g., Huettner, Rosenthal, & Hynd, 1989).

All the above studies used normal adults. In contrast, Wood and colleagues (Flowers et al., 1991; Wood et al., 1991) studied normal adults and adults who had been diagnosed as dyslexic in childhood. Using blood-flow techniques and an auditory-orthographic task in which subjects listened to auditorially presented words and indicated whether words were exactly four letters long, Flowers, Wood, and Naylor (1991) found that reduced activation in Wernicke's area in the left temporal lobe differentiated adults who had been poor versus good readers in childhood. Also, poor readers in childhood had higher blood flow in the angular gyrus than did the good readers in childhood; this finding held, independent of the adult reading level of those diagnosed as dyslexic in childhood. Thus, this research group found differences associated with developmental dyslexia in the same brain structures predicted by the classical, sequential pathway model of reading (see section on neural pathways based on clinicopathological studies earlier in this chapter).

On a phonemic task, high task accuracy was associated with reduced left temporal blood flow in normal readers, but increased left temporal flow in reading disabled adults (Wood, Flowers, Buchsbaum, & Tallal, 1991). Using PET, Wood et al. (1991) found the same pattern of results for the phonemic task. Also, dyslexics performing most accurately showed the greatest activity near Heschl's gyrus in the left temporal region, suggesting that phonemic processing required more effort on the part of dyslexics. This last functional finding is consistent with the structural finding of Leonard et al. (1993) that some dyslexics have multiple Heschl's gyri in the left hemisphere, which is an anomaly that might reduce the efficiency of the functions associated with Heschl's gyrus.

Electrosurgical Studies

Ojemann (1988), for example, uses electrical stimulation to disrupt cortical functioning in awake adult humans having brain surgery and thus to infer the language functions associated with focal sites. The purpose of creating these "functional lesions" is to map an individual's language functions so they can be spared as much as possible during surgery. In contrast to PET and blood-flow studies, electrosurgical techniques identify essential structures without which the behavior cannot occur (Ojemann, 1988).

Based on a study of 55 patients undergoing surgery for intractable epilepsy, Ojemann (1988) found that sites essential for object naming overlapped with sites essential for oral sentence reading, but that some sites were specific to naming and some were specific to reading (e.g., in the temporal, frontal, and parietal operculum regions). The exact location of the naming and reading sites in the left perisylvian region of the temporal lobe varied considerably across patients, demonstrating normal variation at the anatomical level. No reading or naming errors were evoked by stimulating the angular gyrus; this finding is consistent with the PET results of Petersen et al. (1989), but not with the classical model based on the clinicopathological method. To some extent the patterning of sites was associated with language ability, with low verbal IQ patients showing the reversed pattern of high verbal IQ patients as to where sites essential for naming and sites essential for reading were located. This finding suggests that language skill may be related to the *functional* organization and not just to the *structural* organization of the brain.

Ojemann (1991) questioned the classical, serial model, in which language is understood in Wernicke's area in the left temporal lobe and then expressed in Broca's area in the left frontal lobe. He concluded, based on a review of his and others' research results over the past two decades, that language is modular, that is, compartmentalized into separate systems. Each of these systems serves a different function, for example, phoneme identification, naming, and syntactic analysis. Each system has essential structures localized in the frontal and tempoparietal areas as well as neurons widely distributed throughout the left and right cortex. Subcortical structures such as the thalamus and striatum also seem to be involved in language processing. Single neuronal recordings by microelectrode in surgical patients showed that some individual cortical neurons change their activity only in response to reading single words (Ojemann,

Creutzfeldt, Lettich, & Haglund, 1988). It is unknown whether specific activity patterns are associated with individual words. Ojemann (1991) concluded that in both children and adults the *normal variation in functional organization of language is greater than the anatomical variation,* which is observed early in fetal development.

Electrophysiological Studies

The electroencephalography (EEG) brainwave frequency method and the event-related potential (ERP) method are two direct brain measures that are completely noninvasive and can be used with infants and children as well as adults (table 2.1). (See also Languis & Wittrock, 1986, for a description of both of these techniques.) These techniques do not permit inferences about the location of activity in the brain because the brain wave patterns recorded at a particular site on the scalp may have been generated from many sources within the brain and not just that particular site of recording (Harter, 1991). However, power spectra analysis can be used to compute the percentage of delta, theta, alpha, or beta EEG frequency bands in selected time epochs at various scalp locations during task performance. Alternatively, ERPs, short epochs of EEG precisely time-locked to the presentation of a target stimulus, can be collected, computer averaged, and labeled by positive (P) or negative (N) electrical properties and latency in milliseconds from onset of target stimulus (e.g., P300, N400). Either the frequency bands or ERP components can be correlated with specific information processing tasks or with performance of individuals or groups with known characteristics such as dyslexia.

To date, electrophysiological studies have made three major contributions related to reading and writing acquisition. First, they have shown which information processing tasks are identified with the amplitude and latency of each ERP component (see Languis & Wittrock, 1986, for a review). Both amplitude and latency of ERPs are highly similar in identical twins, but not in controls matched to the twins, suggesting a strong genetic basis for ERPs (Polich & Burns, 1987). ERPs also show that language comprehension processes are decomposable into separate subsystems, for example, for semantics and syntax (Neville, Nicol, Barss, Forster, & Garrett, 1991), consistent with Ojemann's (1991) conclusions.

Second, group comparisons have shown that reading disabled and reading abled children differ in the electrophysiological activity of the brain. Conners (1971) identified abnormal visual evoked potentials (VEPs) over the left parietal region containing the angular gyrus in poor readers. Duffy (1981) used brain electrical activity mapping (BEAM) to show that dyslexics had more EEG alpha in the left hemisphere. He also noted that it was not possible to classify subjects accurately as dyslexic or nondyslexic by visual inspection because of *considerable intersubject and intergroup variability*. Byring and Jarvilehto (1985) observed long auditory evoked potential (AEP) latencies in poor spellers and noted that spelling errors involving the whole word unit were associated with low amplitudes of the P50 and P300 AEP. Holcomb, Ackerman, and Dykman (1985) found that reading disabled children had smaller P300 amplitudes than age-matched controls, and smaller P300 amplitudes for three-letter words compared to nonalphanumeric symbols. Power features (based on power analysis of 60 seconds of artifact-free EEGs of normal children aged 6 to 16) discriminated among normal, learning-disabled, and mentally retarded children in subsequent analyses (John, Prichep, Fridman, & Easton, 1988). Harter (1991) reported evidence supporting the hypothesis that poor readers have a better visual processing system for "where" than for "what."

Third, electrophysiological studies have shown that the brain responds differently to orthographic and phonological tasks. For example, Sanquist, Rohrbaugh, Syndulko, and Lindsley (1980) required subjects to match words on the basis of phonological, semantic, or orthographic information. A component centered around 500 msec discriminated match from no-match conditions, whereas a peak in the region of 300 msec discriminated the orthographic from the phonemic and semantic comparisons. Kramer and Donchin (1987) found the greatest increase in the N200 ERP component when orthography and phonology of the tokens did not match, a smaller increase when a mismatch occurred in only one of these dimensions, and the smallest increase when tokens matched on both dimensions. Thus, at one level orthographic and phonological processes may contribute independently to reading, even though at another level they function in concert in the functional reading system.

Unfortunately, few studies have explored the potential of electrophysiology for mapping how brain function changes as a result of learning, particularly in individual children. Exceptions are Andrews (1985), Dunn, Van Dyke, and Hill (1991), and Molfese, Morse, and Peters (1990). For example, Molfese et al. (1990) compared ERP waveforms prior to word training in six infants and ERP waveforms subsequent to training. The positive peaks were markedly longer for all posttest ERPs than for pretest ERPs in both the left and right hemispheres.

Another potential application of electrophysiology is predicting children at risk for reading or writing disability during the preschool years so that intervention can begin early to prevent problems during the school years. Such an approach has been applied successfully to predicting oral language skills during the preschool years from electrophysiological indices in newborn infants. Molfese and Molfese (1985) recorded auditory evoked responses (AERs) from newborn infants, which predicted high versus low language development at age 3. They are currently testing these same children to determine if AERs in newborns predict reading at age 8. If they do, families with a history of dyslexia could have their newborns tested to find out if they are at risk, and intervention to prevent phonological problems could take place in the preschool years.

Spatial and Temporal Processes

Lovegrove (1993) and Lovegrove, Martin, and Slaghuis (1986) reported *behavioral evidence* for a *low-level* deficit in the transient but not the sustained visual system of many, but not all, disabled readers. The visual system has two parallel pathways: a *sustained system,* which is most sensitive to *high spatial* frequencies, *low temporal* frequencies, and *slow* transmission times, and a *transient system,* which is most sensitive to *low spatial* frequencies, *high temporal* frequencies, and *fast* transmission times.

Three kinds of behavioral evidence show that reading disabled children and adolescents have a deficient transient system. First, disabled readers have a different pattern of temporal processing across spatial frequencies than do abled readers on visible-persistence tasks. Second, disabled readers differ from abled readers at low spatial but not high spatial frequencies on measures of pattern-contrast specificity. Third, the greatest differences between disabled and abled readers is at the higher temporal frequencies on measures of temporal-contrast sensitivity.

Lubs et al. (1991) argued that both the sustained and transient systems are involved in reading and found that adult dyslexics were slower in responding on the sustained visual channels. The difference between their results and those of Lovegrove et al. (1986) may be related to developmental differences between child/adolescent samples and adult samples. Lubs et al. also speculated that the temporal processing deficit of dyslexics may affect the auditory speech system, as Tallal (1980) found, as well as the visual system.

Livingstone, Rosen, Drislane, and Galaburda (1991) reported electrophysiological and cytoarchitectonic evidence for dyslexics and controls that supports the hypothesis of Lovegrove et al. (1986) that developmental dyslexics have a deficit in the transient visual system. Dyslexics showed normal responses to slow- or high-contrast stimuli (processed by the slow or sustained system), but diminished visual evoked responses to rapid low-contrast stimuli (processed by the fast or transient system). Abnormalities were found in the brains of dyslexics in the magnocellular pathways used for fast visual processing, but not in the parvocellular pathways used for slow visual processing.

Other research points to *temporal deficits* in motor coordination, naming, and reading latencies of dyslexics. Wolff, Cohen, and Drake (1984) reported evidence that developmental dyslexics have deficits in speed-timing mechanisms that affect perception and memory for sequential information and coordinated action. Wolf and Goodglass (1986) noted that most disabled readers in a longitudinal study of reading development had rate problems on naming and reading latency tasks. Bowers and Swanson (1991) showed that naming speed and phonological awareness contributed independent variance to reading skill. Lovett (1987) demonstrated that some developmental dyslexics are accuracy-disabled in all aspects of reading, whereas others are only rate-disabled and have age-appropriate word recognition skill. These findings, along with those of Tallal (1980) for the auditory processing system, provide converging evidence that temporal mechanisms play a role in reading. (Also see Tallal, Galaburda, Llinás, & von Euler, 1993.)

Orthography and Phonology

A clear consensus exists among reading researchers that visual perception and visual memory (Vellutino, 1979a) and high-level visual processes (Lovegrove et al., 1986) do not differentiate poor versus good readers. However, children who mix up letter order in words may have inefficiencies in processing *orthographic* information, which cannot be equated with an organically based deficit in visual perception, as Orton had proposed (Vellutino, 1979b). Thus a distinction must be made between orthography, which involves visual representations specific to written words, and visual-spatial processing in general, which is not specific to written words (Berninger, 1991). Low-level deficits in the fast visual system discussed above may affect the orthographic processing of printed words more than visual/spatial processing of pictures or three-dimensional objects.

Different brain structures and functions are involved in processing visible language (orthography) than are involved in processing nonlinguistic visual stimuli. Several studies discussed earlier in this chapter lead to that conclusion: the blood-flow studies of Ingvar (1983), the PET studies of Petersen and colleagues (1989, 1990), and the electrophysiological study of Holcomb and colleagues (1985). In addition, clinicopathological and developmental studies provide further support for this conclusion.

As a result of disease or stroke, adult patients can lose their ability to read without losing their visual abilities in general. They can copy and spell words without being able to read them through the *eye*, but can read them through the *ear* by naming words the examiner spells orally, or through the *hand* by naming words as they palpate letter blocks in the hand (Geschwind, 1985). In this visual-verbal disconnection syndrome, the left visual cortex and splenium of the corpus callosum cut off the rest of the visual cortex from the language areas. Although their visual acuity is normal, these patients lose the ability to read words and name colors but do not lose their visual-perceptual, conversational, and object-naming abilities (Denckla & Rudel, 1976).

In developing children, naming graphological symbols (letters and digits) develops independently of naming nongraphological symbols (Wolf, Bally, & Morris, 1986). Performance scale subtests of the Wechsler Intelligence Scale for Children-Revised, which require visual/spatial processing of nonverbal visual stimuli such as pictures and abstract forms, did not emerge in multiple regressions based on a multivariate psychometric battery as predictors of reading real words or nonwords in primary or middle school students (Vellutino, Scanlon, & Tanzman, 1991). Within age groups, performance on a visual recognition task using a novel alphabet that cannot be processed with existing orthographic coding procedures did not discriminate among impaired, average, or good readers (Vellutino, Scanlon, & Tanzman, 1991). This result is not surprising, given Petersen et al.'s (1991) finding that different brain areas process strings of letterlike symbols than process real words or nonwords.

Although there is a clear consensus that phonology is important in learning to read (Brady & Shankweiler, 1991), much remains to be learned about how the subcomponents of the phonological system develop and interrelate with components of the reading system. Evidence indicates that at least four units of phonology probably play a role: *syllable* and *phoneme* (Liberman, Shankweiler, Fischer, & Carter, 1974), *rime* (the part of the syllable that remains when the onset phonemes is [are] deleted) (Trieman, 1985), and *phonetic or name code* for whole word unit (Berninger, Proctor, DeBruyn, & Smith, 1988). The phonetic or name code contains information about segmental phones and the suprasegmental, intonational, contour-marking stress patterns for pronouncing a word.

To date, most of the research on the relationship of phonology to dyslexia has focused on phonemes and rimes. However, Black and Byng (1986) showed that some dyslexics can also have trouble with prosody (suprasegmental coding), and evidence is accumulating to indicate that both phonemic and name codes contribute to reading disorders (e.g., Berninger, 1991; Bowers & Swanson, 1991; Bowers & Wolf, 1993; Felton & Brown, 1990). Phonemic and name codes appear to be localized in different areas of the brain (Ojemann, 1991), but we know little about their functional organization and how they might connect with orthographic codes of different unit size. A specific aim of the research reported in chapter 4 was to investigate the functional organization of phonological and orthographic codes related to reading and writing.

Higher-Level Linguistic and Cognitive Processes

Relatively more attention has been given to the biological basis of low-level language and reading processes, probably because they are easier to analyze as component processes and thus may be easier to localize in the brain. For example, far more research has been directed toward word recognition skills than reading comprehension. The emphasis on word recognition may also be related to the widespread belief that dyslexia is basically a problem in reading single words. Yet teachers and clinicians know that many youngsters have problems with reading comprehension despite adequate word recognition skills. Virtually nothing is known about the structural or functional organization of the brain supporting the generative processes that Wittrock (1990) has shown are critical to reading comprehension.

Behavioral and Cognitive Pathways

Experiments of Mishkin and Appenzeller (1987) and Ungerleider and Mishkin (1982) with primates identified two contrasting visual pathways. The *cognitive pathway,* which has connections from the sensory areas to the limbic structures to the diencephalon to the prefrontal cortex, can learn schemata and structural relations in concepts and is affected by emotions. The *behavioral pathway,* which has connections from the sensory input areas and motor output areas through the striatum, can learn direct stimulus-response associations. This work is important theoretically because it suggests that both the cognitive and behavioral traditions are correct about some aspects of learning: (a) that learning depends on a system guided by knowledge and expectation as argued by the cognitivists and (b) that learning depends on automatic stimulus-response bonds as argued by behaviorists (Mishkin & Appenzeller, 1987). This work has important practical implications for learning-disabled children, some of whom have difficulty with automaticity or paired associate learning (e.g., automatic recognition of a sight vocabulary), but who may have average or better verbal reasoning skills. Other learning-disabled children (e.g., some of those scoring in the borderline range on intelligence tests) may have no difficulty with automaticity but have difficulty with higher level reasoning.

Importance of Biological Constraints in Literacy Acquisition

Many practitioners and researchers do not believe we need to understand the biological basis for reading and writing development; they believe we should focus instead on instructional and other environmental variables that we can directly manipulate. Such a view was more defensible when direct measures of brain structure and function were not available. Now that they are, it makes sense to take them into account, along with environmental variables, for three reasons.

First, the fact that there may be biological constraints at the molecular, neuronal, neural pathway, and system levels reminds us that neither teacher variables alone (such as the quality of the instructional program) or learner variables alone (such as intelligence or motivation) can account for the struggle some children face in learning to read and write. Second, the fact that biological variables constrain rather than determine learning independent of the learning environment serves as a reminder of the importance of the learning environment in fostering learning. Indeed, the research on genetic constraints suggests that the environment actually contributes somewhat more than genetics in learning to read. Third, research from a biological perspective, as reviewed in this chapter, demonstrates the involvement of *multiple brain structures* and the *normal variation* in brain structures and functions that underlie reading and writing acquisition. Reading and writing problems may be related to different biological constraints in different children. There is no single or simple explanation for why children may struggle to learn to read and write. Therefore, investigation of reading and writing acquisition at the functional level of analysis should therefore also take into account individual differences and multiple functions.

Summary

Despite definitional variations of reading/writing disorders, progress is being made in understanding the biological basis of these disorders. The heritability index for dyslexia ranges from 30 to 40 percent, indicating that there are genetic constraints on learning to read. Evidence supports both single major gene transmission on Chromosome 1, 6, or 15, and polygenetic influences in dyslexia. Extragenetic, environmental factors also play a role in learning to read. Sex differences may occur at the extremes rather than at the mean of the distribution of reading skills and may affect writing disabilities more than reading disabilities.

Neuroanatomic constraints associated with dyslexia include (a) microscopic anomalies such as disordered columns and displaced cells in the cerebral cortex, (b) symmetry or reversed asymmetry of structures in the temporal and frontal lobes, (c) missing or multiple gyri (peaks in the folds of the cerebral cortex), and (d) bilateral anomalies. Structural/functional constraints related to components of reading occur throughout the cortex; in the occipital, temporal, frontal, and occipital lobes; and possibly in subcortical structures as well. Biological research has documented the considerable normal variation in brain structures related to reading. Neuroanatomical anomalies are risk factors rather than causal factors in learning to read.

Conclusions about which brain systems are activated during reading depend to some extent on the method used. However, converging evidence indicates that (a) different parts of the brain are activated by visual words (orthography) than by nonlinguistic visual stimuli, (b) and different parts of the brain are activated by auditory words (phonology) than by nonlinguistic auditory stimuli, and (c) different parts of the brain are activated by visual words (orthographic patterns) than by auditory words (phonological patterns). Temporal mechanisms play a role in reading acquisition; dyslexics may have deficits in fast visual processing, speed of motor coordination, and/or speed of naming.

3

Educational Constraints on Reading and Writing Acquisition

As a morphologist, it may sound funny for me to say this, but ultimately the important thing is the function not the structure . . . the structure of the brain does change and . . . such changes occur in response to learning and other environmental factors. . . . But, the important thing is outcome. In some cases who have gotten remediation they have gotten better and in other cases they have not. . . . So the important thing to show in fact is that a particular remediation program, whether it is educational, psychological, or medical works. The rest is less important. It is interesting but not necessarily important.

–Albert Galaburda (1991, p. 173)

Outline

Teacher Training

Certain features of preservice teacher training provide constraints on how and how well children learn to read and write. These include the nature and amount of training teachers receive that is specific to reading and writing, grounded in the basic science foundations of learning and development, and geared to dealing with diversity in the classroom.

Insufficient Course Work Specific to Reading and Writing

Nolen, McCutchen, and Berninger (1990) surveyed the state departments that certify teachers to work in the public schools in each of the 50 states in the United States. In some cases states require specific courses, but in other cases states approve programs, which in turn require specific courses. Only 29 states required prospective elementary school teachers to take any academic coursework in reading;

typically, only one or two courses were required. Likewise, only one or two courses in reading tend to be required by approved programs. None of the states required a course in teaching writing for certification of elementary teachers.

This level of training seems inadequate if we expect teachers to be able to (a) analyze why each child in the classroom may be struggling to learn to read and write or is underachieving relative to ability, and (b) individualize instruction to optimize reading and writing achievement for all students. This level of training for educators also seems alarmingly low compared with the level of training required for physicians. Considering that the mind is as complex as the body, professionals entrusted with development of the mind also need extensive training to be prepared for the enormous challenges they will face. In general, student teaching, the equivalent of an internship, does not provide in-depth experience in diagnosing reading and writing problems and designing alternative interventions tailored to individual children. In-service workshops provide continuing education for teachers but do not eliminate the need for better preservice training. Few of us would want to be operated on by a physician with two courses in surgery and a smattering of continuing education courses. Yet that is the equivalent of what the educators of our children's minds are typically given in regard to reading and writing.

Insufficient Course Work in Basic Science Foundations of Learning and Development

Earlier in this century medical education faced problems similar to those facing teacher education today (Goodlad, 1990). Training of physicians was oriented toward treatment of patients rather than to a conceptual understanding of the disease and healing process. To remedy this situation, Flexner (1910) recommended to the Carnegie Foundation for the Advancement of Teaching that medical education include course work in the basic sciences such as biology and chemistry. His recommendations, which were followed, have been credited with the subsequent improved effectiveness of medical practice, for example, in the control of infectious diseases.

Like medicine at the beginning of the twentieth century, education at the end of the twentieth century is oriented toward practice rather than to a conceptual framework for practice. As medicine benefited from the introduction of basic science training in biology and chemistry, education would benefit from the introduction of basic science training in developmental psychology, cognitive science, and neuroscience. If such courses were required in teacher preparation programs, the effectiveness of educational practice would be improved, because teachers would have a better conceptual understanding of the multiple factors at different levels of analysis that can constrain the learning process. They would learn to analyze learning problems within a theoretical framework of the normal reading and writing acquisition process, any aspect of which might break down or fail to develop normally in an individual child (see Berninger, Hart, Abbott, & Karvosky, 1992).

Insufficient Preparation for Dealing with Individual Differences and Cultural Diversity

Teachers are also not being prepared to deal with the normal variation, whether of constitutional and/or cultural origin, that children bring to the task of learning to read and write. Lyon, Vaasen, and Toomey (1989) surveyed 440 teachers, of whom 93 percent reported no undergraduate training and 82 percent reported no graduate training in dealing with diversity among students. As long as teachers are primarily being trained to ''teach to the group'' and not to accommodate individual differences within the group, the unique needs of individual children will continue to be unmet. Although individualization of learning is a challenge, it is a challenge that can be met if teachers are trained in techniques for individualizing instruction, learning activities, behavioral management, assignments, and evaluation.

Implications for Learning Disabilities

We cannot assume that children who fail to learn at expected levels (even though other children in the classroom do learn at expected levels) necessarily have a learning disability of constitutional origin. Teachers may simply be unprepared to deal with the needs of individual learners (Berninger & Abbott, in press). At the same time, this lack of adequate preparation is not a reflection on the teachers themselves. Many dedicated teachers self-educate themselves or take additional course work at the graduate level and do an exemplary job. The fact that not all teachers are adequately prepared is a professional issue that teacher training institutions and state departments that certify teachers must face together (Nolen et al., 1990) if schools are to *evolve* to meet the needs of all individuals in an increasingly technological society (see Preface).

Teachers' External Attributions for Students' Failure

In an *internal* attribution, people believe their success or failure is the result of their *own* actions, whereas in an *external* attribution, people believe their success or failure is the result of *others'* actions (Rotter, 1966). Teachers tend to make internal attributions when students succeed, crediting their own teaching ability, but to make external attributions when students fail, blaming student characteristics such as low IQ or poor motivation (Johnson, Feigenbaum, & Weiby, 1964) or family characteristics. On the other hand, observers tend to show the opposite pattern of attributions—they blame teachers when students fail, but credit the students when the students succeed (Beckman, 1970).

External attributions about school failure can constrain learning in two ways. First, when made by teachers, such attributions can direct their attention away from factors over which they have control—their own teaching behaviors—to factors over which they have no control, such as the child's IQ or family. Second, when made by others, such as parents or the public, external attributions inappropriately place the entire responsibility for learning on teachers. The truth lies in between; both teaching behaviors and child characteristics can contribute to school failure or success.

The aim of the research reported in chapters 4 through 7 is to identify child characteristics other than IQ and motivation that constrain reading and writing acquisition, namely the developmental skills children bring to the task of learning to read and write. Until now, these developmental skills have generally not been systematically considered in explaining either failure or success in learning to read and write. To the extent that these developmental skills can be identified, teachers may be able to modify their instructional behaviors to accommodate individual differences in these developmental skills. To the extent that teachers do so, either school failure or school success can be attributed to an interaction between internal and external causality.

Misconceptions About the Role of Maturation in Learning

The nativist view, popularized by Gesell (e.g., Gesell, 1925, 1928), claims that behavior is genetically determined, and one must wait for biologically preprogrammed maturation time tables to unfold; specific instructional experiences cannot alter this maturational timetable. Nativist views, which are the ultimate in external attributions of causality, are extremely popular among teachers, especially in the primary grades. The nativist view has led to two widespread educational practices: (a) holding children out of school for an extra year so they can "mature" and be more ready for educational instruction when they are older, and (b) repeating children in a grade so they can be more mature. In this section, research evidence for the validity of these two practices is reviewed. Keep in mind when evaluating this evidence that basic research on extragenetic factors discussed in chapter 2 does not support the nativist view.

Morrison's School Cut-Off Studies

Schools set arbitrary cut-off dates for school entrance based on birthdays. Morrison (1991) and Morrison, Smith, and Dow (1992) capitalized on this "natural experiment" to compare the effects of schooling experience (a group who just made the cutoff for school entrance) and experience not related to formal schooling (a comparable group who just missed the cutoff for school entrance). These groups did not differ significantly in IQ or age (about one month difference) or in achievement levels in specific skills at the onset of the experiment.

These investigators compared those who just met or just missed the cutoff on pretests given at the beginning of first grade or kindergarten, respectively, on posttests given at the beginning of second or first grade, respectively, and on follow-up tests given at the beginning of third or second grade, respectively. Schooling effects were found in that the group who just made the cutoff and was exposed earlier to formal reading instruction performed better in reading and short-term memory skills than did the group who just missed the cutoff and had to wait a year for formal reading instruction. Both groups improved in phonemic skills, but the group who just made the cutoff and had earlier instruction in reading made relatively greater gains. The group who just missed the cutoff did not make greater gains in phonemic analysis or reading when they were in first grade and older (and presumably more mature) than did the group who just made the cutoff and were younger (and presumably less mature) when they were in first grade. Thus, formal instruction in reading facilitated the development of reading and reading-related skills in younger, less mature students. Delaying entrance to school so that a child is older when exposed to formal reading instruction did not facilitate development of reading and reading-related skills.

Despite claims in the literature that the youngest children in a class are at greater risk for learning problems, a number of studies have shown that age is not a major predictor of either earlier or later school success (Morrison & McMahon, 1992). For example, Morrison and McMahon showed that younger first graders (who just made the cutoff), as a group, made normal progress in reading during first grade and did not differ significantly from older first graders, as a group, in the degree of reading improvement over the course of first grade. They also showed that entrance age per se is not a good predictor of academic achievement or risk.

Thus, the nativist or maturationalist view that younger children are not as developmentally ready as older children in a grade to benefit from formal schooling is not supported by empirical research. The practice of delaying entry to school for a year so that children will be older constrains the learning process by delaying exposure to specific instructional experiences that in fact would promote academic learning sooner.

Controlled Research on Retention

Retaining a child in a grade is a very popular educational practice for dealing with not only low academic achievement but also social immaturity. The extent to which it is practiced varies from school to school, but in the United States, 15 to 19 percent of children repeat at least one grade, in contrast to Japan, where less than 1 percent of children repeat a grade. Certain groups are more likely to repeat than others: boys, minorities, poor children, those with late birthdays, and short children. Retention is especially popular with first grade teachers who evaluate its effectiveness on personal anecdotal evidence rather than research with control groups. Research touting the beneficial effects of retention suffers from serious design problems such as lack of a control group (Overman, 1986). Without a control group of children who are promoted, it is not possible to evaluate what progress might have been made had the retained child been promoted. Teachers who retain children often have no knowledge of the child's future achievement and socioemotional adjustment later in schooling. Retention has financial costs for school systems, increasing the cost of educating a student by 8 percent, and emotional costs to students, often reaching far beyond the year that the grade was repeated. (See Carstens, 1985; Smith & Shepard, 1987, 1988, for further discussion of the above issues.)

In a meta-analysis of research on retention using control groups, Holmes and Matthews (1984) compared effect sizes across studies. Promoted children scored, on the average, 0.34 to 0.38 standard deviation units higher than retained children on a variety of outcome measures. Academic achievement, personal adjustment, and attitude toward school were more positive for promoted than retained students. Some children made progress during the year in which they repeated a grade, but even when they did, they did not progress as much as similar children who were promoted. There is no evidence that a retained child is at the top or middle of the class during the repeated year or in subsequent years. Students who received remedial instruction made greater gains than either the promoted or retained students who received no special help. Transitional (pre-first grade) programs are no more successful than retention (Smith & Shepard, 1988). Despite teachers' perceptions that children are not emotionally upset by being removed from age-mates and singled out as having failed, these children do feel shame and experience emotional problems (Smith & Shepard, 1988). Next to blindness and death of a parent, children rated the thought of retention the most stressful thing that could happen to them (Byrnes & Yamamoto, 1984).

A task force of the National Association of School Psychologists (NASP) reviewed the growing body of research on retention. NASP (1988) issued a position statement that effectiveness of retention is not substantiated by sound research and can even be harmful. NASP encourages the use of alternative interventions rather than retention.

Most often children are retained without the benefit of a thorough diagnostic evaluation of why they did not succeed during the past school year. Thus, retention can constrain the learning process by prolonging exposure to the same curriculum that was ineffective the first time and by failing to identify the exact nature of a child's learning problems.

Alternatives to Grade Retention

Three approaches offer viable alternatives to grade retention: (a) promotion with special services, (b) early intervention and prevention, and (c) development of teachers' tolerance and appreciation of diversity. Special services can take the form of tutoring, summer school, or special education. Tutoring and summer school are more effective and less costly than retention (Smith & Shepard, 1988). Despite fears that special education will adversely label children as different, learning-disabled children who receive special education resource services do not differ significantly from average or high achieving students in self-concept or peer acceptance (Vaughan, Haager, Hogan, & Kouzekanani, 1992).

Early diagnosis, regardless of how much subsequent remediation a student receives, is associated with better reading performance five years later (Muehl & Forell, 1973). Unfortunately, children with reading or writing problems often are not referred for evaluation until the intermediate grades after years of failure (Satz, Taylor, Friel, & Fletcher, 1978). Early, intensive, and continuing intervention during the primary grades has been shown to keep student achievement within normal limits even in high-risk urban schools (Slavin, Madden, Karweit, Dolen, Wasik, Shaw, Mainzer, & Haxby, 1991). One exemplary program that makes ample use of individual tutoring and has impressive results is "Success for All," developed by Slavin, Madden, Karweit, Livermon, & Dolan, (1990). Another exemplary program is "Reading Recovery," which was developed by Clay (1985) in New Zealand and has been disseminated and evaluated in the United States by a group at Ohio State University (Pinnell, 1989; Pinnell, Fried, & Estice, 1990). The intent of "Reading Recovery" is to provide early, intensive individualized tutoring during the first year of reading instruction to prevent reading failure from the beginning. Results to date show that it is more effective than Chapter 1 remedial services offered in the public schools (Pinnell, Lyons, DeFord, Bryk, & Seltzer, 1991).

Both "Success for All" and "Reading Recovery" are cutting-edge instructional intervention programs, which may revolutionize the way educators view learning disability—as a condition that can be prevented (Clay, 1987) and that is not necessarily programmed into the genes. However, although most children who participate in the "Success for All" or "Reading Recovery" programs improve, not all do. For example, 10 to 20 percent of the lowest 20 percent of first graders who are tutored cannot be successfully discontinued from the programs (Slavin et al., 1991), suggesting that about 2 to 4 percent of the first grade population may have biologically constrained reading problems. As Slavin et al. (1991) point out, an unanswered question is whether some children may require instruction specific to neurological deficits as well as academic tutoring. It is this question that the intervention research discussed in chapter 7 is trying to address.

One of the reasons that teachers favor retention is that they desire more homogeneous classrooms. They believe it is easier to teach and to be held accountable for their students' achievement when everyone is at the same level. Three reasons explain why such homogeneity is probably more fantasy than fact. First, it is impossible for every child to be achieving on grade level. Test statistics are designed so that grade level is the score above and below which 50 percent of children at that grade level fall. Second, given the findings reported in chapters 4 through 7, normal variation occurs within and among developmental domains at each grade level. Homogeneity does not exist in nature. Third, expert teachers can and do learn to manage and even value the heterogeneity within a class. Smith and Shepard (1988) found that teachers who learned to handle diversity in the classroom were the ones who did not retain children.

Thus, implementing these above alternatives to retention can constrain the learning process in a positive way—by remediating or preventing school failure. However, little research to date on reading and writing acquisition has systematically taken into account a *child's school history,* particularly whether the child was retained, received early intervention/prevention or special education services, or attended summer school, or the *teacher's instructional approach and philosophy for handling diversity.* A child's history of success and failure and the teacher's instructional approach and philosophy exert constraints on learning just as much as the brain structures and functions of the learner do.

Pitfalls of Learning in Groups

Instruction is normally delivered in large groups, with one teacher and twenty to thirty students, or in small groups, with one teacher working with a subset of the larger group. In either arrangement, students may not be maximally engaged in the task at hand. Students may look as though they are paying attention when indeed they are not, or they may look as though they are not paying attention when indeed they are. The only way to know for sure is to ask a question about what was just said to see if the student can answer it correctly. Of course, in a group it is not possible to query every student simultaneously to secure this kind of feedback. Also, small-group instruction, which allows students to respond more frequently, means that other children must work independently for a portion of the school day. Some children may not be focused on the task at hand when working without direct teacher supervision. In contrast, one-to-one tutorials allow the student to respond more frequently during instruction and to obtain more practice of skills with immediate teacher feedback. Group instruction therefore constrains the kind of feedback teachers can give and the amount of time in which a student can actively respond to the teacher and practice skills.

Time-Off Task

Researchers have examined the amount of time during a typical school day in which students are actively engaged in learning, as opposed to passive listening. The general conclusion is that children spend only a small part of the day actively engaged in academic tasks; however, there are individual differences in time engaged in academic tasks, and the amount of academic-engaged time is often strongly and positively correlated with academic achievement (Graden, Thurlow, & Ysseldyke, 1983). For example, in one carefully done behavioral study, of the 390-minute school day, third- and fourth-grade students received 180 minutes of academic instruction, and were engaged in academically responding for an average of 45 minutes, of which an average of 26 minutes involved inappropriate responding. On the average they wrote for 29 minutes, read silently for 10 minutes, and read aloud for less than 1 minute (Graden et al., 1983).

In a related study, Thurlow, Graden, Ysseldyke, and Algozzine (1984) studied the amount of time second-grade students actually practiced reading. In the 240 minutes of scheduled reading time, students actually read orally or silently 10 to 12 minutes. Low-group students engaged in more reading aloud than did those in middle or high reading groups, but still for only about 2½ minutes per day. Individuals differed in amount of practice, with silent reading ranging from 36 seconds to 26 minutes, and oral reading ranging from 0 to 8 minutes daily. These investigators credited the Reverend Jesse Jackson with recognizing the importance of practice in learning:

"We keep saying that Johnny can't read because he's deprived, because he's hungry, because he's discriminated against. We say that Johnny can't read because his daddy is not in the home. Well, Johnny learns to play basketball without daddy. We do best what we do most, and for many of our children that is playing ball. One of the reasons Johnny does not read well is that Johnny doesn't practice reading" (Quoted in Raspberry, 1976).

The Matthew Effect

Biemiller (1977–1978) reported data showing that at the first grade level, good readers get more practice than poor readers during a reading session. In October the most able and average groups read an average of 12.2 and 11.9 words, respectively. In January the most able groups read an average of 51.9 words, the average groups read an average of 25.8 words, and the least able groups read an average of 11.5 words. In April the most able groups read an average of 81.4 words, the average groups read an average of 72.3 words, and the least able groups read an average of 31.6 words. Biemiller attributed the fewer words read by the lower groups to their slower reading speed and to teachers shortening lessons to avoid the difficulty of reading for low-achieving students.

Allington (1984) analyzed teacher logs selected from seven states for good and poor readers in grades 1, 3, and 5 and found that good and poor reading groups did not differ in the number of words read orally, but differed significantly in the number of words read silently, with good readers reading more. He also found that at every grade level good readers completed more contextual reading than did poor readers during the reading instruction session.

Although the studies above may differ in some details, they are all consistent with the notion that good readers become better readers because they continue to get practice, whereas poor readers may continue to be poor readers because of insufficient practice. Walberg and Tsai (1983) and Stanovich (1986) call this educational phenomenon of the rich getting richer and the poor getting poorer "the Matthew effect," based on a verse in the Gospel According to Matthew in the Bible.

Complex Relationship of Learning to Teaching

Educational psychologists differentiate between teaching—what the teacher does—and learning—what the student may or may not do in response to teaching. For example, a theoretical framework proposed by Weinstein and Mayer (1986) distinguishes among (a) teacher characteristics, (b) teaching strategies, (c) learner characteristics, (d) learning strategies, (e) internal cognitive processes during learning, (f) learning outcomes, and (g) performance or demonstration of learning on formal tests. It follows, then, that teaching does not determine learning independent of the learner's strategies and characteristics, both of which can constrain the learning process.

Constructive Processes of the Learner

Learning is no longer viewed as a passive process of storing information the teacher presents; rather, the learner is an active participant in the teaching-learning process (Weinstein & Mayer, 1986) who constructs meanings and plans of actions (Wittrock, in press). Teaching affects achievement only indirectly through student thought processes; teaching affects students' thought processes, which in turn mediate learning and achievement (Wittrock, 1986). Meaning is not given to students by teachers. Students must generate meaning based on relations among concepts in incoming information and between that incoming information and prior information and concepts (Wittrock, in press). Thus, learner strategies—the ability to generate relations among concepts and construct meaning—will constrain the learning process.

Developmental Skills Students Bring to Learning

One of the reasons aptitude-treatment interaction (ATI) research (see Corno & Snow, 1986) has not been more successful in identifying effective instructional strategies for particular aptitudes may be that aptitude has been treated as a global construct rather than a profile of abilities. An alternative approach to aptitude is to identify developmental domains that impact on school learning and then describe profiles of relative development across these domains for each individual (see Berninger & Abbott, in press, table 1). With this ultimate goal in mind, the aim of the research reported in chapters 4 through 6 was to identify relevant developmental domains so that assessment and remediation of reading and writing disabilities, as discussed in chapter 7, can be related to an individual's profile across these developmental domains. Learner characteristics, such as the developmental skills students bring to the task of learning to read and write, can constrain the learning process.

The Zebra Syndrome: Viewing Instructional Issues as Black and White

Over the past three hundred years a number of methods of reading instruction have been proposed, including the alphabet (ABC) method, the phonic method, the phonogram (word family method), the whole word (also known as sight vocabulary or look-say) method, and the sentence method (for a history of reading instruction, see Aaron & Joshi, 1992; Mills, 1970; for a description of these methods see Glossary). Which of these methods is in vogue changes from time to time. What does not change is the tendency to think about the best method in terms of "either/or" logic rather than "both/and" logic. For example, the current controversy is over which approach is better—whole language, which is a *meaning-based* approach that teaches the whole word method for word recognition, or phonics, which is a *sound-based* approach that teaches decoding for word recognition. This kind of black and white thinking, which is referred to as the zebra syndrome, pits alternative methods against each other rather than considering how these alternatives might be integrated within an instructional model. A supreme example of the zebra syndrome, which received wide publicity, was Flesch's (1979) thesis that Johnny can't read because meaning-based instruction is used in the schools. To remedy reading problems Flesch offered a simple solution: phonics and more phonics. A less known but more insightful analysis is why Rudolph can't read (Sebesta, 1981), which provides a more balanced view—that good reading instruction uses a variety of methods including those based on meaning and sound.

The zebra syndrome, with its either/or logic, constrains learning because students are at the mercy of the way the pendulum of currently favored reading methods is swinging when they are in elementary school. Students are also at the mercy of the personal philosophy of their teachers about reading instruction, which is generally formed on the basis of their own experience in learning to read and on their preservice undergraduate training. Some teachers may have had trouble learning phonics because of problems in phonemic awareness (P. Lindamood, personal communication, May 1990); for them reading may be a psycholinguistic guessing game (Goodman, 1976) and they present it as such to their students. Other teachers, who learned to read with phonics drills, may think that every child needs these drills to learn to read. Teacher trainers in academics are just as likely as practitioners in the schools to suffer from the zebra syndrome and present a black and white view of how to teach reading. Rarely are prospective teachers taught how to incorporate the best elements of both a whole language and a code approach or how to individualize a reading program to meet the unique profile of developmental skills of an individual learner.

Regular Education: Teaching May Not Be Directed to All Levels of Language

Cases in our clinic illustrate how instruction that focuses on one component of reading at the expense of other components can interact with learner characteristics. Assessment showed that one child had a reliable connection for whole printed words and whole spoken words but not for letters and phonemes; hence, at the time of the assessment he could learn better with a whole word than a phonic approach (see chapter 4); however, his instruction at school consisted solely of phonics instruction with words out of sentence context. Assessment showed that another child had a reliable connection for letters and phonemes but not for whole printed and whole spoken words; hence, at the time of assessment he could learn better with a phonic than a whole word approach (see chapter 4); however, his instruction at

TABLE 3.1 Teaching to All Levels of Oral and Written Language

I. **Sublexical Level** (smaller than the word)
   A. Phonics—learning letters and their corresponding sounds in isolation
   B. Word Families—learning the frequent phonograms or syllable patterns of written and spoken language (e.g., -at, -en, -in, -op, -ug)

II. **Lexical Level** (word units)
   A. Sight words (learn to read through look-say or whole word method, or learn to spell through memorization)
   B. Vocabulary meaning (semantic features and definitions of words in isolation)

III. **Translexical Level** (linguistic units larger than the single word)
   A. Comprehension and production of syntactic structures within an utterance or a sentence
   B. Comprehension and production of discourse structures larger than the single utterance or sentence in conversation, drama, poetry, narratives, essays, etc.

school consisted solely of whole language instruction with connected text and no explicit instruction in word attack skills. The profiles of developmental skills related to reading were mismatched with the instructional program for both of these boys. Both children would have had a better match between learner characteristics and instructional strategy if they could have changed places. Thus, the match of learning profile and instructional program may depend as much on luck as a lottery does.

Mismatches such as these could be avoided if teachers routinely taught reading and writing within the context of an instructional model that included instruction directed toward all levels of language. On the basis of basic research on language processes from a biological perspective, these levels should include *phonological* (sound), *lexical* (whole word), *syntactical* (grammatical structures), *semantic,* (meaning for single words or combination of words) (Shankweiler & Crain, 1986) as well as *discourse* (Frederiksen, 1979) processes. Table 3.1 outlines the levels of language to which instruction should be directed. The importance of teaching to all levels of language will be elaborated in chapter 7.

Special Education: Individualized Educational Plans May Not Be Individualized

Schools in the United States are required by federal law to identify children with learning disabilities and to write and implement individualized educational plans (IEPs). Often these IEPs are implemented in special education resource rooms, a pull-out program that provides remediation services, for example, for 30 minutes to 2 hours daily. Although the idea of individualized education plans may seem ideal, IEPs do not ensure that appropriate individualized instruction will be provided. Haynes and Jenkins (1986) conducted a large-scale field study of reading instruction in special education resource room programs. They found that (a) the nature of the reading instruction varied considerably across programs and was not linked systematically to students' characteristics, (b) remarkably low amounts of reading instruction occurred, and (c) instructional process variables did not seem to be related to student achievement. Jenkins, Pious, and Peterson (1988) documented that services for dealing with individual differences in learning among low achieving students are fragmented in public schools. One reason for this fragmentation is the lack of a well-articulated and validated theoretical framework for linking assessment of individual differences in learning with instructional interventions.

Research Support for Teaching to Multiple Levels of Oral and Written Language

Over the years, much research has pitted one method of reading instruction against another. These studies are generally not helpful for three reasons.

First, it is difficult to generalize from studies comparing methods independent of teacher characteristics, which are rarely reported. Chall and Feldman (1966) showed that teachers who follow a particular method vary considerably in how they implement that method, and there can be considerable discrepancy between what teachers say they use and what observation shows they actually use. Stahl (1992), for example, has shown that educators mean many different things by phonics instruction, and phonics instruction can be good or bad. The same method may be implemented more effectively when it is new and teachers are enthusiastic about it than when it is established and routinized (Pinnell, 1989).

Second, research on methods of reading instruction usually do not make sense apart from historical context, that is, the methods that were being used at a particular time. For example, at a time when meaning-first methods prevailed, Chall (1965) reviewed the effectiveness of meaning-first and sound coding-first methods of reading instruction up to the fourth grade. Based on empirical evidence, she concluded that code-methods, which teach the alphabetic principle of letter-sound correspondence, were superior to meaning-based methods, at least in beginning reading. However, she predicted astutely that educational practice would dictate what the conclusion might be in the future. For example, if phonics instruction were overused or used inappropriately (e.g., not matching the nature of phonics instruction with the developmental reading level of the student), she predicted that ''. . . we will be confronted in about ten or twenty years with . . . the 'natural' approach—one that teaches 'whole words' and emphasizes 'reading for meaning and appreciation' at the very beginning.'' She correctly predicted both the subsequent inappropriate use of phonics (e.g., Stahl, 1992) and the current whole language movement.

Third, studies comparing teaching methods do not account for learner characteristics. For example, Traweek, Cartwright, and Berninger (1992) tested and confirmed the hypothesis that individual differences in orthographic and phonological coding were a significant predictor of reading achievement outcome at the end of first grade, but the instructional program per se was not. Presumably, children with problems in orthographic and/or phonological coding had trouble abstracting letter-sound correspondences inductively from experience with whole words in whole language programs, and had trouble applying rules of letter-sound correspondence deductively in phonics programs.

Four lines of research have provided empirical support for inclusion of multiple methods aimed at different levels of language in teaching reading or remediating reading problems. First, Vellutino and Scanlon (1987) compared experimental analogues of phonics (subword level of alphabet mapping), sight words (whole word level), and both phonics and sight words. In most cases, children who received both treatments, whether they were good or poor second- or sixth-grade readers, performed better than those who received only one treatment.

Second, Lovett and colleagues, in an ongoing research program, have drawn upon a variety of intervention strategies ranging from letter-phoneme regularities and spelling patterns at the sublexical or subword level to whole word approaches for exception words at the lexical level to syntactic and semantic contexts at the translexical or transword level. For example, Lovett, Ransby, Hardwick, Johns, and Donaldson (1989) found that both word recognition and decoding training (lexical and sublexical levels) and oral and written language training (lexical and translexical levels) resulted in greater improvement in word recognition skills than did classroom survival skills, but the word recognition and decoding training resulted in item-specific learning rather than gains in letter-sound knowledge. Lovett (1991) speculated that prior training in phonological awareness is needed to abstract and transfer letter-sound knowledge.

Lovett, Ransby, and Barron (1988) compared the effects of three treatments in *accuracy-disabled* readers who were achieving at least 1.5 years below grade level and *rate-disabled* readers who were age-appropriate in word recognition but not in reading speed. The first treatment stressed phonological skills and rapid naming of printed words in isolation. The second treatment stressed higher level language skills, words in context, and semantic and syntactic units larger than the single word. The third treatment involved a contact control group, which was given comparable individual attention without any reading instruction; instead, they were taught study skills and organizing strategies. Training in word recognition and decoding (lexical and sublexical levels) had a relative advantage for both accuracy- and rate-disabled students, but training in oral and written language at the lexical and translexical levels benefited the rate-disabled children only.

Third, Olson and colleagues, in an ongoing research program, have shown that feedback from a variety of levels of segmentation at the word and subword levels can be effective in improving word recognition. They developed a computerized system that provides synthetic speech feedback for words in which corresponding orthographic segments of varying size are highlighted: whole word, syllable, subsyllable, and letter. In a study using only single words, the onset/rime segmentation (e.g., d/ish) showed an advantage over postvowel segmentation (e.g., di/sh) (Wise, Olson, & Trieman, 1990). In another study using only single words, feedback for the whole word (e.g., reader) and syllable (e.g., read/er) was more helpful than feedback for grapheme-phoneme correspondence (e.g., r/ea/d/er) (Wise, 1987, 1991). In long-term training studies with connected text, computer feedback in general resulted in about twice the gains as a control condition without any feedback, but pretest-posttest gains in number of words read correctly was greatest for subsyllable feedback (onset/rime) and next greatest for whole word feedback, suggesting that feedback at multiple segment sizes can be helpful (Wise, Olson, Anstatt, Andrews, Terjak, Schneider, Kostuch, & Kriho, 1989).

Fourth, in addition to studies of instructional methods, studies of readers' strategies provide support for multiple levels. Firth (1972) identified two strategies: (a) a link between a whole word letter string and stored phonetic transcription of its string, and (b) a link between a letter or letter cluster and pronunciation of subsyllables and syllables. In Firth's study, good beginning readers used both strategies, but poor beginning readers used only the first strategy.

The above research indicates that multiple levels of language at the subword, word, and transword levels play a role in reading acquisition. This research also serves as a reminder that the most appropriate question is not which method of teaching reading is the best, but rather how can a method of reading instruction be designed to facilitate all levels of language related to the various components of the reading acquisition process. To the extent that reading or writing instruction is not directed to all the relevant levels of language, instruction itself may constrain the reading and writing acquisition process.

Importance of Educational Constraints

If educational constraints such as the ones discussed in this chapter are not considered, reading and writing problems might be attributed solely to biological determinants. Biological and educational constraints are confounded in static, one-shot measures of reading and writing achievement and of developmental skills related to reading and writing. The opportunity to learn must be carefully assessed before attributing reading and writing problems solely to biological constraints (Berninger & Abbott, in press).

Summary

A number of educational constraints, in addition to the biological constraints discusssed in chapter 2, affect reading and writing acquisition: (a) insufficient teacher preparation; (b) attribution of student failure solely to learner characteristics rather than to teaching behaviors; (c) delay of entrance to school or retention of students in a grade instead of identifying the nature of the learning problem and remediating it; (d) deficits in the constructive processes of the learner, or the developmental skills learners bring to the task of reading and writing acquisition; and (e) the zebra syndrome of black and white, that is, either/or thinking, about instructional methodologies for reading and writing acquisition. Because of these potential educational constraints, one should be cautious in attributing all learning problems to biological constraints.

Research on Reading and Writing Acquisition from the Developmental Neuropsychological Perspective

4

Introduction to Part II and Multiple Connections and Multiple Procedures for Reading and Spelling Single Words

Many psychologists dream of describing minds so economically that psychology would become as simple and precise as physics. But one must not confuse reality with dreams. It was not the ambitions of the physicists that made it possible to describe so much of the world in terms of so few and simple principles; that was because of the nature of our universe. But the operations of our mind do not depend on similarly few and simple laws, because our brains have accumulated many different mechanisms over aeons of evolution. This means that psychology can never be as simple as physics, and any simple theory of mind would be bound to miss most of the 'big picture.' The science of psychology will be handicapped until we develop an overview with room for a great many smaller theories.

–Marvin Minsky (1986, p. 322)

Outline

Introduction to Part II

A major purpose of the research reported in chapters 4 through 6 was to add to current knowledge of the phenotypes for component reading and writing skills and developmental skills related to reading and writing acquisition; as discussed in chapter 2, better understanding of the phenotypes may lead to better understanding of the genotypes for reading and writing disabilities. The concepts of normal variation, levels of analysis, and multiple constraints introduced in chapter 1 and elaborated upon in chapter 2 are fundamental to this research. The model of reading acquisition in chapter 4 and the model of writing acquisition in chapter 6 reflect the perspective of the developing rather than skilled reader or writer. Just as children are not merely little adults, reading and writing acquisition are not simply scaled-down versions of skilled reading and writing.

None of the theories underlying this research are simple in the sense of being based on a single variable. Rather, the intent was to focus on developing a few smaller, but somewhat complex, theories within the context of a broader multivariate framework. Psychologists have been told for many years that parsimony (the simplest explanation) is a virtue. This research was equally concerned with not making nature simpler than it really is (see quotation at beginning of this chapter). The basic research discussed in chapters 4 through 6 has practical significance and can be applied to theory-based assessment, prevention, and remediation of reading and writing disabilities, as discussed in chapter 7. As with part I, the reader is encouraged to make ample use of the Glossary, which defines the numerous technical terms from linguistics, psychology, and education.

Limitations of Dual Route Theory for Explaining Beginning Reading

According to the dual route theory (e.g., Coltheart, 1978), there are two independent and noninteractive routes for reading single words: the direct route, which is used to read phonically irregular words, and the indirect route, which is used to read phonically regular words. The direct route is thought to involve a path between the visual code and the semantic code without intervening phonological recoding; the indirect route is thought to involve a path between the visual code and the phonological code, followed by a path from the phonological code to the semantic code (Barron, 1986). The direct route is a lexical or whole word path and is based on word-specific representations, whereas the indirect route is a sublexical or subword path based on rule-governed mechanisms (Carr & Pollatsek, 1985). The direct route is often characterized as visual, in contrast to the indirect route, which is often characterized as phonological (Doctor & Coltheart, 1980). Some have claimed that beginning readers rely on the indirect route, and skilled readers rely on the direct route (Doctor & Coltheart, 1980). This claim reflects the perspective of adult skilled readers who have the phenomenological experience of recognizing the meaning of words automatically on the basis of their visual patterns without having to consciously decode them into sound. However, Barron (1986) showed that both routes may be used in beginning reading, and Van Orden (1987) showed that the indirect, phonological route is also used in skilled reading.

There are four major problems with dual route theory in explaining beginning reading from the perspective of the developing child. First, the assumption that readers rely on a visual *or* phonological path represents disjunctive either/or logic analogous to the zebra syndrome pervading thinking about teaching methods (see chapter 3). More realistic is a both/and conjunctive logic, in which both visual and phonological representations of words play a role in how printed words become represented in memory (Berninger, Abbott, & Shurtleff, 1990). Also, considering the evidence that visual and orthographic processes are not identical (see chapter 2), an orthographic and not a visual path is involved in reading single words.

Second, the assumption that beginning readers use only an indirect, phonological route does not mesh with the well-known fact that many beginning readers readily acquire a set of sight vocabulary. This fact led Gough and Hillinger (1980) to propose that the first stage of reading acquisition is paired associate learning between distinctive visual features in the word and the word's name. Likewise, Frith (1985) proposed that the first stage of reading is logographic, in which salient graphic features are matched with a word's name.

Third, dual route theory does not take into account the multiple orthographic units on which phonological units might operate— syllables and short words (Shallice & Warrington, 1980); graphemes, consonant clusters, subsyllabic units, syllables, and morphemes (Shallice, Warrington, & McCarthy, 1983); or letter, letter cluster, and whole word units (Barron, 1986).

Fourth, it is unlikely that there are separate mechanisms for regular and irregular words. (See Berninger, 1990, for discussion of the two ways regularity/irregularity are defined: in terms of phonics rules of grapheme-phoneme correspondence or in terms of letter cluster-rime analogies to known words). Rather, degree of irregularity affects ease of pronunciation of written words—mildly irregular words with a single exception to letter-sound correspondence are read better than highly irregular words with several exceptions to letter-sound correspondence (Shallice, Warrington, & McCarthy, 1983). Few words are completely phonically irregular—onset phonemes (the first sound or sound blend of a syllable) are usually regular even if rimes (the remaining part of the syllable) are not, and rimes may be orthographically regular even if not phonologically regular (Berninger, 1990). For example, consider the "h" in house, which is phonically regular, and the "ouse" in house, which is phonically irregular (the silent "e" does not make the preceding vowels long vowels) but is orthographically regular ("ouse" is a permissible letter sequence and occurs in other words such as mouse). Brain damage does not selectively eliminate either the lexical route for irregular words or the sublexical route for regular words (Humphreys & Evett, 1985). There is no evidence that the brain sorts words into regular or irregular bins before applying a word recognition mechanism (Berninger & Abbott, 1992b).

Limitations of Boder's Model for Explaining Reading Disability

Boder (1973) proposed a system for diagnosing three kinds of dyslexia based on the kind of spelling errors made. *Dysphonetic* dyslexics read globally by visual gestalts because an auditory deficit interferes with learning letter-sound relationships. *Dyseidetic* dyslexics read analytically because a visual memory deficit interferes with processing the gestalt of the whole word. *Mixed* dyslexics show evidence of both dysphonetic and dyseidetic strategies. Moats (in press) reviewed the reliability and validity of the Boder classification system and concluded that they were not sufficiently adequate to use the Boder subtypes for research purposes. By analogy, these subtypes should not be used for clinical diagnosis, either.

Boder (1973, p. 682) made this strong claim: "One of these three patterns is found in all severely retarded readers . . . and none are found among children who read and spell normally." Two studies cast doubt on this claim and the model in general. Bruck (1988) showed that reading-disabled and reading-abled children do not differ in the processes they use to read and spell words, but do differ in the degree to which they have mastered those processes. Thalberg and Corker-Free (unpublished data, 1988) tested but did not confirm the hypothesis that students with a strong auditory memory rely on an auditory spelling strategy and that students with a strong visual memory rely on a visual spelling strategy. None of the four schemes they applied to analysis of error patterns supported the validity of Boder's conceptual scheme.

Furthermore, it is not always possible, as Boder claims, to categorize errors as purely visual or purely auditory. For example, a child might produce "b" for "d" because of (a) confusion of a visually similar letter form or (b) confusion of an auditorily similar phonemic sound. Context effects may be more important than visual or auditory modality in generating errors. Liberman, Shankweiler, Orlando, Harris, and Berti (1971) showed that reversals are more likely in than outside the context of a word. Reversals are most likely due to problems in orthographic symbol-sound association rather than to orthographic symbol or sound alone (Vogel, 1989).

Boder's diagnostic scheme, which is widely used by neuro-psychologists, may also be on shaky grounds in inferring processing strategy on the basis of error analysis. Errors may not be reliable or valid indicators of processing strategies, and may reflect normal developmental trends rather than individual differences in processing strategies. For example, Berninger and Alsdorf (1989) found that specific kinds of visual errors tended not to be stable constructs across different standardized measures, and only certain auditory/language errors involving phonemic or morphophonemic codes had concurrent validity for spelling errors. Reliability of spelling-error patterns depended on the informational properties of stimulus words and on reading level. Errors of high and average achievers were more influenced by the informational properties of stimulus words than were the errors of low achievers. These investigators concluded that clinicians should be cautious in inferring processing strategies from error analysis unless they use (a) converging evidence of the same error type on multiple measures and (b) age-norms for error types, because errors reflected normal developmental trends as well as individual differences.

In sum, Boder's scheme suffers from the same conceptual problems as does dual route theory: (a) disjunctive logic of attributing reading problems primarily to visual *or* linguistic problems (although her mixed category does acknowledge, unlike dual route theory, the possibility of both visual and auditory problems), and (b) failing to consider the multiple orthographic units on which phonological processes might operate. In addition, Boder's scheme does not make a clear distinction between orthographic and visual processes or between phonological and auditory processes, which Petersen et al. (1989) for example, (see chapter 2), have shown is important. Also, it is based on error analysis, which may not be a reliable or valid way to infer processing strategies.

Limitations of Connectionism for Educational Practice

The paradigm of connectionism, which is increasingly influential in cognitive psychology, has led to computer simulations in which a single computational procedure is applied to all words, regular or irregular, and real words or nonwords (e.g., Seidenberg & McClelland, 1989). Words are not represented as entries in a lexicon, but rather in terms of weights or connections between the orthographic input unit and hidden units (between input and output units), and between hidden units and phonological output units in a distributed memory network. Learning occurs through modification of those weights based on experience in reading words. Connectionism has been criticized for not adequately accounting for results of experiments on word recognition with human subjects, particularly for reading nonwords (Besner, Twilley, McCann, & Seergobin, 1990). Also, the large number of learning trials that connectionist architecture requires (e.g., 50,000 trials to reach 95 percent accuracy in oral reading of text) limits its generalizability to human learning, which usually occurs in far fewer trials. However, hybrid models that combine symbolic learning with connectionist input-output pairings show promise for handling learning from instruction in fewer learning trials (Schneider & Graham, in press). In addition, the claim that only one computational procedure underlies the reading of real words and nonwords is questionable. Berninger and Abbott (1992b) showed that different codes and code interactions explained the variance in reading real words and in reading nonwords.

Van Orden, Pennington, and Stone (1990) proposed the covariant learning hypothesis, which is a subsymbolic connectionist model with rulelike but not rule-governed mechanisms. Subsymbols are microfeatures that emerge momentarily and, when activated, behave as single, functional entities in invariant patterns in a dynamic system. Orthographic and phonological subsymbols are connected to each other by modifiable weights and can function at any unit size, which can vary from time to time, for example, whole word, single letter, or letter group; however, the orthographic-phonological mapping must be of appropriate unit size. Learning occurs as the weights between the subsymbols are adjusted through whole word crosstalk or subword crosstalk; whole word and subword crosstalk can occur independently of each other. Connection weights grow faster when there is consistent crosstalk than when there is inconsistent crosstalk. The matrix of connection weights resulting from crosstalk reflects the continuous, rather than categorical, orthographic-phonological covariance of the language.

Crosstalk follows a predictable developmental pattern: Initially, connections are formed on a stimulus-specific basis after sufficient experience with specific input-output pairs, but eventually the correlational structure distributed across input-output pairs begins to make performance appear rulelike at the subword level. Conceptually, this model is appealing, but the claim that orthographic-phonological covariances can be abstracted solely from experience with words does not mesh with the well-known fact that many children benefit from explicit instruction in grapheme-phoneme correspondences (e.g.,

Adams, 1990; Brown & Felton, 1990; Foorman, Francis, Novy, & Liberman, 1991). Also, dyslexics do not seem to be able to abstract patterns of letter-sound covariance from item-specific learning (Lovett, Warren-Chaplin, Ransby, & Borden, 1990).

Reconceptualizing the Reading Acquisition Process Within the Framework of a Heterarchy of Functional Systems

Developing Crosstalk Between the Visible Language and Oral Language Systems

In keeping with the society of mind theory (see chapter 1), the clues to reading acquisition lie in the earlier layers of the mind formed during childhood and not in the currently functioning layers of mind of the adult skilled reader. Thus the first step in modeling the reading acquisition process is to analyze the functional systems of the brain of the prereading child that will reorganize to support a new functional reading system. As Ellis (1985) has argued, reading and writing modules are not preformed in the infant brain waiting for the right environmental contingencies to elicit them, but rather grow out of and are constructed from other cognitive capabilities, such as visual, semantic, and phonological skills.

Nonreaders already have a highly developed visual system and a highly developed oral language system at the time formal reading instruction is introduced. Their visual system is specialized for (a) recognizing faces, (b) perceiving nonhuman objects and abstract forms such as geometric shapes, and (c) analyzing two-dimensional pictures and three-dimensional scenes. Their oral language system is specialized for understanding and producing (a) single words, (b) utterances including multiple words, and (c) connected text across conversational turns. They have also developed systems for communicating *within* these systems (e.g., recognizing a face within a group of people in a room; requesting confirmation of a single word in the preceding utterance of the conversational partner) and *between* systems (e.g., naming a person or object; describing a picture).

Nonreaders have not yet developed systems for crosstalk between the visual and oral language system regarding printed words. The central task of learning to read is for these two systems to learn to talk to each other about printed words; that is, construct new neural connections, so that printed words can be translated into linguistic representations. However, at the time beginning readers are trying to construct such a communication system, the visual system and the

TABLE 4.1 Neuropsychological and Educational Relevance of the Multiple Connections Model

Orthographic Coding	Phonological Coding	Crosstalk (Code Connection)	Teaching Method
		Lexical Level	
Whole word	Phonetic	Whole word-name	Look-say
		Sublexical Level	
Letter	Phonemic	Letter—Phoneme	Phonics
Letter cluster	Syllable	Letter Cluster—Syllable	Structural analysis
Letter cluster	Rime	Letter Cluster—rime (analogy)	Word families
Letter cluster	Blends, digraphs, diphthongs	Letter cluster—phoneme(s)	Phonics

oral language system are undergoing functional reorganization, which has a bearing on the kinds of communication links or crosstalk that may occur (Berninger, Chen, & Abbott, 1988).

Within the visual system an orthographic coding system is emerging that is specific to whole printed words, component letters in printed words, and letter clusters in printed words (Berninger, 1987). Within the oral language system, a phonological coding system is emerging that codes not only whole words but also component phonemes and syllables (Berninger, Proctor, DeBruyn, & Smith, 1988; Liberman, Shankweiler, Fischer, & Carter, 1974) and onsets and rimes within syllables (Trieman, 1985). This phonological coding system is related to the semantic coding system within the oral language system: Whole spoken words activate both phonetic and semantic codes (Berninger, 1989); a phoneme is the smallest unit of sound that makes a difference in meaning without having meaning of its own (Liberman, Cooper, Shankweiler, & Studdert-Kennedy, 1967); syllables and rimes mark morphemic structure that modifies meaning of root words (Leong, 1986).

According to the multiple connections model, the development of multiple orthographic codes and of multiple phonological codes affects the process of crosstalk about printed words: Crosstalk occurs

TABLE 4.2 Comparison of Dual Route Theory, Covariance Learning, and Multiple Connections Model[a]

I. *Dual route theory*

Route to lexicon	Example	Teaching method
visual (whole word)	reading	sight word
phonological (subword)	/r//ea//d//i//ng/	phonics

II. *Covariant learning hypothesis*

Crosstalk at different unit sizes	Teaching method
r-/r/ (in reading and ring)	repeated exposure to
ing-/ing/ (in reading, eating, ring)	a set of words, e.g.,
ea-/ea/ (in reading, eating)	reading, ring,
d-/d/ (in reading, dog)	eating, dog

III. *Multiple Orthographic-phonological coding*

		Teaching method
whole word-phonetic	reading-/reading/	look-say
letter-phoneme	r-/r/, d-/d/, i-/i/	phonics
letter cluster-	read-/read/,	structural
syllable	ing-/ing/	analysis
letter cluster-rime	ead-/ead/	word families
letter cluster-digraphs/ diphthongs	ea-/ea/, ng-/ng/	phonics

[a]Orthographic symbols are not enclosed in / /, but the corresponding phonological recoding is enclosed in / /.

for codes of the same unit size as shown in table 4.1 (Berninger, 1990; Berninger, Chen, & Abbott, 1988). The multiple connections model is educationally relevant in that a different method of teaching word recognition underlies each of the possible connections between corresponding orthographic and phonological codes (see table 4.1 and Berninger, 1990). In contrast to the dual route theory, which implies that methods of teaching word recognition are visual or phonological, the multiple connections model assumes that all methods of teaching word recognition require an integration of visual (orthographic) and phonological codes (table 4.2). In contrast to the covariance learning hypothesis, which assumes that the orthographic-phonological correspondences at different unit sizes can be abstracted inductively from repeated exposure to the same words, the multiple connections model makes those unit sizes explicit *and* assumes that the correspondences are learned through explicit, deductive instruction as well as inductively (table 4.2).

Foundations in Developmental Psychobiology

The multiple connections model is also grounded in four general principles of developmental psychobiology: normal variation, alternative pathways, redundancy, and critical developmental periods.

Normal Variation

For biological structures and functions, normal variation is the rule and not the exception; for example, eye and skin color, blood type, and the exact location of the speech center in the brain exhibit normal variation (see chapter 2). Normal variation refers to diversity without pathology and does not imply that functions are necessarily distributed in a "normal" bell-shaped curve. Two kinds of normal variation are potentially important for reading and writing acquisition: *interindividual differences* along a continuum within a domain (Berninger, 1986), and *intraindividual differences* across domains (Berninger & Hart, 1992, 1993). Normal variation is consistent with an interactionist model that rejects extreme empiricism (only experience matters) or nativism (only biological maturation matters) (Wolff, 1981).

Redundancy

The biological advantage of redundancy is that a back-up system exists if one system fails or fails to develop. Redundancy is a built-in design feature of many organ systems of the body—we have two lungs, two kidneys, two arms, two cerebral hemispheres, and so on. Redundancy may also exist in functional brain systems. For example, there may be multiple code connections underlying single word recognition. As shown in table 4.2, the multiple connections model makes explicit predictions about built-in redundancy in the reading system, whereas the dual route theory does not allow for redundancy. There is empirical evidence for redundancy in the reading system. The combination of a whole word-phonetic/semantic code composite variable and a letter-phoneme composite variable accounted for significantly more variance in oral reading than did either of these variables alone at the end of first grade (Berninger, Chen, & Abbott, 1988). This finding is at odds with the claims of dual route theory that beginning reading relies only on an indirect route (letter-phoneme connection) (e.g., Doctor & Coltheart, 1980). This finding is consistent with Barron's (1986) claim that both routes may operate in beginning reading.

Alternative Pathways

If one neural pathway is blocked or dysfunctional, alternative pathways may become functional that allow a function to be performed. The first pathway may have been sufficient, but not necessary, for the function. Alternative neural pathways for the same function open up the possibilities that different individuals may (a) accomplish the same function in different ways at the same point in time, or (b) follow different developmental paths to the same learning outcome (Berninger & Abbott, 1992a). There is empirical support for both possibilities. If one orthographic-phonological code connection is dysfunctional, beginning readers seem able to rely on the remaining ones with no deficit (Berninger, Chen, & Abbott, 1988) or only mild deficit (Berninger & Abbott, 1992b). From the beginning to the middle to the end of first grade, children in the same instructional group reached comparable learning outcomes but varied in how they processed stimulus information in printed words and translated that information into linguistic representations (Berninger & Abbott, 1992a).

Critical Developmental Period

As discussed in chapter 1, there is probably a critical developmental period early in formal schooling during which reading is most easily acquired and remediated. As explained in chapter 2, this critical developmental period may result from both genetic and instructional constraints. In one study, early intervention during this critical developmental period in at-risk second-grade children resulted in significant gains in word attack skills for 90 percent of the children (Berninger & Traweek, 1991). In general, the earlier the identification of a reading problem, the better the prognosis, regardless of the amount of subsequent intervention (Muehl & Forell, 1973).

Evidence for Multiple Orthographic Codes in the Hierarchical Orthographic System of Beginning Readers and Writers

Johnson (1978) reviewed the concept of codes in the cognitive psychology literature. Codes are procedures for transforming stimulus information into unitary mental representations. Codes are content free and not the same as the perceptual processes in which informational content is recognized; the content of a code is available only after the decoding process is complete. Orthographic coding, the procedures for transforming stimuli into mental representations, should therefore be distinguished from orthographic images (Ehri, 1980), the mental representation of a specific printed word.

Printed words can be coded at different levels or unit sizes. Huey (1908) observed that words can be read by letter, groups of letters, whole words, or all of these units, depending upon the reader's purpose. Johnson (1986) showed that pattern-level processing of whole word units precedes component-level processing of letters in time, as long as the pattern can be unitized. Johnson, Turner-Lyga, and Pettegrew (1986) showed that the pattern is processed on a component-by-component basis if it cannot be unitized. Barron (1986) pointed out that beginning readers can represent multiple orthographic units, including letters, letter clusters, and whole words.

Berninger (1987) compared orthographic coding of whole word units, single letters, and letter clusters in the same children when they were nonreaders at the end of kindergarten, and when they were readers at the end of first grade. At the end of kindergarten, they coded whole word patterns better and more quickly than letters in words, which they coded better and more quickly than letter clusters in words. At the end of first grade, the same relative pattern for the multiple codes occurred. Berninger, Yates, and Lester (1991) replicated this relative patterning (only accuracy data were available) in first, second, and third graders. Using a modified Stroop Test (single-letter, letter-cluster, and whole word color-inconsistent stimuli), these investigators showed greater interference for word units (the more automatic orthographic coding unit) than for single letter and letter cluster units (the less automatic units) in developing readers in the second, fourth, and sixth grades.

The multiple orthographic codes are hierarchical in that a whole word is composed of letter clusters, which are composed of single letters. However, this kind of hierarchical organization does not imply a power status in that whole word units dominate the word recognition system.

Evidence for Multiple Phonological Codes in the Hierarchical Phonological System of Beginning Readers and Writers

Studdert-Kennedy (1974) reviewed the literature on speech perception and concluded that acoustic verbal stimuli are processed at four different levels: (a) auditory; (b) phonetic; (c) phonological; and (d) lexical, syntactic, and semantic. At the *auditory* level, preliminary analysis of the frequency and intensity of the incoming acoustic signal takes place. At the *phonetic* level, the first linguistic coding occurs of sound information in lexical or whole word units. At the *phonological* level, the linguistic coding is more abstract than at the phonetic level; words are coded into phonemes, which relate sound to meaning. A phoneme carries no meaning of its own but is the smallest unit of sound providing a minimal contrast among words that makes a difference in meaning (Liberman et al., 1967). (Prelexical access is phonetic, but postlexical access is phonological, that is, phonemic, Foss & Blank, 1980.) At the lexical, syntactic, semantic level, meaning is a product of semantic codes associated with single lexical items and computation of syntactic/semantic relationships among lexical items. Studdert-Kennedy (1974) did not review the *text or discourse* level at which speech and print can also be analyzed (e.g., Frederiksen, 1979) in terms of the stated propositions in utterances or sentences and the linking of propositions through cohesive devices, unstated presuppositions, and implications of stated propositions.

There has been considerable conceptual confusion in the reading literature because terms borrowed from the psycholinguistic literature have not been used precisely (Berninger, 1989, 1990; Berninger, Abbott, & Shurtleff, 1990; Berninger, Proctor, DeBruyn, & Smith, 1988). Reading researchers have tended to use the term *phonological* to refer nonspecifically to any sound code (LaBerge & Samuels, 1974). For example, phonological coding has been used to refer to phonemic segmentation of spoken words, phonological recoding of printed words, and phonetic coding in working memory (Wagner & Torgesen, 1987). Technically speaking, *phonetic, phonemic,* and *phonics* are not interchangeable terms. Phonetic refers to sound patterns in spoken words. There is *no phonetic method of teaching reading* purely in terms of speech sounds; rather, there is a *phonics* method of teaching reading that teaches the correspondence between graphemes (letters) and phonemes (abstract classes of component sounds in words). In this book, phonetic and phonemic coding refer to two different levels of phonological or sound coding in general; however, in Studdert-Kennedy's (1974) scheme, phoneme processing occurs only at the phonological level.

In this book the term *phonological* refers to the processing of sound information in *spoken words* unless otherwise indicated. It does not refer to phonological recoding of printed real words or nonwords (what educators call *decoding*), because that process also taps orthographic coding processes (discussed later in this chapter). Multiple phonological codes have been identified and include phonetic or name codes for whole words, syllables, and subsyllables (phonemes and rimes). Research has identified the normal developmental sequence of these codes. Preschoolers can understand and produce whole words at the phonetic level. Kindergarten children can rhyme (Vellutino & Scanlon, 1987); that is, they can segment monosyllabic words into onsets and rimes and match rimes across words. They can also segment polysyllabic words by syllable (Liberman et al., 1974). First graders can segment by phonemes (Liberman et al., 1974). Phonemic coding is thought to emerge as a consequence of the need for more efficient memory storage as vocabulary size increases (e.g., Lindblom, 1989); it may develop further as a consequence of learning grapheme-phoneme correspondences in the course of reading acquisition (e.g., Morais, Carey, Alegria, & Bertelson, 1979). Thus, phonemic coding enables reading acquisition but also is enabled and develops as a consequence of reading acquisition (Perfetti, 1985).

Like orthographic codes, phonological codes are hierarchical in that the phonetic or name code is composed of syllabic, phonemic, or rime subcomponents, and syllable codes are composed of phonemic and rime subcomponents. Again, however, this hierarchical relationship of the multiple codes does not imply that the name code for the whole word has a power status that dominates the other codes.

Evidence for Multiple Orthographic-Phonological Code Connections from the Cognitive Literature

At least six code connections probably exist. These code connections cannot be measured directly and must be inferred from a synthesis of behavioral evidence in the cognitive literature. In addition to the five orthographic-phonological code connections in table 4.1, one code connection involves the orthographic and semantic system. None of these code connections alone is sufficient for one to recognize all the printed words of the language, but taken together they make it possible to identify all words, both regular and irregular.

There are two *lexical level code connections*. Whole printed words can map onto whole spoken codes, referred to as *phonetic* or *name codes,* or onto meaning codes, referred to as *semantic codes.* Posner, Lewis, and Conrad (1972) demonstrated that name and meaning codes exist independent of one another. In Petersen et al.'s (1989) model (fig. 2.4, chapter 2), these connections are represented as separate pathways from a visual (orthographic) code to an articulatory code and from a visual (orthographic) code to a semantic code.

Evidence for the *whole printed word-whole spoken word code connection* in beginning reading is the ease with which many children acquire a sight vocabulary through the look-say method and pronounce familiar words automatically without applying decoding rules. Additional evidence (Berninger, 1989) is that beginning and developing readers pronounced real words in which every letter could be phonemically coded as quickly as they pronounced real words in which every letter could not be phonemically coded; they took significantly longer to pronounce nonwords, which have to be decoded (Berninger, 1989). These results suggest that both regular and exception words can be recognized by mapping a name code for the whole word onto the printed word, whereas unfamiliar words must be recognized by the slower process of mapping letters onto phonemes and/ or letter clusters onto rimes to construct name codes.

Evidence for the *whole printed word-meaning code connection* in beginning reading was reported by Barron and Baron (1977). An articulatory task interfered with a concurrent sound categorization task but not with a concurrent meaning task. Also, Berninger (1989) found that beginning and developing readers took significantly longer to make semantic judgments about nonwords than real words, suggesting that they had direct access to semantic codes for real words but needed extra time to detect the absence of a semantic code in a nonword. These same children took less time to name real words than nonwords—not only because they had to decode the nonwords, but also because the presence of the semantic code for a real word facilitates the naming process. Berninger concluded that for "automatized" sight words, the phonetic code for naming words is probably accessed earlier in time than is the semantic code for assigning meaning, but once the phonetic code is accessed, it activates the semantic code and thus primes the path from the whole printed word to the semantic code.

Because a real word has both a phonetic and semantic code, it is not possible to measure phonetic coding of real words independent of semantic coding. So the lexical code connection is sometimes referred to as the *whole word-phonetic/semantic code connection* (Berninger & Traweek, 1991). The whole printed word-phonetic code connection plays a more obvious role in oral reading, whereas the whole printed word-semantic code connection plays a more obvious role in silent reading; but both may be activated in either oral or silent reading. The lexical code connections contribute to the recognition of known words or unfamiliar words taught through the look-say method; they are critical to the development of automaticity or rapid, effortless identification of a word without slow, effortful decoding of a word. The lexical code connections alone are not sufficient for learning to read because they do not provide a mechanism for word attack or decoding unknown words.

There are *four sublexical code connections*. Letters map onto phonemes; letter clusters map onto syllables, rimes, or phoneme(s).

In Petersen et al.'s (1989) model (fig. 2.4) these connections are represented by the pathway from the visual (orthographic) coding to phonological coding.

The *letter-phoneme code connection* underlies discovery of the alphabet principle, which is critical to beginning reading (Gleitman & Rozin, 1977), and the phonics method of teaching word recognition. This sublexical code connection, unlike the lexical code connections, provides clues to decoding unfamiliar words, but it does not specify the articulatory gestures for oral production of words. A phoneme is an abstract sound class that subsumes phones (the articulated sound segments); does not map linearly onto phones, acoustic signals, or articulatory gestures; and technically cannot be pronounced in isolation. Phones are context-dependent, and their articulation is influenced to some extent by surrounding phones. For example, the words *bed, bug,* and *rub* all contain the grapheme b, but the articulated phone varies slightly in each case even though each is an allophone of the abstract phoneme class /b/. (See Gleitman & Rozin, 1977, for further discussion of these issues.)

Thus, Liberman, Shankweiler, Liberman, Fowler, and Fischer (1977) concluded that it is impossible to read by sounding out letters one by one in left-to-right order. The name for the whole word has to be constructed from clues provided by the phonemic string. Although the letter-phoneme connection does not provide a complete program for pronouncing a whole word, this code connection has the advantage of offering clues for the construction of a phonetic code for the whole word and of relating sound to meaning. The letter-phoneme connection is necessary but is not sufficient alone for word recognition because (a) it does not provide a pathway for automaticity or direct pronounciation of the whole word; and (b) not all letters can be coded into a phoneme in some words, either because a letter is silent or because it does not conform to conventional phonics rules.

The *letter cluster-syllable code connection* underlies abstraction of the orthographic regularities of the language, that is, the correspondence between letter sequences and the invariant pronunciation of syllables (Venezky, 1979). Although words may be phonically irregular in terms of letter-phoneme correspondence, they may still be orthographically regular in that letter order conforms to permissible letter sequences in English and thus to a predictable correspondence between spelling and sound. Orthographic regularity is not the same as phonic regularity (Venezky, 1979). For example, a word can be phonically irregular but orthographically regular (e.g., eighth), or phonically regular but orthographically irregular (e.g., ssilf).

Orthographic regularities are important because they focus attention on the morphophonemic codes that modify semantic codes via tense or number markers or affixes. Where English violates phonics rules, it usually preserves correspondence between written and spoken morphology (e.g., "sign," which is derived from "signal," Chomsky, 1979). Although there is no comprehensive, explicit set of orthographic rules as there is for phonics rules, Venezky (1970) specified a set of orthographic structure rules that can account for most English spellings.

The letter cluster-syllable connection alone is not sufficient for word recognition because, unlike the letter-phoneme connection, it does not provide clues to the pronunciation of unknown written syllable patterns. A syllabary is not as effective as phonics in teaching beginning word recognition (Gleitman & Rozin, 1977). However, automatic word recognition may depend on using the orthographic regularity in words, as proposed by Venezky and Massaro (1979), and not only on direct access to a phonetic code. Some disabled readers may have trouble with orthographic rather than phonic regularity, or with both phonic and orthographic regularity. Assink and Kattenberg (1991) showed that poor readers differed from good readers in processing sublexical orthographic information, which for the poor readers did not improve with repeated exposures to the words. Further research is needed to determine whether problems in abstracting the orthographic regularity of the language may be related to a deficit in the transient visual system (see chapter 2).

The *letter cluster-rime code connection* underlies use of analogies or words that share similar spelling patterns in word recognition. Both skilled readers (Glushko, 1979) and beginning readers (Goswami, 1988) may use analogies to known words rather than phonics rules of grapheme-phoneme correspondence to recognize unknown words. Analogies may be regular, in that the rime pattern is pronounced the same in each word (e.g., *gave* and *save*) or irregular, in that the rime pattern is not pronounced the same in each word (e.g., *gave* and *have*). Goswami (1989) found that in beginning reading, end analogies (e.g., *beak* and *peak*) are more effective than beginning analogies (e.g., *beak* and *bean*) in achieving transfer to unknown words. End analogies may be more effective because words are segmented between the onset (initial phoneme) and rime (rest of syllable without the onset) (Wise et al., 1990). The letter cluster-rime code connection allows transfer of knowledge of subword patterns from known to unknown words. However, it is not sufficient alone because it does not allow the reader to code phonemically the onset of the syllable, but it probably contributes along with the letter cluster-syllable connection to abstracting the orthographic regularity of the language.

The *letter cluster-phoneme(s) connection* underlies phonics rules for consonant blends at the onset (e.g., *bl*ack) or end (e.g., fa*st*) position of a syllable, for consonant diphthongs at onset (e.g., *th*at) or end position (e.g., si*ng*) in a syllable, and for vowel digraphs (e.g., fr*ie*nd) and diphthongs (e.g., j*oy*) in medial or end positions of a syllable. Consonant blends are recoded into two phonemes, whereas consonant diphthongs are recoded into one phoneme, which is not the same sound associated with either component letter. Vowel digraphs are recoded into one phoneme, the sound associated with one of the letters, whereas vowel diphthongs are recoded into one phoneme, which is not the same sound associated with either component letter. Letter cluster-phoneme(s) connections are not sufficient alone for word recognition because they do not allow automatic recognition of the whole word; they do, however, allow for the complexities of phonics rules that single letter-phoneme connections do not.

Evidence for Multiple Orthographic-Phonological Code Connections from the Clinical Neuropsychological Literature

Four kinds of developmental dyslexia have been observed (C. Hynd, 1986) as well as hyperlexia (Siegel, 1984), a reading disorder characterized by precocious word recognition skills but severe deficits in reading comprehension and oral language. Each of these may be related to relative inefficiencies in different functional code connections (Berninger, Lester, Sohlberg, & Mateer, 1991). The *developmental surface dyslexic,* who can read phonically regular words or nonwords better than phonically irregular real words, has a dysfunctional whole word-name code connection. The *developmental direct dyslexic or hyperlexic,* who can pronounce words but not with understanding, has a dysfunctional whole word-semantic code connection. The *developmental phonological dyslexic,* who can read familiar, phonically irregular words better than unfamiliar, phonically regular words, has a dysfunctional letter-phoneme and/or letter cluster-syllable/subsyllable code connection. The *developmental deep dyslexic,* who has trouble decoding unfamiliar words out of sentence context and can read better in context but confuses semantically similar words, may have dysfunctions in all the code connections except the whole word-semantic code connection (Berninger & Hart, 1992).

Evidence for Multiple Orthographic-Phonological Code Connections from the Developmental Neuropsychological Perspective

Segmental orthographic and phonological coding tasks have been used to investigate multiple orthographic-phonological code connections of corresponding unit size from the developmental neuropsychological perspective outlined in this book. To date the focus has been primarily on three of these connections: whole word-phonetic/semantic code, letter-phoneme, and letter cluster-syllable. The orthographic tasks, which were derived from the work of Johnson (1978, 1986), required children to represent briefly presented words in memory and then to make decisions about whole word, letter, or letter cluster units (Berninger, 1987; Berninger, Yates, & Lester, 1991). The phonological tasks required children to retrieve or generate phonetic/semantic codes and, based on the work of Liberman et al. (1974), to segment spoken words into phonemes, without pronouncing the phoneme in isolation, or into syllables.

According to the *developmental mismatch hypothesis* (Berninger, 1987; Berninger, Chen, & Abbott, 1988), code connections will not become functional if corresponding orthographic and phonological codes of the same unit size are not developed to comparable levels. Two mechanisms can contribute to corresponding codes not being developed to comparable levels: (a) genetically constrained normal variation in orthographic and phonological coding skills, which affects a child's experience with written and spoken language and may result in one or more codes being relatively overdeveloped or underdeveloped; and (b) mismatches in the developmental timetable for corresponding codes becoming functional. Given the developmental patterns for the orthographic and phonological codes discussed earlier, whole word coding emerges first for both written and oral language, creating a match at the lexical level for acquiring a sight vocabulary. However, phonemic coding may emerge later than letter coding, creating a mismatch for the letter-phoneme code connection; and letter cluster coding may emerge later than oral syllable coding, creating a mismatch for the letter cluster-syllable code connection.

The evidence for the developmental mismatch hypothesis is strongest for the letter cluster-syllable code connection. In a study of unreferred first graders (Berninger, Chen, & Abbott, 1988), dysfunctional code connections were operationally defined as large discrepancies of 1 standard deviation or more between corresponding orthographic and phonological codes. Large discrepancies were more frequent for letter cluster coding and syllable coding (40 percent of the sample) than for whole word coding and phonetic/semantic coding (26 percent of the sample) or for letter coding and phoneme coding (24 percent of the sample). When there was a discrepancy between corresponding codes, it was more likely to be due to impaired letter cluster coding than to impaired syllable coding, but it was equally likely to be due to impaired letter coding as to impaired phonemic coding.

According to the *multiple connections model* (Berninger & Abbott, 1992b; Berninger, Chen, & Abbott, 1988; Berninger, Lester, Sohlberg, & Mateer, 1991; Berninger & Traweek, 1991), multiple orthographic-phonological code connections contribute to word recognition. Berninger, Chen, and Abbott (1988) compared first graders with large discrepancies (≥ 1 standard deviation) or small discrepancies ($< 1/3$ standard deviation) between corresponding orthographic and phonological skills. For the whole word-phonetic/semantic code connection and the letter cluster-syllable code connection, children with small discrepancies read significantly better than those with large discrepancies. The number of large discrepancies affected mean oral and silent reading achievement, which was above the mean (range, $+0.2$ to $+0.5$ standard deviation units) for children with one or zero large discrepancies, but was substantially below the mean (range, -0.7 to -01.2 standard deviation units) for children with two or three large discrepancies. Thus, the reading system was able to tolerate one dysfunctional code connection and was most likely to be impaired by two or more dysfunctional code connections. In this unreferred, school-based sample of 42 children, one third had no large discrepancies, about two fifths had one large discrepancy, about one fifth had two large discrepancies, and about one fourteenth had three large discrepancies.

Berninger and Abbott (1992b) further tested the multiple connections model in an unreferred, school-based sample of 300 first, second, and third graders. They addressed two basic questions: (a) whether each of the three orthographic codes (whole word, letter, and letter cluster) and each of the three phonological codes (phonetic/semantic, phonemic, and syllable) contributed unique variance to the criterion measures of reading real words, reading nonwords, and spelling real words; and (b) whether corresponding codes must be closely matched or just relatively comparable in level of development.

To answer the first question, they used multiple regression to evaluate the statistical significance of the main effect of each orthographic and each phonological code and the interaction between corresponding orthographic and phonological codes. All the codes accounted for significant variance in the criterion measures. For *reading real words,* all the codes also accounted for significant unique increments of variance. For *spelling real words,* all the codes except for whole word coding also contributed significant unique increments of variance.

For *reading nonwords,* all the codes except letter coding also accounted for a significant unique increment of variance. This finding is important because it shows that *nonword reading is not a purely phonological task;* two orthographic coding skills contributed unique increments of variance to nonword reading above and beyond that contributed by three phonological coding skills.

Of the interaction terms, only the letter cluster-syllable interaction term explained a significant increment of unique variance and only for nonword reading and spelling real words. Thus, the level of development of letter cluster coding and syllable coding may need to be more finely tuned than the relative level of the other corresponding codes.

To address the second question, Berninger and Abbott (1992b) used more stringent criteria than Berninger, Chen, and Abbott (1988) had used to determine dysfunctional code connections. To be considered dysfunctional, a code connection had to meet two criteria: (a) level of development of one code was significantly different from that of the corresponding code based on the Mahalanobis statistic (Stevens, 1986), and (b) one or both of the codes fell in the bottom 5 percent of the normal distribution.

On the basis of these operational definitions, almost 70 percent of the sample had all three code connections functional, about 10 percent had only two code connections functional, 2 percent had only one code connection functional, and 0.3 percent had no functional code connection; the rest were indeterminate because they met one but not both criteria. On the average, the group with *all code connections functional* read real words about 0.90 standard deviation better, read nonwords about 0.86 standard deviation better, and spelled about 0.67 standard deviation better than did the group with only two code connections functional. On the average, the group with *two code connections functional* read only slightly better but spelled about 0.5 standard deviation better than the group with only *one code connection functional.* On the average, the group with one code connection functional read real words over 1 standard deviation better, read nonwords about 0.80 standard deviation better, and spelled about 0.50 standard deviation better than did the one child with zero code connections functional, who was barely able to read or spell.

Thus, reading and spelling achievement drops as the number of functional code connections decreases. Compared with the previous study, which used less stringent criteria, this study suggested that just one dysfunctional code connection can reduce the level of reading and spelling achievement. However, in both studies the most dramatic differences in achievement were between children with all corresponding code connections functional and those with only one or zero code connections functional; typically, the magnitude of the difference was more than 1 standard deviation.

Evidence for Heterarchical Organization of Functional Reading and Spelling Systems for Single Words

Functional systems are based on horizontal and vertical crosstalk within societies or between societies via higher level coordination mechanisms. According to the society of mind theory, the higher level coordination between societies is not orchestrated by a single executive or homunculus, but rather by a complex managerial system that evolves over the course of development to allow different agencies to perform their functions and resolve conflict when necessary (see chapter 1). It follows that the executive system may orchestrate functional systems differently, depending on the task at hand.

To explore how the same systems might contribute differently depending on the task at hand, structural equation modeling (Bentler, 1991) was applied to analyze covariance structures among latent factors underlying different coding systems, and latent factors underlying achievement in component reading and writing skills. Structural equation modeling combines the advantages of factor analysis and multiple regression (Biddle & Marlin, 1987). Like factor analysis but unlike multiple regression, this technique can model latent factors based on the covariance of the measured variables; like multiple regression but unlike factor analysis, it can describe the degree of relationship among predictor latent factors and between predictor latent factors and criterion latent factors (Lunneborg & Abbott, 1983).

Berninger, Abbott, and Shurtleff (1990) tested competing theoretical models for two reading tasks—making judgments about the meaningfulness of words and naming single words—and one spelling task—written reproduction of briefly presented words. In one model the visible-oral language covariance was set to zero; in the other model this covariance was freely estimated. The visible language system was based on two indicators—whole word and letter coding—and the oral language system was based on two indicators—phonetic/semantic coding and phonemic coding. Allowing a covariance between the visible and oral language factors improved the fit at the beginning but not the end of first grade. The visible and the oral language systems differentiated as children gained in reading and spelling skill, showing that the functional organization of the brain is flexible and does change. At the beginning of first grade, the direct effects of both the visible and oral language factors were significant for all tasks; at the end of first grade, the direct effect of the visible language factor was significant only for naming (oral reading), but the direct effect of the oral language factor was significant for all tasks. Thus, individual differences in visible language exerted effects on some but not all literacy skills, suggesting that the executive management depended on the task at hand.

Multiple group structural equation modeling, which tests whether the fit of a model is significantly different at different grade levels, was used to test developmental changes in the systems related to reading (Berninger & Abbott, 1992b) and spelling (Abbott & Berninger, 1993) single words. The orthographic coding factor was always based on the same indicators—whole word, letter, and letter cluster coding, and the phonological coding factor was always based on the same indicators—syllable and phonemic coding. The criterion factor was either reading single words based on two indicators—reading real words and reading nonwords (fig. 4.1), or spelling single words based on three indicators—spelling real words from dictation and in narrative and expository compositions (fig. 4.2).

At all grade levels, the paths from both the orthographic and the phonological factors contributed to the fit of the models for reading (Berninger & Abbott, 1992b) and spelling (Abbott & Berninger, 1993). However, the management of those systems tended to differ, depending on skill development level and the criterion task. For reading, at the first grade level, the path from the orthographic coding factor was stronger than the path from the phonological coding factor; but at the second and third grade levels, the path from the phonological coding factor was stronger than the path from the orthographic coding factor. In contrast, for spelling, consistently at each grade level, only the path from the orthographic coding factor was significant. Again, the executive management of the orthographic and phonological coding systems depended on the task at hand.

At first glance, the results at the first grade level for spelling in Abbott and Berninger (in press), which show a significant path from the orthographic factor, seem at odds with the results at the end of first grade for spelling in Berninger et al. (1990), which did not show a significant path from the visible language factor. This discrepancy is probably related to the difference in the spelling tasks across

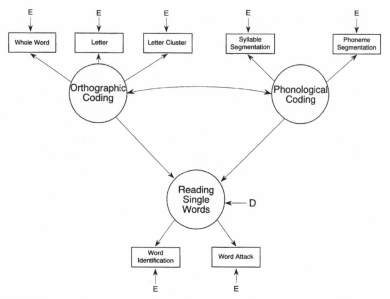

FIGURE 4.1

Structural equation modeling of latent factors (circles) based on indicators (rectangles) for reading single words. Figures 4.1 and 4.2 have the same predictor factors but differ in the criterion factor.

studies. The spelling task in the first study required only short-term representation and reproduction of words varying in phonic and orthographic regularity and in availability of a semantic code. The spelling task in the second study required spelling real words from dictation and in functional communicative contexts, which requires retrieval of representations of words from long-term memory. Thus, the path from the orthographic factor to spelling was significant only when long-term memory for spelling words was tapped.

The results for naming single words at the first grade level are also somewhat different across the studies. In both studies the path from the visible language or orthographic factor was significant, but the studies differed as to whether the oral language path was significant. When the oral language factor was based on phonemic and phonetic/semantic indicators, the oral language path to oral reading was significant; but when the oral language factor was based only on phonemic and syllabic indicators, the oral language path to oral reading was not significant. Thus, in beginning readers, oral reading of single words seems to require connection to both whole word (phonetic/semantic) and subword (phonemic) codes in the oral language system and not just to subword (phonemic and syllabic) codes alone.

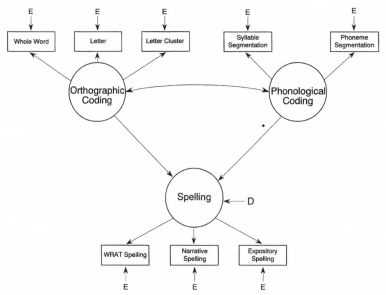

FIGURE 4.2
Structural equation modeling of latent factors (circles) based on indicators (rectangles) for spelling single words. Figures 4.1 and 4.2 have the same predictor factors but differ in the criterion factor.

Evidence for Multiple Procedures for Processing and Producing Single Words

Procedures for Meaning, Sound, and Orthographic Representation

Kolers and Roediger (1984) argued that both stimulus information and procedures of mind for operating on that stimulus information are represented in memory. Berninger (1988a) investigated the acquisition of three procedures of mind for printed words in beginning readers—lexical decision, naming, and written reproduction. Lexical decision requires children to judge whether stimuli (real words, pronounceable nonwords, or letter strings) are real words that are meaningful. Naming requires children to pronounce real written words or pronounceable nonwords. Written reproduction requires children to reproduce a briefly presented written stimuli (real words, pronounceable nonwords, or letter strings) from memory. Each of these procedures showed a different developmental pattern of acquisition, indicating that they are not identical.

At the beginning, middle, and end of first grade, accuracy was always greater on lexical decision—a receptive task—than on naming or written reproduction—both production tasks. The superiority of lexical decision cannot be attributed to the higher probability of guessing correctly on lexical decision, a yes/no choice task; accuracy was based on consistently correct responses over three replications of the same stimuli in a block of randomized stimuli. The relative superiority of receptive judgments shows that children acquire knowledge about printed words before they can recode printed words into sound.

Berninger (1988a) also manipulated the kind of stimulus information available for the procedures by including four word types: phonically regular real words, phonically irregular/orthographically regular real words, pronounceable nonwords, and letter strings. Consistently at the beginning, middle, and end of first grade, accuracy on lexical decision was best for phonically regular real words, next best for letter strings, next best for phonically irregular real words, and worst for phonically regular nonwords. Thus, beginning readers had abstracted some implicit knowledge of orthographic regularity that allowed them to reject correctly orthographically irregular letter strings better than they could correctly reject phonically regular nonwords without meaning.

This last finding is consistent with Pick's (1978) report that first graders rejected orthographically illegal letter strings as not being real words and Pearson and Barron's (1989) finding that nonreaders in first grade had abstracted partial spelling knowledge of words before formal reading instruction began. (For further details about this last study, see Berninger, 1990.) This abstraction of orthographic knowledge may occur in the hidden units in tertiary association areas of the cortex, which are not directly connected to the environment but provide extra computational space for abstracting associations among stimuli (Hinton & Sejnowski, 1986). Computations in these hidden units may be responsible for the knowledge children acquire about words before they can overtly produce them (Berninger, 1988a). In keeping with Luria's (1973) model (see table 1.2, chapter 1), academic learning may require maturation of the tertiary association cortex to support such computations in hidden units before production systems for observable units in the environment become functional.

At the end of first grade, significant interactions occurred between procedures and specific stimulus words for nonsense words, but not for the phonically regular or irregular real words. This finding suggests that procedures for operating on words and data structures for representing stimulus words are more amalgamated when a word is already represented in memory but are more autonomous when a word is novel, not represented in memory, and has to be decoded.

Whole Word and Subword Mechanisms

Although beginning and developing readers may have a repertoire of multiple orthographic-phonological code connections, several studies support a developmental trend from relative reliance on whole word mechanisms to relative reliance on subword mechanisms. Freebody and Byrne (1988) administered measures of reading irregular real words, which tap a whole word mechanism, and of reading nonwords, which tap subword mechanisms for decoding. They identified second and third graders who were high in both skills, who were better in one or the other, and who were poor in both skills. In this cross-sectional study, the readers better in the whole word mechanisms were superior in reading comprehension in grade 2, but the readers better in the subword mechanisms were superior in reading comprehension in grade 3. In a subsequent longitudinal study, Byrne, Freebody, and Gates (1992) found that readers better in the whole word mechanisms declined in word reading from third to fourth grade, but readers better in subword mechanisms improved.

Berninger, Yates, and Lester (1991) compared second, fourth, and sixth graders on reading regular and irregular real words, which can rely on whole word or subword mechanisms, and reading nonwords, which can rely only on subword mechanisms, on standardized achievement tests. A significant interaction between grade and word type occurred on age-corrected standard scores with comparable means and standard deviations. Second graders tended to read real words better than nonwords, fourth graders read real words and nonwords equally well, and sixth graders read nonwords better than real words. These results are consistent with the research by Byrne and colleagues above and the developmental trend predicted by the co-variant learning hypothesis (Van Orden et al., 1990) from relative reliance on whole word mechanisms to increasing reliance on subword mechanisms.

Comparison of Dual Route Theory, Boder's Model, Connectionism, and Multiple Connections/Multiple Procedures

Connectionist models postulate one learning algorithm underlying all word recognition, and have an implicit naive optimism that word recognition will always proceed normally just on the basis of experience with words, without explicit instruction in rule-governed mechanisms. In contrast, dual route theory postulates at least two mechanisms in word recognition and allows for a mechanism in which rules can be applied to decode new words not experienced before. However, in contrast to dual route theory and Boder's model, which tend to view these mechanisms as either visual or auditory, the connectionist models have made a contribution in acknowledging the orthographic-phonological correspondence in word recognition.

The multiple connections model is similar to dual route theory in its recognition of two major classes of word recognition mechanisms—lexical and sublexical, and is similar to the covariant learning hypothesis in its recognition that orthographic-phonological covariances can be abstracted at different unit sizes. However, the multiple connections model, unlike dual route theory and Boder's model, assumes that every word recognition mechanism has an orthographic *and* a phonological or linguistic component. The multiple connections model is inconsistent with any model, such as dual route theory or Boder's model, that conceptualizes word recognition as visual or auditory and fails to distinguish between visual and orthographic processes and between auditory and phonological processes. From the perspective of the multiple connections model, both paths in dual route theory involve an orthographic code *and* a phonological or linguistic code. The direct path involves a whole word orthographic code leading to a whole word phonetic or semantic code, whereas the indirect path leads from a letter code to a phonemic code or from a letter cluster code to a syllable, rime, or phoneme code.

The multiple connections model is more educationally relevant than connectionism. Educators cannot directly manipulate the *hidden* units where orthographic-phonological connections are constructed. Educators can, however, design learning activities that stimulate development of specific orthographic or phonological codes in *observable* units of spoken and printed words, and thus increase the probability that connections between codes of corresponding unit size will be formed; they can also explicitly teach children the multiple ways to link units of written language with units of spoken language (Berninger & Traweek, 1991).

Summary

The limitations of dual route theory, Boder's model, and connectionism are discussed. Learning to recognize printed words is conceptualized within a heterarchy of functional orthographic and phonological coding systems. Evidence is presented for the multiple connections model with at least six orthographic-phonological code connections of corresponding unit size and for the developmental mismatch hypothesis, in which code connections fail to form because corresponding orthographic and phonological codes are not developed to comparable levels. Evidence is also presented for multiple procedures for processing meaning and producing oral and graphic output. Studies supporting a developmental trend from whole word (whole word-phonetic code, whole word-semantic code) to subword (letter-phoneme, letter cluster-syllable/rime/phoneme) mechanisms in word recognition are reviewed. Thus, the phenotype for beginning reading should take into account multiple orthographic codes, multiple phonological codes, multiple orthographic-phonological code connections of corresponding size at both the whole word and subword levels, and procedures for meaning and for oral and graphic production of printed words. Although the multiple connections model is consistent with current knowledge of brain structure, it is based solely on behavioral data and should be confined to theory-building at the functional level of analysis.

5

Levels of Language and Intraindividual Differences in Levels of Language in Reading Comprehension and Composition

The term level of analysis *has been used in psychology to refer to the level of structural organization . . . the level of explanation . . . and the level of processing. . . .*

–John Cacioppo and Gary Bernston (1992, p. 1020)

Outline

Meanings of Levels

The term *level* has had multiple meanings in the research literature. According to Luria (1973), in 1874 Jackson introduced the concept of *levels of structural organization* in the nervous system. Jackson observed that the layers of the brain are more organized, less modifiable, and more automatic at the lower than the higher layers. He noted that the highest layers are more complex, special, and integrated with the most numerous interconnections. An example of different *levels of explanation* is Vellutino's (1979a) distinction between immediate and ultimate causality (see chapter 1). *Level of processing* refers to the depth of processing in a memory paradigm that compares recall when task instructions do and do not require semantic encoding (e.g., Craik & Lockhart, 1972).

The *levels of analysis* approach described in chapter 1 is used by linguists as well as neuroscientists. Linguists apply different coding schemes, which vary in the size of the production unit coded, to the same language sample. A general linguistic principle is that different units of analysis (e.g., sublexical sound units, lexical semantic units, and translexical syntactic/semantic units or pragmatic units) are usually related in some fashion, but not perfectly, with one-to-one correspondence (Berninger & Garvey, 1981).

Levels are implicit in the *componential approach* that aims to identify isolable-information processing components that when executed in sequential or parallel manner accomplish higher order tasks. For example, Posner, Lewis, and Conrad (1972) identified three isolable subsystems for processing single lexical units in skilled reading: (a) visual codes, (b) name codes, and (c) meaning codes. Frederiksen (1981) postulated different levels of component reading processes: (a) encoding of graphemes and multiletter units, (b) decoding, (c) lexical access, (d) syntactic and propositional analysis, and (e) interactions among these components at different levels.

In this chapter, *level* reflects elements of several of the above uses of the term. It is used to refer to level of organization at the functional rather than structural level of the brain (see chapter 1). It is also used to refer to level of processing within the functional language system, but not in the sense used by memory researchers. Rather, in keeping with the linguistic tradition, *level* refers to the different-sized units at which language is processed and produced.

Neuropsychological Evidence for Levels of Language

Different levels of language function appear to have different neuroanatomical correlates on MRI scans. Length of the insular cortex was associated with naming skills (lexical level), but right frontal width was associated with passage comprehension (text or translexical level) (Semrud-Clikeman et al., 1991). Different levels of language function also appear to be disrupted by electrical stimulation at different brain sites. Ojemann (1991) reported that some sites were specific to phonemic tasks (sublexical level), whereas others were specific to naming (lexical level) or syntactic analysis (translexical level). To date, research on the genetics of reading disability has not defined the phenotype in terms of multiple levels of oral and written language or intraindividual differences in the level to which the different levels of language are developed.

Importance of Levels for a Systems Approach to Reading and Writing Acquisition

Verbal intelligence is not a homogeneous construct (Hunt, 1983). Although reading researchers have long acknowledged that reading acquisition depends on oral language (e.g., Just & Carpenter, 1987), only recently have they begun to investigate how different language skills may contribute in different ways to reading acquisition. Olson, Davidson, Kliegl, and Davies (1984) showed that individual differences in specific oral language skills are related to individual differences in reading ability. Carr, Brown, and Vavrus (1985) pointed out the need for research on the structure of the oral language system into which component reading skills are organized during the process of learning to read. Such an approach requires inclusion of multiple language measures rather than a single language measure.

Vellutino, Scanlon, Small, and Tanzman (1991) included multiple oral language measures (e.g., of phonemic, vocabulary, and syntactic/grammatical skills) in a study of reading in the primary and middle school grades. Syntactic/grammatical (phrase/sentence level of oral language) and phonological skills (sublexical level of oral language) contributed significant variance beyond that contributed by listening comprehension (text level of oral language) and word identification (lexical level of written language) to reading comprehension (text level of written language). Vocabulary (lexical level of oral language) and phonological segmentation (sublexical level of oral language) tended to be the best predictors of word identification.

However, these investigators cautioned that the relative weighting of different oral language skills contributing to reading may change over the course of development. For example, syntactic skills are a strong predictor of reading skill during the preschool years (Scarborough, 1990), are not a reliable predictor of reading comprehension during the primary grades (Vellutino, Scanlon, Small, & Tanzman, 1991, table 1, younger students), and are a reliable predictor of reading comprehension during the middle school grades (Vellutino, Scanlon, Small, & Tanzman, 1991, table 1, older students).

Other investigators are also finding that both sublexical (phonemic) and lexical (naming) skills are related to reading acquisition (e.g., Berninger, Proctor, DeBruyn, & Smith, 1988; Felton & Brown, 1990; Lovett, Benson, & Olds, 1990). (See Berninger, 1991, for discussion of the importance of synthesizing the research on *phoneme* skills and the research on rapid, automatized *naming* of visual stimuli.)

Leong (1988; 1991) applied linear structural equation modeling to indicators of multiple levels of written language—orthographic/phonological, morphological, and sentence—underlying reading in the intermediate grades. The indicators were on-line, computer-administered measures scaled for accuracy and latency. In both a Phase I and a Phase II replication, the model fit best in fourth grade, reasonably well in fifth grade, and not so well in sixth grade. One explanation of the results is that the levels of language studied—sublexical, lexical, and sentence—are the important ones in fourth and fifth grade, but another level of language not studied—higher order discourse structures—begins to be important in sixth grade.

Taken together, the above studies and research discussed in chapter 4 indicate that at least three levels of language should be considered in research on reading: *sublexical* (phonological skills such as syllable, phoneme, and rime segmentation of units smaller than the word), *lexical* (phonetic and semantic codes for word units), and *translexical or text* (processing of phrases, sentences, and discourse units of text larger than the single word). These same levels of language should also be considered in research on writing.

Levels of Language in Beginning Reading

Ehri and Roberts (1979) investigated levels of written language in learning to read and showed that what children learn about words depends on the level of written language emphasized. Training that focused on words in isolation (lexical level) resulted in greater knowledge of orthographic features of words, whereas training that focused on words in context (sentence level) resulted in greater knowledge of semantic features of words. Letter-sound relationships at the lexical level, but not at the sublexical level, were related to learning the meaning of words.

Berninger, Proctor, DeBruyn, and Smith (1988) tested six predictions derived from a model of the multiple levels of oral language processing and production related to learning to read in a sample of children who did not receive formal instruction in reading until first grade. According to this model, the oral language system is *partially hierarchical* in that the text level (translexical) is dependent to some degree on the outcome of the lexical level, which in turn is dependent to some degree on the outcome of the sublexical level. The battery used to test the model contained six oral language measures: three levels of oral language—sublexical phonemic, lexical vocabulary meaning, and translexical text comprehension skills—using two response types—receptive tasks with minimal motoric requirements and expressive tasks with response construction requirements. It also contained measures of two reading components: decoding/encoding printed words (pronouncing single words) and reading comprehension.

The *first prediction* was that each level of oral language skill would be related to at least one component reading skill. At the end of kindergarten, receptive and expressive phonemic skills and receptive vocabulary skills were correlated with both component reading skills, but at the end of first grade, all six measures of oral language were correlated with both component reading skills.

The *second prediction* was that multiple levels of oral language would account for more variance in component reading skills than would a single level of oral language. At the end of kindergarten, a combination of two oral language skills never predicted more variance in reading than did a single skill alone; at the end of first grade, expressive phonemic and expressive vocabulary accounted for significantly more variance in both component reading skills than did phonemic skills alone. This result demonstrates that multiple levels of oral language may become important only when formal reading instruction begins, and that the sublexical and lexical levels are the most important levels in beginning reading.

The *third prediction* was that the pattern of relationships between levels of oral language and component reading skills would change from the end of kindergarten to the end of first grade because the functional oral and written language systems reorganize as a consequence of learning to read. Steiger's (1980) statistical technique for correlated correlations, which does not require the assumption of multivariate normality, was used to test the pattern hypothesis. The magnitude of the relationship between four oral language skills—expressive phonemic, expressive vocabulary, receptive text, and expressive text—and one reading skill—word decoding/encoding—increased significantly from the end of kindergarten to the end of first grade. Although receptive and expressive oral language text skills were correlated with reading comprehension at the end of first grade, the magnitude of the relationship between text level oral language skills and reading comprehension did not improve significantly from the end of kindergarten to the end of first grade. Again, the results indicate that the sublexical and lexical levels may be the most important in beginning reading, consistent with results for the second prediction and results reported by Vellutino, Scanlon, Small, and Tanzman (1991).

The *fourth prediction* was that sublexical and lexical oral language skills are related to decoding/encoding of printed words, but that lexical and translexical oral language skills are related to reading comprehension. Correlations between gain scores on an oral language skill and gain scores on a component reading skill provided support only for sublexical and lexical skills being related to decoding/encoding of printed words, but with a twist. Gain scores on expressive phonemic skills were *negatively correlated* with gain scores in decoding/encoding of printed words. Children who were superior in phonemic segmentation at the end of kindergarten tended to make large gains in decoding/encoding of printed words and modest gains in phonemic segmentation once formal reading instruction was introduced. Children who were average or lower in phonemic segmentation at the end of kindergarten tended to make large gains in phonemic segmentation and modest gains in decoding/encoding of printed words once formal reading instruction was introduced. Gain scores in receptive vocabulary were positively correlated with gain scores on decoding/encoding of printed words.

The *fifth prediction* was that levels of oral language in a partially hierarchical system would be moderately correlated, rather than perfectly correlated, as would be the case in a system without unique levels of language, or uncorrelated, as would be the case in a completely hierarchical system. Pairwise correlations between all combinations of six oral language skills were moderately significant for the most part; correlations between receptive phonemic and receptive or expressive text skills at the end of kindergarten, and receptive phonemic and expressive vocabulary skills and receptive and expressive text skills at the end of first grade were not significant.

The *sixth prediction* was that the independence of the levels of oral language would be more evident if receptive and expressive task requirements were held constant. Partial correlations for two oral language skills with a third oral language skill removed were compared separately for the receptive and expressive measures. At the end of kindergarten, phonemic and lexical skills were uncorrelated (expressive measures only), and the phonemic and text skills were uncorrelated (receptive measures only). At the end of first grade, phonemic and lexical skills were uncorrelated (receptive and expressive measures), lexical and text skills were uncorrelated (receptive and expressive measures), and phonemic and text skills (expressive measures only) were uncorrelated. Thus, the semi-independence of the levels of oral language in a partially hierarchical system emerges in kindergarten but is most evident at the end of first grade, after a year of formal reading instruction. This finding shows the reciprocal influence of written language development on the functional organization of the oral language system.

Levels of Language and Intraindividual Differences in Developing Reading

Word identification constrains reading comprehension in beginning reading (Vellutino, Scanlon, Small, & Brown, 1991). That is, if a child cannot identify the words, comprehension will probably suffer. However, it does not follow from this fact or the fact that individual differences in *oral language* at the word and subword levels are most important in beginning reading that the sentence level is not important in beginning reading. Sentence level skills (a) contribute to the computation of meaning and (b) provide context that does not necessarily aid word identification (see Aaron & Joshi, 1992) but may facilitate self-monitoring of comprehension.

Berninger (1987) used a paradigm in which sentences were presented one word at a time and one sentence at a time under equated time conditions (Forster, 1970; Potter, Kroll, & Harris, 1980) to study word-level and sentence-level procedures in beginning sentence comprehension. The task was to decide whether or not a sentence was meaningful. Sentences contained only real words. Nonsense sentences (e.g., "A little dig can run fast") differed from meaningful sentences (e.g., "A little dog can run fast") by only one word (the orthographic foil, or critical word). The one word rendering a sentence nonsensical differed by just one letter or letter order from a word that would have been sensible in that context.

Consistently, at the beginning, middle, and end of first grade, mode of sentence presentation affected speed but not accuracy of comprehension. Sentences were comprehended significantly faster when presented normally than when presented one word at a time. Presenting all the words in a sentence at the same time allowed children to read forward or backward in the sentence to use context to resolve conflicts more quickly when orthographic foils occurred. In contrast, when sentences were presented one word at a time, children could access prior text only in working memory, and did not have access to complete context until the last word in the sentence was presented.

Thus, beginning readers were able to use contextual information provided by sentence-level procedures to comprehend more quickly but not more accurately. Context was not beneficial if the child failed to detect the orthographic foil. Context was beneficial only in speeding up the process of rendering a judgment about the sentence.

Berninger (1993) administered the same experiment to second, fourth, and sixth graders. Results for the second graders and for the fourth and sixth graders combined were analyzed separately because presentation rate of stimulus sentences had to be adjusted for differences in reading rates of less skilled and more skilled readers. The second graders, like the first graders, comprehended sentences faster, but not more accurately, when the sentence level was highlighted on normal sentence presentation. In contrast, the fourth and sixth graders comprehended sentences more accurately, but not faster, when the word level was highlighted on one-word-at-a-time presentation. Subsequent analyses ruled out the possibility that the difference between the second and the combined fourth and sixth grade samples was due to the difference in rate of presentation rather than to developmental changes in word-level and sentence-level procedures.

The developmental changes are probably related to developmental changes in *automaticity* (rapid identification of a word without effortful decoding), *modularity* (insulation from other sources of information), and *working memory* (where sentences are stored and processed). Younger readers have less automatic, less modular word recognition skills (e.g., Stanovich, 1990) and less working memory capacity (Berninger & Swanson, in press).

Because their word recognition skills are less automatic, younger readers are more likely to apply decoding skills to each word, whether sentences are presented normally or one word at a time; hence, there is no advantage for accuracy for a mode of presentation that highlights attention to the single word. Because their word recognition skills are less modular, and context information is more likely to penetrate, they are able to use that context information to complete computation of sentence meaning faster—as long as all context information is available on the printed page and prior context is not only available in limited-capacity working memory. Thus, comprehension is faster when the sentence is presented normally and all context is available and working memory is not taxed.

Accuracy is better in older readers when sentences are presented one word at a time, for two reasons. First, older readers have more automatic whole word recognition than do younger readers; they are more likely to focus attention on the single lexical item and apply subword decoding skills to detect orthographic foils when the single lexical item is highlighted within the sentence. Second, older readers have more modular word recognition and are better able than younger readers to ignore contextual information that might cause them to decide an orthographic foil is a semantically plausible word; thus they do not have an accuracy advantage for normal sentence presentation. Mode of presentation does not affect speed of older readers' comprehension, as it does with younger readers, because older readers have more working memory capacity; thus, they are better able to consult prior text in working memory than are younger children to check out a conflict between orthographic features and context. Hence, older readers do not have a speed advantage when sentences are presented normally, reducing the load on working memory, compared with the one-word-at-a-time presentation.

Intraindividual differences in processing sentences at the word and the sentence level were also analyzed by examining dissociations between these levels. A dissociation was defined as a discrepancy of 1 standard deviation or more between the standard scores on the one-word-at-a-time condition and the one-sentence-at-a-time condition. Four possible dissociations were considered: each combination of two sentence types—meaningful and nonsense—and of two dependent measures—accuracy and reaction time (RT). *On-line dissociations* were defined as one or two dissociations, which may reflect temporary fluctuations in relative word-level and sentence-level capabilities. *Developmental dissociations* were defined as three or four dissociations, which are more likely to reflect stable characteristics of the learner in relative word-level and sentence-level capabilities.

In the second grade, on-line dissociations were more frequent than developmental dissociations: 35 percent had one dissociation,

20 percent had two dissociations, and 5 percent had three dissociations. Likewise, in the fourth and sixth grades, on-line dissociations were the most frequent: 28 percent had one dissociation, 30 percent had two dissociations, 3 percent had three dissociations, and 5 percent had four dissociations. The overall incidence of at least one dissociation was comparable across grade levels: 60 percent, second grade; 66 percent, fourth/sixth grade.

Dissociations were likely to go in either direction with better word-level processing or better sentence-level processing equally likely. The children with developmental dissociations were examined further. The second grader was more accurate but slower in word-level than sentence-level processing. Of the fourth graders, one was more accurate and faster in word-level than in sentence-level processing; one was more accurate and faster in sentence-level than word-level processing; and one was more accurate but slower in word-level processing than sentence-level processing.

Another second grader, who showed only two large discrepancies—less accurate and slower in word-level than in sentence-level processing on meaningful sentences, showed a dissociation between the word and sentence levels in another way. Although his comprehension accuracy was above chance, ranging from 63 percent to 69 percent depending on mode of sentence presentation, he could not pronounce in isolation any of the critical words (orthographic foils) rendering a sentence nonsensical. In isolation he made many paralexic errors, for example, saying "salmon" for "fish," "jump" for "hop," "tired" for "sleepy," "10 o'clock" for "time," "kitten" for "cat," "puppy" for "dog," "puddles" for "wet," and "red light" for "stop." How could he comprehend at all when his decoding/encoding of printed words was so impaired? The following distinction between lexical analysis and lexical selection provides a clue.

Massaro and Oden (1980) identified *multiple lexical procedures* for processing single words: *lexical analysis* (a bottom-up process that affects stimulus encoding) and *lexical selection* (a top-down process that makes lexical judgments based on accumulating sentence context). During lexical analysis, the features of the stimulus word are processed; during lexical selection, the word's identity in a given context is chosen (Oden & Spira, 1983). The output of lexical analysis interacts with lexical selection, but only lexical selection interacts directly with sentence context (Rueckl & Oden, 1986). Based on Swinney's (1979) finding that a target word with multiple meanings primed both meanings even though only one meaning made sense in the sentence, Perfetti and McCutchen (1987) postulated an initial, impenetrable stage in which all multiple meanings are activated and only *linguistic context*—immediate lexical neighbors—is involved, and a subsequent stage in which the appropriate contextual meaning is selected and only *text context* is involved.

Thus, the multiple lexical procedures contribute in two ways to sentence procedures. First, lexical analysis contributes feature analysis of the stimulus word and constrained semantic priming of near lexical neighbors. Second, lexical selection contributes by deciding a word's identity based on output from lexical analysis (feature analysis and semantic priming) and interactions with sentence-level procedures, providing accumulating contextual information. Sentence-level procedures provide context that affects word identification through lexical selection rather than through lexical analysis.

The boy described above was unusual in that his semantic priming operated normally, as evidenced by the paralexic errors reflecting near lexical neighbors; and his lexical selection operated normally, as evidenced by his above chance comprehension of words in sentence context. However, he had a severe deficit in lexical analysis of features in stimulus words, as evidenced by his inability to decode/ encode printed words out of sentence context. Thus this boy showed classic signs of developmental deep dyslexia (see chapters 2 and 4), which may result when the orthographic and/or phonological feature analysis component of lexical analysis is severely impaired but semantic priming and lexical selection are normal. (See Berninger & Hart, 1992, for further discussion of the theoretical significance of this case and its implications for children who can comprehend silently better than they can read orally.)

Berninger and Hart's (1993) individual subject analyses of 300 primary grade children offer additional evidence for the dissociation of word- and sentence-level procedures. They used absolute, relative, and combined absolute and relative criteria for defining disability in reading comprehension, word identification (pronouncing real words in isolation), and word attack (pronouncing nonwords in isolation) (Berninger, Hart, Abbott, & Karovsky, 1992).

When they used an *absolute criterion* (achievement in the bottom 5 percent of the normal distribution) for a disability in reading comprehension, only 64 percent also had disabilities in word identification, only 57 percent also had a disability in word attack, and only 50 percent also had disabilities in both word identification and word attack. When they used a *relative criterion* (underachievement significantly below that predicted by verbal IQ based on the Mahalanobis statistic, Stevens, 1986) for disability in reading comprehension, only 50 percent also had a disability in word identification, only 56 percent also had a disability in word attack, and only 50 percent also had disabilities in both word identification and word attack. In fact, one child, who was underachieving in reading comprehension, was over-achieving in word identification (significantly above that predicted by verbal IQ based on the Mahalanobis statistic) and was achieving at expected levels in word attack! When *combined absolute and relative criteria* (bottom 5 percent of normal distribution and underachieving relative to verbal IQ) were used for a disability in reading compre-hension, only 28 percent also had a disability in word identification, only 14 percent also had a disability in word attack, and only 14 percent also had disabilities in both word identification and word attack.

Berninger and Hart (1993) also examined the relationship in the reverse direction. That is, if an individual child had a disability in word identification or word attack, what was the probability of also having a disability in reading comprehension? When the *absolute criterion* was used, of those with a disability in word identification, only 56 percent also had a disability in reading comprehension; and of those with a disability in word attack, only 64 percent also had a disability in reading comprehension. When the *relative criterion* was used, of those with a disability in word identification, only 47 percent also had a disability in reading comprehension; and of those with a disability in word attack, only 53 percent also had a disability in reading comprehension. When the *combined criteria* were used, of those with a disability in word identification, only 53 percent also had a disability in reading comprehension, and of those with a disability in word attack, only 40 percent also had a disability in reading comprehension.

Thus, a disability in reading comprehension, which taps word- and text-level procedures, is not always accompanied by a disability in word identification or word attack, which taps word-level proce-dures only. Conversely, a disability in word identification and word attack (word-level only) is not always accompanied by a disability in comprehension (word level and text level). Group analyses may sup-port the conclusion that ability to read single printed words constrains reading comprehension (e.g., Perfetti & Hogaboam, 1975), but indi-vidual analyses support the conclusion that (a) not all problems in reading comprehension are related to problems in word identification or attack, and (b) not all problems in word identification or attack result in problems in reading comprehension.

The reason for the fact that *word reading skills constrain but do not determine reading comprehension* is that intraindividual differences in other levels of language also contribute to reading connected text. Thus, sentence- and text-level skills should be incorporated into the instructional program from the very beginning stages of reading development, even though subword- and word-level skills are the primary contributors to early reading, as discussed earlier in this chapter. This developmental neuropsychological perspective contrasts sharply with Chall's (1979) stage model of reading, which postulates an initial word-decoding stage, followed by a stage in which children read to develop fluency rather than to acquire new information, followed by a stage in which children begin to read for knowledge. From a developmental neuropsychological perspective, subword, word, and transword procedures contribute to beginning reading, and both *sound* (subword and word levels) for decoding/encoding printed words and *meaning* (word and transword levels) are fundamental to reading acquisition from the beginning on. The reason is that the oral and the written language systems in the brain of beginning readers are designed to develop crosstalk at multiple levels.

Levels of Language and Intraindividual Differences in Developing Writing

Berninger, Mizokawa, Bragg, Cartwright, and Yates (in press) examined intraindividual differences in levels of written language of developing writers in the intermediate grades. They tested the hypotheses that (a) an individual child's abilities to spell words, construct sentences, and compose paragraphs on production tasks are not necessarily developed to the same level; and (b) an individual child's abilities to make judgments about words, sentences, and paragraphs on receptive metalinguistic tasks are not necessarily developed to the same level. These investigators reasoned that during writing acquisition, children learn to sequence the hierarchical units of written language—the letters in words, the words in sentences, and the sentences in paragraphs. Therefore, they measured children's *production of local (adjacent) letter connections* in words spelled from dictation, *word connections* in composed sentences, *sentence connections* in composed paragraphs, and children's judgments about the *sequencing of letters* in words, *sequencing of words* in sentences, and *sequencing of sentences* in paragraphs. Stimuli for the production and metalinguistic judgment tasks at the same level of language were comparable to the extent possible.

Study 1 included only children reading at least at grade level. The dependent measures were the proportion of correct productions or decisions about letter sequences in words, of correct productions or decisions about word sequences in sentences, and of productions or decisions about relevant sentence sequences in paragraphs. None of the levels of language was correlated with another level of language within the production or metalinguistic judgment tasks. That is, skill at the text (paragraph) level could not be predicted from skill at the word or sentence level; skill at the sentence level could not be predicted from skill at the word or text level; skill at the word level could not be predicted from skill at the sentence or text level.

In Study 2, children showing a normal range of reading ability participated in the same experiment with minor modifications. Partial correlations, with effects due to reading ability removed, replicated the findings of Study 1—the word, sentence, and text levels were not correlated with each other. There were intraindividual differences in levels of language, in that an individual child's ability at one level of language could not be predicted from his or her ability at other levels of language.

Whitaker, Berninger, Johnston, and Swanson (in press) investigated intraindividual differences in levels of language on initial and revised drafts of a letter written by intermediate grade students. Developmental maturity was coded for word, sentence, and text levels of the initial and revised drafts using a comparable scale ranging from 1 to 5. The word-level scheme coded sophistication of word choice— lower scores were assigned to more frequently used words, higher scores to less frequently used words. The sentence-level scheme coded grammatical complexity—lower scores were assigned to simple clauses, higher scores to compound clauses with linking words, and the highest scores to complex clauses with subordinate clauses. The text-level scheme coded text organization—lower scores were assigned to listing propositions, higher scores to using cohesive devices to link propositions, and the highest scores to using propositions with cohesive devices to support main ideas.

The developmental maturity of word skills was not correlated with the developmental maturity of sentence or text skill, and the developmental maturity of sentence skill was not correlated with the developmental maturity of text skill. This pattern of results held for both the initial and revised drafts. However, skill at a particular level of language was highly correlated across drafts (range, 0.77 to 0.84), indicating that the level of language is a stable construct.

Thus, taken together, the studies discussed above provide converging evidence (Garner, Hake, & Eriksen, 1956) across samples, tasks, and the nature of the coded dependent measure, that skill at one level of written language does not predict skill at another level of written language. Table 5.1 summarizes these differences across samples, tasks, and the nature of the dependent measures. In all studies,

TABLE 5.1 Intraindividual Differences in Levels of
Written Language in Composition

I. *Production and Metalinguistic Judgments* (Berninger et al., in press: Study 1, *N* = 72 intermediate grade students of good reading ability; Study 2, *N* = 102 intermediate grade students of varying reading ability)
   A. Production tasks
      1. Spell words (proportion of words with correct *letter sequences*)
      2. Construct sentences (proportion of sentences with grammatically acceptable *word sequences*)
      3. Compose paragraphs (proportion of linguistically coherent *sentence sequences*)
   B. Metalinguistic judgment tasks
      1. *Decisions about letter sequences* in spelled words (proportion correct)
      2. *Decisions about word sequences* in sentences (proportion correct)
      3. *Decisions about sentence sequences* in paragraphs (proportion correct)
   C. Finding: Within a task, skill at one level of language (word, sentence, paragraph) did not predict skill at another level of language.

II. *Drafting and Revising* (Whitaker et al., in press) (*N* = 48 intermediate grade students of varying reading ability)
   A. First draft of letter
      1. Developmental maturity of *word choice*
      2. Developmental maturity of *sentence syntactical complexity*
      3. Developmental maturity of *text organization*
   B. Revised draft of letter
      1. Developmental maturity of *word choice*
      2. Developmental maturity of *sentence syntactical complexity*
      3. Developmental maturity of *text organization*
   C. Finding: Within draft, skill at one level of language did not predict skill at another level of language.

124

there was sufficient range within levels of language for significant correlations to emerge, and there was good interrater reliability for the coding schemes for each level. These *intraindividual differences in levels of language* appear to be sufficiently reliable across drafts to be stable learner characteristics (Whitaker et al., in press).

Levels of Language in Reading and Writing Acquisition of Disabled Students

Learning-Disabled Students

Berninger, Mizokawa, and Bragg (1991) administered the experiment in Study 1 of Berninger, Mizokawa, Bragg, Cartwright, and Yates (in press) to eight learning-disabled children evaluated in the Clinical Training Laboratory at the University of Washington. They analyzed the results for the referred sample at the individual unit of analysis using means and standard deviations for conditions of the writing experiment administered to the unreferred sample of intermediate-grade children (Berninger et al., in press, Study 1). Writing disabilities were defined as performance 1 standard deviation or more below the mean for grade (or the sample, if grade differences were not significant) on an experimental condition. Reading disabilities were defined as 1 standard deviation or more below the average standard score for age on standardized reading tests. Five general principles emerged from analysis of these clinical cases.

First, children show intraindividual differences as to whether their writing disabilities are at the word, sentence, or paragraph levels. For example, one boy was significantly below average on all the word- and sentence-writing tasks, but was average or above average on the paragraph-writing tasks.

Second, reading and writing skills usually develop in concert, but developmental dissociations or uneven development can occur. For example, one girl was reading below grade level, but showed no deficits in any writing task; however, one boy who was reading at grade level showed deficits in four of the six writing tasks.

Third, some writing disabled children may not lack knowledge of written language, but rather lack the ability to translate that knowledge into written productions. Although the unreferred children in the intermediate grades were consistently and dramatically better on production than metalinguistic judgment tasks (Berninger et al., in press), some referred learning-disabled children were consistently better on metalinguistic judgment tasks than on production tasks.

Fourth, just as some reading-disabled children are rate disabled rather than accuracy disabled (Lovett, 1987), some writing-disabled children are rate disabled rather than accuracy disabled. For example, one child showed no deficit in accuracy on any writing task but showed a deficit in speed of sentence and paragraph production.

Fifth, one kind of writing disability is specific to the word level, but varies as to whether both production and metalinguistic judgment are involved (two children), or whether only production is involved (two children).

Nonvocal, Nonwriting Students Who Are Physically and Communicatively Challenged

Can individuals who are severely motorically impaired and cannot talk or use their hands develop normal intelligence, oral language, and written language skills? Piaget (1952) made the strong claim that the infant's sensorimotor activities are the origin of intelligence and a prerequisite for development of operational thought. Segalowitz (1980) proposed that individuals who lack the sensorimotor capability to act on the world to develop Piagetian operational thought may construct alternative models of the world that are primarily verbal. Berninger (1988b) used Siegler's (1981) adaptation of Piagetian tasks, for which developmental norms from preschool to college age are available, to show that a child, an adolescent, and an adult with severe cerebral palsy and a grossly abnormal sensorimotor period, who could not sit without support, crawl, walk, talk, or use their hands for play with objects or writing, had acquired operational thought.

Berninger, Gans, St. James, and Connors (1988) compared adult patients with *severe cerebral palsy,* who never had normal motor function, and adult patients with *spinal cord injury,* who had normal motor function during the formative stages of intellectual development but lost it during or after adolescence, on the Modified WAIS-R for patients with speech and/or hand dysfunction. An abnormal sensorimotor period was more likely to compromise procedural knowledge (operations that act upon symbols) than declarative knowledge (verbal representations of propositions). Thus, Piaget's strong claim that the sensorimotor period is the origin of *all* intelligence needs to be modified (Berninger, 1988b; Berninger & Hart, 1992). It is reasonable to expect that some nonvocal, nonwriting individuals who have sustained severe damage to the motor systems in the brain may acquire normal oral and written language, at least to some degree.

Berninger and Gans (1986) compared the language profiles of the nonvocal, nonwriting adult, adolescent, and child studied by Berninger (1988b). These individuals could communicate only through electronic devices using small sticks attached to the fist or by wands attached to head bands to operate a computer keyboard. All had measured intelligence in the normal range on psychometric instruments for which response requirements had been adapted to their response capabilities. Profiles were constructed for four levels of receptive oral language—phonemic segmentation, vocabulary knowledge, sentence understanding, and passage understanding; for three levels of receptive written language—reading single words, sentences, and paragraphs; and for one level of written language production—spelling single words.

All individuals showed intraindividual differences in levels of language. Grade equivalents for receptive oral language in the adult ranged from 3.7 to above the 12th; he was age-appropriate in receptive oral language at the phonemic, syntactic, and discourse levels, but below average for adults in receptive vocabulary knowledge. His reading and spelling skills ranged from grade 4 to grade 6. Receptive oral language skills in the adolescent ranged from grade 1 to high school grade equivalents. Receptive phonemic, vocabulary, and syntactic skills were delayed for age, but his discourse skills were age-appropriate. His reading and writing skills ranged from grade 2 to grade 4. Receptive phonemic skills in the child were delayed for age, but his receptive vocabulary, syntactic, and discourse skills were advanced for age. His written language skills ranged from the mid-first grade to the beginning second grade level.

All these individuals showed at least average or better receptive oral language skills at the discourse or text level, and they could use the verbal code to represent and remember information about the world, as Segalowitz (1980) proposed. Most showed deficits at other levels of oral language, yet none showed exactly the same pattern of relative strengths and weaknesses in the verbal domain. Like children without brain damage, these individuals with brain damage to the motor system showed evidence of intraindividual differences in oral language. Thus, the developmental neuropsychological perspective can be applied to developing individuals with nonprogressive brain damage as well as to developing individuals without brain damage.

Summary

There is neuropsychological and behavioral evidence for multiple levels of language within the oral language, reading, and writing systems. Within a given individual, the various levels of language are not necessarily developed to the same level. Intraindividual differences across levels of language can affect the reading and writing acquisition of normally developing, learning-disabled, and physically and communicatively challenged students. Profiles of intraindividual differences across levels of oral and written language have not been considered in describing the phenotype for reading disabilities, but they should be.

6

Multiple Constraints and Shared Subsystems in Writing Acquisition

We have all heard of writing and reading described as encoding and decoding, respectively. This metaphor suggests that writing begins with ideas stored in some representation and consists of substituting some other representation, according to an algorithm or code. Reading, then, consists of the inverse procedure of someone who is in possession of the same code. . . . Mathematically, two functions are inverses if the second function, applied to the output of the first, leads back to the starting point. Similarly, as you read my writing, you should reconstruct essentially the message that I am

trying to convey. . . . Yet I believe
that young children do not begin
with this assumption and that
although they can read and write,
their reading and writing are not
inverses.

–Charles Read (1981, p. 105)

Outline

Overview of Research on Writing Development

The view that writing and reading are not inverses (Read, 1981) is consistent with the observation that children cannot always spell the words they can read, or that children may be able to comprehend written text but not necessarily to compose coherent written text. Less research has been done on writing than on reading; however, there is a rapidly growing body of research on writing. It is being reported in diverse literatures, including cognitive psychology, developmental psychology, neuropsychology, educational psychology, psychoeducational assessment, teacher education, teaching of English, special education, linguistics, and medicine. This research on writing uses a wide range of methods, including qualitative/descriptive, and quantitative/experimental approaches.

Much of this literature has had a *pedagogical orientation* for regular or special education students (e.g., Englert, Raphael, Anderson, Anthony, & Stevens, 1991; Harris & Graham, 1992; McArthur, Schwartz, & Graham, 1991). Scardamalia and Bereiter (1986) reviewed instructional interventions with normally developing students and Newcomer and Barenbaum (1991) reviewed instructional interventions with learning-disabled students.

Other literature has an *assessment orientation,* either with group-administered tests to *assess schoolwide achievement* (e.g., National Assessment of Educational Progress, 1980) or with individually administered tests to *diagnose writing disabilities* (e.g., Berninger, Mizokawa, & Bragg, 1991). In the past, assessment of writing focused on the *writing product,* but there has been a paradigm shift to focus on the *writing process* that generates that product (Fitzgerald, 1987).

Still other literature has a *developmental orientation* and deals with the basic processes in writing development such as (a) the higher level cognitive and linguistic processes involved in composing, (b) the writer's cognitive and linguistic knowledge, and (c) the linguistic structures of text. Beal (1989), Bereiter, Burtis, and Scardamalia (1988), Englert, Stewart, and Hiebart (1988), Hayes and Flower (1980), Hidi and Hildyard (1983), McCutchen (1986), and Perfetti and McCutchen (1987) are among the investigators who have contributed to our understanding of the development of writing skill.

Finally, a literature with a *neuropsychological orientation* is emerging. Although much of this research is based on acquired writing disorders (e.g., Roeltgen & Heilman, 1984), some of it is based on writing disorders in developing children (e.g., Berninger & Colwell, 1985; Berninger & Rutberg, 1992; Levine, Oberklaid, & Meltzer, 1981; Sandler, Watson, Footo, Levine, Coleman, & Hooper, 1992).

Researchers in a particular tradition tend to ignore contributions from the other traditions and are slow to integrate findings across diverse traditions (Scardamalia & Bereiter, 1986). The research reported in this chapter represents an attempt to move beyond writing research grounded in a single approach to research drawing upon multiple approaches, especially the neuropsychological, linguistic, and cognitive orientations from a developmental perspective.

Modifying Hayes and Flower's Model of Skilled Writing to Explain Beginning and Developing Writing

The most influential cognitive model of the skilled writing process was proposed by Hayes and Flower (1980). This model, which was based on protocol analysis of adult writers "thinking aloud" as they composed, identified three processes—planning, translating, and reviewing—that operate in the context of the writer's long-term memory and the task environment during written composition. This model's contribution was moving the field away from a *sequential view of writing* (in which planning always preceded translating, which always preceded reviewing), to a *recursive view of writing* (in which planning, translating, and revising can interact with one another at a given point in time) (Scardamalia & Bereiter, 1986). That is, during translating, one may be planning what to say next and reviewing and revising what has just been written; all planning is not completed before translating commences, and reviewing and revising are not necessarily postponed until translating is completed.

In applying the Hayes and Flower model to beginning and developing writing, we concluded that developing writing is not merely a scaled-down version of skilled writing, just as children are not merely little adults. Based on our research findings, Berninger and Swanson (in press) proposed seven modifications of the Hayes and Flower model to explain beginning and developing writing. These modifications, which are discussed next, do not minimize the contribution of Hayes and Flower to understanding the adult, skilled writing process; the modifications do highlight the importance of examining writing acquisition from the perspective of the developing child.

1. Translation has two components that may develop at uneven rates. Hayes and Flower identified three components of planning—idea generating, organizing, and goal setting—and two components of reviewing—evaluating and revising—but they did not specify any components of translating in adult, skilled writing. Although Hayes and Flower did not distinguish between *idea generation,* which was in the planning process in their model, and *text generation* in the translation process, this distinction seems necessary for beginning writers who may be able to generate ideas but have difficulty finding the language to express those ideas.

Berninger, Yates, Cartwright, Rutberg, Remy, and Abbott (1992) identified two components of translating in beginning writers—text generation and transcription—and showed that these components do not always develop at the same rate. Whereas *text generation* is the transforming of ideas into language in working memory, *transcription* is the translating of those language representations in working memory into written symbols on the printed page. Some children can generate more elaborate text in working memory than they can transcribe into written language, while others can transcribe better than they can generate text. Compositional fluency (number of words produced within a constant time interval) and compositional quality (mean of two independent ratings of content and text organization on a scale of 1 to 5) were significantly but only moderately correlated (average $r = .60$ across narrative and expository compositions). The modest magnitude of the correlation for measures that are weighted relatively more on transcription (compositional fluency) or on text generation (compositional quality) suggests that the transcription and text generation components develop at about the same rate in many beginning writers, but at different rates in others. Indeed, examination of individual writing protocols showed that when a dissociation in these components of translation occurred, transcription was more likely to lag behind text generation than text generation was to lag behind transcription; but both kinds of dissociations occurred (Berninger, Yates, Cartwright, Rutberg, Remy, & Abbott, 1992).

2. Individual differences in oral language and in levels of written language affect the text generation component of translation. Hayes and Flower did not consider how individual differences in oral language or written language skills may affect the process of translating ideas into written language. They studied writing at a stage of development when such individual differences may no longer be a major source of constraint, but our results show that individual differences in language skills play a role in the translation of beginning and developing writers.

Abbott and Berninger (1993) used multiple group structural equation modeling to demonstrate a significant path from the oral language system, based on subword, word, sentence, and text level skills, to compositional quality in first, second, and third graders. This finding showed that individual differences among children in the oral language system contribute to individual differences in the composition of primary grade students.

As discussed in chapter 5, intraindividual differences exist in the levels to which different written language skills are developed within the same child in the intermediate grades. An individual child's word skill does not predict that child's sentence or text skill, and an individual child's sentence skill does not predict that child's text skill.

Berninger et al. (in press) showed that these individual differences in levels of written language can influence text generation of intermediate grade children. Metalinguistic judgment at the word level was correlated with written production at the word level, and metalinguistic judgment at the sentence level was correlated with written production at the sentence level.

3. Both planning and reviewing have temporal and spatial dimensions. In their model, Hayes and Flower did not clearly articulate distinctions between (a) advanced or preplanning before translating and on-line planning during translating, (b) on-line revising during translating and posttranslation revising after translating, (c) planning directed toward the whole text and planning directed toward a local part of the text, and (d) revising directed toward the overall text organization and revising directed toward a local part of the text. These distinctions involve both temporal dimensions (before, during, or after translation) and spatial dimensions (whole text or a portion of it). Advanced planning operates at the whole text level before translating, whereas on-line planning operates on a local portion of text during translating. On-line revising is more likely to operate on a local portion of text during translating than is posttranslation revising, which can operate on the whole text or a local portion of it after initial translating.

These distinctions are important for several reasons in drawing conclusions about the planning and revising abilities of beginning and developing writers (Berninger & Swanson, in press). First, advanced planning and on-line planning are separate processes (Whitaker et al., in press). Although advanced planning may emerge relatively later in writing acquisition than translating and reviewing/revising, beginning writers seem to do some on-line planning. Their on-line planning involves not only strategies for searching long-term memory for content (e.g., Scardamalia & Bereiter, 1986) but also strategies for deciding what to write next in relation to what they have already written (Berninger & Swanson, in press). Second, posttranslation revision is an emerging ability at some levels of language in intermediate grade writers (Whitaker et al., in press), but operates at all levels of language in junior high writers (Berninger, Whitaker, Feng, & Swanson, 1993). Spontaneous on-line revision, on the other hand, occurred at a very low rate from grades 1 through 9, even though children, who used pencils without erasers, were always given explicit instruction to cross out and rewrite whenever they wanted to revise. Thus, posttranslation revision and on-line revision seem to be on their own developmental trajectories.

4. Planning, translating, and revising are not fully operative in beginning writing but emerge systematically during the course of writing development. Hayes and Flower modeled writing at a stage of development when the cognitive processes of planning, translating, and reviewing/revising are mature skills. Models of writing development, on the other hand, need to consider that these processes are not mature and may emerge at different rates. Our research to date shows that translating emerges before posttranslation revising, which emerges before advanced planning. That is, children are authors before they are editors. This conclusion—based on research with 300 primary grade students, 300 intermediate grade students, and approximately 300 junior high students—is represented schematically in figures 1 to 3 in Berninger and Swanson (in press). This conclusion may need to be modified as results of studies with different measures of planning, translating, and reviewing/revising and different methodologies (e.g., instructional research) become available.

Within the translating process, transcription develops before text generation. Traweek developed a scheme for coding the written productions of kindergarten and first grade children (Traweek, Cartwright, & Berninger, 1992). In the first stage children drew pictures to represent their ideas. In the second stage, children used *invented spellings to write single words,* an indicator of *transcription.* Early in the third stage, children used invented and conventional spellings to produce a *single simple sentence or clause or a complex sentence combining independent and dependent clauses,* showing that *text generation* had emerged. Later in the third stage, usually by the end of first grade, children could write *more than one sentence or clause on a theme,* showing that their *text generation* ability was expanding.

5. Developing writers' metacognitions about writing are not organized around the three processes in Hayes and Flower's model. Hayes and Flower included monitoring in their model. Monitoring is a metacognitive control process or executive function, which is not the same as metacognition or knowledge about a cognitive process. We were interested in whether metacognitive knowledge about the writing process might play a role in writing acquisition. Thus, we administered a questionaire, "Thinking about Writing," with items about planning, translating, and revising, to a sample of intermediate (Whitaker et al., in press) and junior high grade students (Berninger, Whitaker, et al., 1993).

Principal components analyses did not support a tripartite structure in which items loaded on planning, translating, and revising factors at either grade level. In the intermediate grades, the responses tended to be random and did not correlate with external criteria of the planning, translating, and revising processes. In the junior high grades, however, responses to items about translating and revising were significantly correlated with external criteria of translating and revising, respectively, suggesting that metacognitions about these cognitive processes were beginning to be related to writing. Responses in the junior high grades loaded on two factors—one tapping general knowledge about the writing process and another tapping sensitivity to audience. Thus, metacognitive knowledge seems to influence the writing of junior high students but at this developmental level is not organized around planning, translating, and reviewing/revising.

6. **Working memory, and not only long-term memory, is involved in writing development.** The distinction between short-term memory, a transient system for coding incoming stimulus information from the environment, and long-term memory, a permanent storage system, is well known. Evidence has also been accumulating for a working memory system (Swanson, in press), which is important in reading and writing acquisition (Swanson & Berninger, in press). In the case of reading, incoming stimulus information and information from long-term memory are stored in working memory until procedures for computing meaning are completed. In the case of writing, plans and goals, information from long-term memory, procedures for generating and transcribing text, and monitoring strategies are stored in working memory while a composition is constructed.

Relatively more research has been done on the role of long-term memory than working memory in writing. For example, Hayes and Flower (1980) included long-term memory but not working memory in their model of skilled writing. Much research on the development of writing has focused on searching long-term memory for the content of compositions (e.g., McCutchen & Perfetti, 1982; Scardamalia & Bereiter, 1986) rather than on the contribution of working memory to the composing process. Although this relative neglect of working memory in writing research is beginning to change (e.g., McCutchen, in press; Swanson & Berninger, in press), there is still more research on working memory in reading (e.g., Just & Carpenter, 1992) than in writing.

The research that does exist on the contribution of working memory to written composition in developing writers supports three conclusions (Swanson & Berninger, in press). First, individual differences in working memory are more predictive of individual differences in composition of intermediate grade writers than of primary grade writers and continue to be predictive of individual differences in composition of junior high writers. The measure of working memory included in the primary grade battery did not contribute unique variance to composition (Berninger, Yates, Cartwright, Rutberg, Remy, & Abbott, 1992), but the measure of working memory in the intermediate grade battery did contribute unique variance to both compositional fluency and compositional quality (Berninger, Cartwright, Yates, Swanson, & Abbott, 1993; Berninger & Swanson, in press). The measure of working memory included in the junior high battery contributed unique variance to three criterion measures of compositional quality (Berninger, Whitaker, Feng, & Swanson, 1993). In the intermediate grades, working memory influenced translation at the text level, whereas in the junior high grades, working memory influenced translation at the word and text levels and began to influence advanced planning and revision (Berninger & Swanson, in press). Thus, working memory plays an increasing role in writing as writing skill improves.

Second, working memory contributes unique variance to composition beyond the variance contributed by reading. This finding was replicated in three different samples of intermediate grade students with different measures of reading and writing (Swanson & Berninger, in press) and lends support for Read's (1981) claim that writing is not merely the inverse of reading. Reading ability alone is not sufficient to explain writing ability.

Third, individual differences in working memory are more related to text generation than to transcription, whereas individual differences in short-term memory are more related to transcription than to text generation (Swanson & Berninger, in press). During the intermediate grades, working memory and short-term memory loaded on different factors. Also, factor scores for working memory correlated with those for text generation but not with those for transcription (spelling), and factor scores for short-term memory were correlated with those for transcription but not with those for text generation (Swanson & Berninger, in press).

7. Gender differences in writing and writing-related skills exist but affect the transcription component more than the text generation component of translation. Hayes and Flower (1980) did not consider gender differences in writing, but it is often reported that girls are superior to boys in writing ability. Berninger and Fuller (1992) examined the developmental origins of these gender differences. In the primary grades, boys outperformed girls on oral verbal fluency (generating exemplars of semantic categories), but girls outperformed boys on written orthographic fluency (writing the alphabet in sequence from memory). Girls also outperformed boys in compositional fluency (the number of words produced within a time limit). Of the three best predictors of compositional fluency in the primary grades—orthographic coding, fine motor finger function, and speeded orthographic-motor integration—only the latter showed a significant gender difference, with boys more impaired on the average. Berninger and Fuller concluded that the developmental origin of disabilities in compositional fluency was not related to orthographic coding or to fine motor function alone, but rather to the *integration* of orthographic coding and fine motor finger function, which constrains the transcription component of translation.

In the intermediate grades, effects for verbal fluency disappeared, but girls still outperformed boys on orthographic fluency and compositional fluency (Berninger & Swanson, in press). In the junior high grades, girls outperformed boys on advanced planning, translating, and posttranslation revision, but these gender differences disappeared for translating and posttranslation revising when effects due to compositional fluency (the number of words produced within a time limit) were removed statistically (Berninger, Whitaker, et al., 1993). Thus, during the junior high grades, gender differences exist in low-level compositional fluency, but not in compositional quality or posttranslation revision processes (Berninger & Swanson, in press).

Taken together, the results for gender differences in writing show the importance of studying writing development from the perspective of the developing child. If gender differences early in writing development related to transcription and production of words under time constraints had not first been identified, Berninger, Whitaker, et al. would not have removed effects due to word production within time limits. They would have mistakenly assumed that males and females differed in all writing processes in the junior high grades.

Multiple Constraints Model of Writing Acquisition

Typically, children are not referred for assessment of writing problems because they have trouble with high-level cognitive functions in written composition such as planning, translating for a particular text structure (e.g., compare and contrast), revising, or adapting to an audience. They are usually referred because they have problems completing written assignments in general, for example, independent seatwork or science, social studies, or book reports; or they have problems taking written tests or notes from lectures. That is, they have developmental output failure (Levine et al., 1981), which cannot be fully explained by a cognitive approach to writing.

Levine et al. showed that chronic problems with producing written output are associated with neurodevelopmental and linguistic dysfunction. For example, Berninger and Colwell (1985) found that fine motor dysfunctions were associated with penmanship (handwriting) problems in primary grade students (age 7), but with written composition problems in intermediate grade students (age 10). Berninger, Mizokawa, and Bragg (1991) reasoned that inefficiencies in low-level skills affecting handwriting early in writing development may contribute to future writing disabilities in high-level skills, either directly because of the enormous sustained effort needed to produce written words, or indirectly because of the aversion to writing that generalizes from early frustration with it.

Based on clinical, teaching, and research experience, Berninger, Mizokawa, and Bragg (1991) therefore postulated a model of multiple constraints on writing development from the perspective of the developing writer. This model postulates three levels of constraint on the developmental skills children bring to the task of learning to write—neurodevelopmental, linguistic, and cognitive. Table 6.1 on page 140 summarizes the developmental skills thought to be important for each of these levels of constraint and the measures we used to investigate each level. According to this model, children in the primary grades who are at most risk for writing disabilities are those with structural or functional delays or deficits in (a) the *primary zones* for coding sensory information for auditory or visual stimulus words or for producing motor output, or (b) the *secondary zones* for sensory-motor integration that preserves some modality-specificity (see table 1.2 in chapter 1 for overview of Luria's model). Children in the intermediate grades who are at most risk for writing disabilities are those with structural or functional delays or deficits in the secondary or tertiary zones of the functional oral and written language systems (see table 1.2, chapter 1). Students in the junior high grades who are at most risk for writing disabilities are those with structural or functional delays or deficits in the programming/regulating unit (see table 1.2).

TABLE 6.1 Multiple Constraints on Writing Acquisition

Operational Measures

Neurodevelopmental constraints[a]

Orthographic coding   University of Washington Orthographic Coding Test (Berninger, Yates, & Lester, 1991). A written word is presented for 1 second and then removed. Child must decide if second word matched first word exactly, if a letter was in the word, or if a letter cluster was in the word. Score is percent of correct decisions.

Finger function   Finger Succession Task (Berninger & Rutberg, 1992). Child holds both hands in the air out of view and with one hand touches thumb to each finger in sequence; score for each hand is time for 5 cycles.

Orthographic-motor integration   Alphabet Task (Berninger & Fuller, 1992; Berninger, Yates, et al., 1992). Child prints alphabet in lower case letters in order. Score is number correct in the first 15 seconds.

Linguistic constraints[b]   (Described in Berninger, Cartwright, et al., 1993)

SUBWORD OR WORD LEVEL

Expressive orthographic coding   Expressive orthographic coding (Berninger, in press). A word is presented for 1 second and removed. Child writes whole word or designated letter or letter cluster. Score is percent correct.

Speeded receptive orthographic coding   Colorado Perceptual Speed Test (Decker & DeFries, 1981). Child matches a target string of alphanumeric symbols with one of four alternatives. Score is average percent correct in three 1-minute trials.

Orthographic image (orthographic address)   Homophone/Pseudohomophone Choice (Olson et al., 1989). Child selects real word in a pair that also has a nonword pronounced the same. Score is percent correct.

Orthographic image (semantic address)   Homophone choice (Stanovich et al., 1991). Child chooses the homophone that answers a riddle. Score is percent correct.

Phonological coding   Phoneme/rime/syllable deletion (Berninger, in press). Child repeats nonword, then says it again without specified sound segment. Score is percent correct.

         Phoneme localization (Vellutino et al., 1991). Child indicates whether a pair of words differs at the beginning, middle, or end of word. Score is percent correct.

[a]Primary grades.
[b]Intermediate grades.

TABLE 6.1 *Continued*

Operational Measures

| | Phoneme articulation (Vellutino et al., 1991). Child tells the sounds that are different in a pair of words that differ in only one phoneme. Score is percent correct. |

WORD LEVEL

Phonetic/semantic — WISC-R vocabulary subtest (Wechsler, 1974). Child explains word meanings. Score is standard score for age.

Phonetic memory — Memory for nonwords (Vellutino et al., 1991). Child repeats string of nonwords after an interference task. Score is number of correct nonwords.

Verbal working memory—words — Rhyme and semantic association tasks (Swanson, 1992, in press). Child answers a process question and then repeats a string of rhyming words or semantically related words. Score is number of sets completed correctly.

TRANSWORD LEVEL

Verbal working memory—sentences — Listening-recall or -generation spans (Berninger, Cartwright, et al., 1993). Child listens to a set of sentences, answers a process question, then recalls the last word in sentence or generates a sentence with the last word. Score is number of process questions answered correctly and the number of words recalled or sentences generated correctly.

Verbal working memory—text — Narrative and expository text recall (Berninger, Cartwright, et al., 1993). Child listens to connected discourse, answers process question, and recalls text. Score is number of propositions correctly recalled.

Cognitive constraints[c] — (Berninger, Whitaker, et al., 1993)

Advanced planning — Planning task prior to first draft of letter. Students are asked to write plans to help them write first draft of a letter under either a self-directed or an examiner-directed cued condition. Score (1–5) reflects developmental maturity of planning.

Posttranslation revising — Revising task after the first draft. Students are asked to revise their first draft of a letter under a self-directed condition or an examiner-directed cued condition. Score (1–5) reflects developmental maturity of revising at different levels of language.

[c]Junior high grades.

141

Evidence for Neurodevelopmental Constraints in Beginning Writing

Berninger, Yates, et al. (1992) described the full battery given to the primary grade students. Results that support the claim that neurodevelopmental constraints affect writing acquisition during the primary grades are briefly summarized. Measures of orthographic coding, finger function, and orthographic-motor integration (table 6.1) correlated significantly with and contributed unique variance to *handwriting fluency* (the number of words correctly copied within a constant time interval). Measures of visual-motor integration (analysis and production of geometric forms), orthographic-motor integration, and knowledge of letter-sound correspondence (nonword reading) correlated significantly with and accounted for unique increments of variance in *dictated spelling accuracy*. (Measures of orthographic coding and phonological coding contributed to the knowledge of letter-sound correspondence based on nonword reading; see chapter 4). Orthographic coding, finger function, and orthographic-motor integration also correlated with *compositional fluency*. Orthographic coding and orthographic-motor integration also correlated with *compositional quality*. Verbal IQ explained a unique increment of variance in the quality but not the fluency of composition, probably because quality is relatively more influenced by the text generation than is fluency, which is relatively more influenced by transcription.

Thus, the claim that there are neurodevelopmental constraints on writing acquisition in the primary grades was supported. However, low-level neurodevelopmental skills exerted the most constraint on component writing skills requiring transcription (handwriting fluency, spelling, and compositional fluency). High-level verbal reasoning exerted the most constraint on text generation in beginning writing.

Canonical correlations revealed two dimensions underlying the entire battery of predictor measures of developmental skills and criterion measures of component writing skills. These were identified as an *orthographic-linguistic dimension,* which included low-level coding processes and high-level verbal reasoning, and an *automaticity dimension,* which involved fluent retrieval rather than effortful analysis. These dimensions suggest that translation in beginning writing depends not only on the coordination of orthographic and phonological abilities involved in transcription, and of the linguistic abilities

TABLE 6.2 Relationship Between Individual Differences in Levels of Oral Language and Component Writing Skills in Intermediate Grade Writers

Levels of Language	Component Writing Skill(s)
Subword phonemic skills	Spelling
Word meaning	Spelling and compositional quality
Sentence working memory	Compositional fluency and compositional quality
Text working memory	Compositional quality

involved in text generation, but also on the degree to which this coordination is automatized, freeing up attentional resources for the higher level, less automatic aspects of writing. (See McCutchen, 1988, for discussion of the role of automaticity in writing.)

Evidence for Language Constraints in Developing Writing

Berninger, Cartwright, et al. (1993) described the full battery given to the intermediate grade students. Individual differences in different levels of oral language were related to individual differences in different component writing skills (table 6.2). *Phonemic skills* (analysis of subword sound segments) correlated significantly with and added unique increments of variance to spelling. *Word skills* (defining vocabulary meaning) correlated significantly with spelling and compositional quality. *Sentence skills* (listening to a set of sentences and generating sentences using the last word of each orally presented sentence) correlated significantly with and added unique variance to compositional fluency and compositional quality. *Text skills* (listening to a narrative or expository text and recalling it) correlated significantly with compositional quality. None of the language skills correlated with handwriting.

These results show that individual differences in language skills at the subword and word level play a role in transcription (spelling), but that individual differences in language skills at the word, sentence, and text levels play a role in text generation (composing paragraphs). These results support the claim of the model that individual differences in different levels of language constrain text generation in developing writers in the intermediate grades.

Evidence for Cognitive Constraints in Developing Writing

For a fuller description of the experiment with advanced planning, translating, and posttranslation revising tasks, see Whitaker et al. (in press) for the intermediate grade sample, and Berninger, Whitaker, et al. (1993) for the junior high grade sample. At both grade levels, students were first asked to plan a letter to a Russian exchange student about what school is like in America. Next, they were asked to write a first draft of the letter. Finally, they were asked to revise the letter and produce a second draft. Coding schemes with good interrater reliability were developed to evaluate maturity on a scale of 1 to 5 for advanced planning and for translating at the word, sentence, and text levels; the coding schemes for translating were applied to both the initial and revised drafts.

Intermediate grade children showed individual differences in advanced planning ability. Some generated abstract goals; many simply listed ideas using a "retrieve and write" strategy rather than a "knowledge transforming" strategy (see Bereiter et al., 1988); some were unable to do advanced planning and simply wrote a first draft of the letter. However, the individual differences in advanced planning were not correlated with the quality of translating on the first draft, suggesting that advanced planning at this stage of writing development does not yet control the translating process as in skilled writing (Hayes & Flower, 1980).

Intermediate grade children also showed evidence of individual differences in posttranslating revising ability on the coding schemes at the word, sentence, and text levels. However, the second drafts were rated significantly higher, on the average, only at the text and not at the sentence or word levels. This finding does not mean that intermediate grade writers were more likely to change text organization than a sentence or word when revising. The coding scheme rated the developmental maturity of the revised draft at the word, sentence, and text levels; it did not code the nature of the revision. Rather, this finding indicates that the net effect of the revision, even if it involved changing a word or sentence, was the quality at the text level. Given the coding scheme used for the text level, the revisions probably included more connectors or an improved topic sentence than did the first draft; revisions did not include less frequent (more distinctive) words or use of more complex sentence construction, that is, subordinate rather than simple or coordinate clauses.

Junior high students, on the other hand, not only showed evidence of individual differences in advanced planning ability, but also these individual differences were significantly correlated with individual differences in translation, as reflected in the quality of the first draft. Thus, advanced planning begins to control the translating process at this stage of development, as in skilled writing (Hayes & Flower, 1980).

Junior high students also showed evidence of individual differences in posttranslating revising ability at the word, sentence, and text levels. In contrast to the intermediate grade students, the junior high students' second drafts were significantly better at all three levels of language coded—word, sentence, and text. Thus, posttranslation revision emerges in intermediate grade writers, but operates to some degree at all levels of language in junior high writers.

To evaluate the claim of the model that planning and reviewing processes are major sources of constraints in junior high writers, all measures in the experiment were entered as independent variables into a multiple regression: advanced planning, number of words-first draft, sentence complexity-first draft, text quality-first draft, number of words-second draft, sentence complexity-second draft, and text quality-second draft. The dependent variable was an external criterion of writing ability (quality of an expository composition). Only the number of words in the first draft and the text quality of the second draft contributed unique increments of variance. This result suggests that for junior high students, posttranslation revision ability is a key cognitive variable in writing competence, but that compositional fluency (number of words produced within time limits) is still a critical variable, as it was for the primary grade students. Although planning was correlated with translating in the junior high writers, it did not yet contribute a unique increment of variance to writing ability.

Thus, the model is supported in that posttranslation revision is a major source of constraint on the writing process at this developmental stage. However, advanced planning emerges as a source of constraint on the writing process in that it was correlated with the translating task, but it was not yet a major source of constraint in that it did not contribute a unique increment of variance to translating, as did posttranslation revision.

Evidence for Relative Weighting of Constraints Across Development

Berninger, Mizokawa, and Bragg (1991) presented this model of multiple constraints on writing acquisition as a stage model in which neurodevelopmental constraints operated earlier in development than did linguistic constraints, which operated earlier in development than did cognitive constraints. However, they left open the possibility that these constraints may operate throughout writing development; for example, they recommended that diagnosticians determine whether neurodevelopmental and linguistic constraints as well as cognitive constraints operate in junior high students.

In contrast, Berninger, Yates, et al. (1992) and Berninger and Swanson (in press) emphasized that these constraints may operate throughout writing development, but that the relative weighting of these constraints changes over the course of development; they deemphasized the stage nature of the model. For example, low-level, neurodevelopmental skills affecting transcription accounted for 66 percent of the variance in *handwriting fluency* in the primary grade students, but only 22 percent of the variance in handwriting fluency in the intermediate grade students, and only 16 percent of the variance in junior high students. Neurodevelopmental skills affecting transcription *and* text generation accounted for 46 percent of the variance in *compositional fluency* (number of words generated and written within time limits) in primary grade students, but only 14 percent of the variance in compositional fluency of intermediate grade students, and only 17 percent of the variance in compositional fluency of junior high students. A similar pattern of results was found for compositional quality (Berninger & Swanson, in press, table 1).

Thus, neurodevelopmental skills are a major source of constraints in beginning writing, but continue to be a source of constraints, to some degree, in developing writing. Scardamalia, Bereiter, and Goleman's (1982) claim that production factors related to the mechanics of writing do not interfere with the quality of written composition after the primary grades needs to be qualified, because the low-level processes related to transcription may affect quality of writing after the primary grades. Graham (1990) showed that production factors can interfere with the quality of composition of learning-disabled intermediate grade students. Our results for an unreferred, school-based sample show that low-level processes related to transcription may affect the writing of children who are not learning disabled after the primary grades.

Functional Writing Systems

Luria (1973) introduced the idea that the same brain structures can participate in more than one functional system, and the same functional system can draw upon multiple local structures distributed throughout the brain. Likewise, the same component processes may participate in more than one functional system, and the same functional system can draw upon multiple component processes. For example, Ellis (1985, 1987) proposed that the reading and writing systems draw upon and are constructed from component visual, phonological, and semantic processes.

We investigated the possibility that functional systems for different component writing skills may share or draw upon some of the same processes, but also draw upon different processes unique to a particular component writing skill. For example, reading and spelling are to some extent dissociable systems (Moats, in press) because they draw upon some of the same component processes, but also unique processes. We reasoned that if a component writing skill draws upon a process, then a measure of that process would contribute a significant increment of variance to explaining the variance in that component writing skill. If different component writing skills draw upon the same process, then measures of that process should contribute significant increments of variance to each of those component writing skills. If, however, the measure of a process contributes to one component writing skill but not to another, then the skills draw upon unique processes. We examined four component writing systems: handwriting fluency, spelling, compositional fluency, and compositional quality.

Shared Processes Among Component Writing Systems

For a description of the measures used in these analyses, refer to table 6.1. In the *primary grades,* the different component writing systems drew upon some of the same processes (Berninger, Yates, et al., 1992). *Orthographic-motor integration* contributed a significant increment of variance to handwriting fluency, spelling accuracy, compositional fluency, and compositional quality. *Finger function* contributed a significant increment of variance to handwriting fluency and compositional fluency. *Orthographic coding* contributed a significant increment of variance to handwriting fluency, compositional fluency, and compositional quality and to nonword reading, which in turn contributed a significant increment of variance to spelling.

Likewise, in the *intermediate grades,* the different component writing systems drew upon some of the same processes (Berninger, Cartwright, et al., 1993). *Speeded receptive orthographic coding* contributed a significant increment of variance to handwriting fluency, compositional fluency, and compositional quality. *Expressive orthographic coding* contributed a significant increment of variance to handwriting fluency, spelling dictated real words, and spontaneous spelling in expository compositions. *Orthographic-motor integration* (the alphabet task also used in the primary grades) contributed a significant increment of variance to handwriting fluency, compositional fluency, and compositional quality. *Homophone choice* (semantic address to an orthographic image) contributed a significant increment of variance to spelling dictated real words and spontaneous spelling in narrative and expository compositions. *Homophone/pseudohomophone choice* (orthographic address to an orthographic image) contributed a significant increment of variance to all spelling measures (spelling real words and nonwords from dictation, spontaneous spelling in narrative and expository compositions).

Phoneme articulation contributed a significant increment of variance to spelling real words and nonwords from dictation. The *verbal working memory span* (listening-generate) contributed a significant increment of variance to compositional fluency and compositional quality.

Unique Processes Among Component Writing Systems

Based on the results reported above, in the primary grades, only two processes were shared by all the component writing systems: orthographic-motor integration and orthographic coding. Although handwriting fluency and compositional fluency shared the finger function process, spelling did not. Although compositional quality shared the verbal reasoning process, handwriting fluency and compositional fluency did not. Of the component writing systems, only spelling shared visual processes not specific to the orthography of the written language, that is, ability to analyze and reproduce geometric designs. This latter finding suggests that beginning spellers may learn words by treating them as novel visual patterns. However, spelling also drew upon the orthographic coding process.

In the intermediate grades, no one process was shared by all the component writing systems, and the various component writing systems tended to draw upon unique processes more than had been the case in the primary grades. Handwriting fluency but not spelling accuracy drew upon speeded receptive orthographic coding. Conversely, spelling accuracy but not handwriting fluency drew upon orthographic images with orthographic address. Spelling real words from dictation drew upon phonemic articulation, which taps phonemic invariance across word contexts (a concept introduced by Byrne & Fielding-Barnsley, 1990), but spelling real words in compositions drew upon phonetic memory, which requires coding sound information independent of meaning. Apparently different aspects of the phonological system were tapped, depending upon whether the task was to focus only on spelling a single word in isolation, or to juggle the many goals of functional communication, only one of which is spelling.

In the intermediate grades, only compositional fluency tapped finger function. Apparently the resources of the system underlying planning and executing sequential finger movements were most likely to contribute uniquely when the writer had to juggle the multiple goals of functional communication rather than to write a single word in isolation. As with the primary grade children, finger function contributed uniquely to compositional fluency, which is highly constrained by transcription, and not to compositional quality, which is relatively more constrained by text generation. Both compositional fluency and compositional quality, which are affected by text generation to varying degrees, shared verbal working memory, whereas the handwriting and spelling measures, which are affected by transcription only, did not share verbal working memory.

Developmental Changes in Processes Related to Component Writing Systems

Abbott and Berninger (1993) applied multiple group structural equation modeling to analyze developmental changes in the relationships among writing-related processes and component writing systems. For the *handwriting fluency factor,* consistently across grades 1 to 6, only the path from the orthographic coding factor was significant. The path from the fine motor finger function factor was not significant but the fine motor finger function factor contributed to the overall fit of the model. This result shows that handwriting is not just a motor act but rather is a linguistic act for which coding of alphabet symbols is fundamental.

For the *spelling factor,* consistently across grades 1 to 3, only the path from the orthographic coding factor was significant. The path from the phonological coding factor was not significant but contributed to the overall fit of the model. Consistently across grades 4 to 6, the paths from both the orthographic coding factor and the phonological coding factor were significant. However, the standardized path coefficient for the orthographic coding factor was substantially larger than the standardized path coefficient for the phonological coding factor. These findings show that orthographic coding is of fundamental importance for spelling, as it is for handwriting. Also, phonological coding contributes more directly to spelling in the intermediate grades than in the primary grades.

For the *compositional fluency factor,* in grade 1 only the path from the reading factor was significant, but in grades 2 and 3, both the path from the oral language/verbal intelligence factor and the path from the reading factor were significant. This finding shows that some knowledge of letter-sound relationships, which underlies beginning word recognition skills in reading, is needed for transcription in beginning writing. Once some transcription skills are acquired, oral language skills also contribute to written composition. It was not possible to model the relationship among the oral language/verbal intelligence, reading, and compositional fluency factors in the intermediate grade students, because the covariance between the oral language/verbal intelligence and reading factors was so high.

For the *compositional quality factor,* in grades 1 to 3, the paths from both the oral language/verbal intelligence factor and the reading factor were significant; however, in the second and third grades, the reading factor made an incremental contribution. Thus, knowledge of letter-sound relationships constrains quality of composition, which also draws upon the oral language system. Again, it was not possible to draw conclusions for the intermediate grades because of the high covariance between the oral language/verbal intelligence and reading factors.

Shared and Unique Processes of the Functional Reading and Writing Systems

Ellis's (1985, 1987) proposal that the reading and writing systems are constructed on the basis of other systems also implies that the reading and writing systems draw upon common as well as unique processes. Abbott and Berninger (1993) and Berninger and Abbott (1992b) applied multiple group structural equation modeling to spelling and reading, respectively, in primary grade children. As reported in chapter 4, for reading, only the path from the orthographic coding factor was significant in grade 1, and only the path from the phonological coding factor was significant in grades 2 and 3. For spelling, at all three grade levels, only the path from the orthographic coding factor was significant. Yet in all grade levels, both the orthographic and phonological coding factors contributed to the fit of the models, indicating that the functional systems for reading and spelling single words draw upon the same processes, but depending on the level of skill acquisition and task at hand, those processes are organized differently in terms of which contributes directly and which contributes indirectly.

Berninger, Cartwright, et al. (1993) analyzed the processes shared and not shared by the functional reading and writing systems in intermediate grade children. Both *reading and spelling of single real words* drew upon the same orthographic processes: homophone choice (orthographic images with semantic address), homophone/ pseudohomophone choice (orthographic images with orthographic address), and expressive orthographic coding. However, *reading and spelling nonwords* did not share the orthographic process involving orthographic images with semantic address (homophone choice), and *reading and spelling nonwords* did not share the expressive orthographic coding.

Both reading and spelling of single words drew upon the phonological system, but not the same phonological skills. *Reading real words and nonwords* drew upon three phonological skills: phoneme articulation (tapping phonemic invariance across word contexts), phoneme localization (a receptive analogue of phoneme articulation), and phonological (syllable/rime/phoneme) deletion. *Spelling real words and nonwords* drew only upon phoneme articulation.

Reading comprehension and quality of written composition drew upon mainly different processes. *Reading comprehension* drew upon the phonological system (phoneme localization), the orthographic system (homophone/pseudohomophone choice), the verbal working memory system at the word (semantic association) and transword (phrase) levels, and verbal IQ. *Written composition,* on the other hand, drew upon speeded receptive orthographic coding, speeded orthographic-motor integration, verbal working memory at the sentence level (listening-generation span), and verbal IQ. The only shared process was verbal reasoning; the rest of the processes were unique to the reading comprehension or written composition systems.

Summary

The reported research findings illustrate the importance of examining writing development from the perspective of the developing child rather than the adult. The findings also show the importance of taking into account different levels of analysis in modeling the writing acquisition process. Early in writing acquisition in the primary grades, both low-level neurodevelopmental processes and high-level cognitive processes exert constraints on writing acquisition, but the relative weighting is greater for neurodevelopmental constraints. Later in writing acquisition in the intermediate grades, linguistic constraints are weighted greater. Even later in writing acquisition, in the junior high grades, cognitive constraints are weighted greater.

Individual differences within different developmental domains permitted modeling of relationships among functional working brain systems related to literacy acquisition. Results suggest that a system approach (see chapter 1) should be used for defining phenotypes for reading and writing disorders (see chapter 2) in the context of all the relevant component reading, component writing, and reading- and writing-related processes rather than on the basis of isolated skills. The findings also provide support for the notion of functional writing systems that draw upon some of the same processes but also upon unique processes. Component reading and writing systems draw upon some of the same processes but also upon unique processes, lending credence to the claim that reading and writing are not inverses of one another (see quotation at the beginning of this chapter).

Implications of the Developmental Neuropsychological Perspective for Assessing, Preventing, and Remediating Reading and Writing Disabilities

We should not get in the habit of thinking that the organization of the brain is something innate and fixed in time. Teaching does reprogram the brain. It provides new organization, information flow, and temporal patterns. The fact that individuals differ in brain processes should not necessarily be thought to imply such differences are immutable.

–Michael Posner (1979, p. 340)

Outline

Origin of Reading and Writing Disabilities from a Developmental Neuropsychological Perspective

The claim has been made that learning to read is an unnatural act (e.g., Gough & Hillinger, 1980), which requires formal instruction in school. In contrast, learning oral language is considered a natural act, which just happens in the home setting. This point of view overlooks the contribution both of the brain and of cultural experience to learning either oral or written language.

Brain Development

Development of receptive and expressive oral language and speech depends on Luria's Neurodevelopmental Stages 1, 2, and 3 (table 1.2), which is why they are normally acquired between birth and age 5 (see chapter 1). Development of receptive written language and expressive written language, on the other hand, also depends on Luria's Neurodevelopmental Stages 4 and 5 (table 1.2), which is why they generally emerge at about age 5 to 6 and continue to develop during the

elementary school years. Brain machinery is as equipped for understanding and producing written language as it is for understanding
and producing oral language, even if the oral and written language
systems develop on different time tables.

Cultural Traditions

Up to this point in human evolution, cultural traditions have been
relatively more geared to promoting oral than written language acquisition. Over the course of evolution, oral communication has been
more critical than written communication for survival (see Preface),
and human culture has developed ways to promote development of
oral language in infants and young children as they interact with
adults and other children that make the process seem natural rather
than contrived. The field of developmental sociolinguistics has provided extensive descriptive detail of how this "motherese" teaches
children oral language as they interact with dyadic conversational
partners who provide individually tailored feedback (e.g., Snow &
Ferguson, 1977). Oral language is not acquired without any instruction or teaching; it is acquired from active interactions with individuals, with frequent turns and responses to turns rather than from
passive reception of instructional language from an adult speaking to
a large group, as happens in learning written language in school.

There is no inherent reason why written language cannot also
be acquired as naturally as oral language, as long as the brain systems
that support written language are sufficiently mature. (In other words,
it is inappropriate to expect a 2-year-old to read and write, although
it is not inappropriate to read to the 2-year-old on a daily basis.)
Human culture is still evolving ways to foster natural development
of written language, which only recently has begun to be crucial for
survival. At present, written language is usually taught in large group
settings, without frequent turns and responses to turns, which may be
the most economical way in the short run but not the most efficient
or effective way in the long run to teach written language.

The crucial studies have not yet been done to prove that oral
language is learned more naturally than written language, in which
the amount of time exposed to learning experiences and spent prac-
ticing skills is equated for oral and written language. Considering
current cultural traditions, children probably receive far more instructional input and practice of skills in oral than written language. Although middle-class parents may spend a great deal of time reading

books to their children (Adams, 1990), they probably spend more time talking and listening to them. The behavioral studies reported in chapter 3 suggest that children get far more practice in talking than in reading or writing. Cultural traditions have not yet been established for developing written language in the context of one-to-one functional communication with dyadic partners (as is the case with oral language) in school settings.

In fact, given our current cultural practices, children may actually acquire written language skills with less instruction, practice, and individual interaction than they receive for oral language. In sum, written language development might be as natural as oral language development *if* young children were given comparable amounts of individually tailored feedback, practice, and one-to-one interaction in learning written language as they are given in learning oral language. Thus, from a developmental neuropsychological perspective, reading or writing disabilities may originate from (a) failure to provide sufficient adult-child dyadic interaction involving reading or producing written text, especially in the beginning stages of written language acquisition, and practice in reading and writing and/or (b) delayed or deviant development of brain structures supporting written language or related oral language skills.

Assessment Issues

Dealing with Heterogeneity

Although in the past dyslexia was treated as a unitary disorder, there is increasing recognition that reading and writing disabilities encompass a variety of disorders, and that not all reading or writing disorders are caused by a single deficit (e.g., Lyon, 1985a, 1985b; Lyon & Moats, 1988; Lyon, Moats, & Flynn, 1988). The typical approach to dealing with heterogeneity has been to search for *subtypes*— homogeneity within the heterogeneity—based on static, one-shot assessment measures. There are two approaches to subtyping: (a) the *clinical-inferential approach* (visually inspecting interrelated test scores) and (b) *multivariate classification approaches* (Q-factor analysis or hierarchical cluster analysis) (Lyon, 1985b).

A third approach is the theory-based, developmental neuropsychological approach that has not searched for subtypes or patterns of homogeneity within the heterogeneity for two reasons. First, it has elevated the *individual* to a special status; theoretically, no two individuals have exactly the same profile of reading and writing skills and developmental skills related to reading and writing (see chapter 1). Second, it recognizes the principle of *noncontingent, normal variation,* whereby different domains of developmental skills develop independently of one another but within a developmental domain there is normal variation; therefore, deficits do not cluster together as in syndromes but rather show unique patterns across individuals (Berninger & Hart, 1992, 1993). At the same time, it acknowledges that *prototypical profiles,* with the same *relative* pattern of strengths and weaknesses in component reading and writing skills may occur.

Importance of Assessing Low-Level Skills Shown to Be Related to Reading and Writing

One implication of the developmental neuropsychological perspective is that both product and process variables should be assessed. Product variables include achievement in component reading and writing skills; process variables include learner characteristics that influence the process of reading and writing acquisition. The research reported in chapters 4 to 6 showed that these process variables include not only high-level skills such as verbal reasoning but also low-level skills such as orthographic and phonological coding. The latter should not be confused with visual or auditory skills, which may also be low-level sensory processes but are not specific to the written or oral language systems, respectively. Neuroimaging and clinicopathological studies reviewed in chapter 2 showed that different brain structures are involved in orthographic and visual processing and in phonological and auditory processing.

Behavioral evidence substantiates the distinction between orthographic and visual processing. As discussed in chapters 4 and 6, orthographic measures were correlated with reading and writing. However, performance subtests of the Wechsler Intelligence Scale for Children-Revised (WISC-R) (Wechsler, 1974), which require visual processing of nonlinguistic stimuli, were not good predictors of reading achievement in either unreferred (Vellutino, Scanlon, & Tanzman, 1991) or referred (Greenblatt, Mattis, & Trad, 1990) samples. In children referred for assessment of learning disabilities, none of the performance scale subtests of the WISC-R (picture completion, picture arrangement, block design, object assembly, or coding) were correlated with reading achievement on the Wide Range Achievement Test (WRAT) (Jastak, Bijou, & Jastak, 1978); of the performance subtests, only block design was correlated with spelling achievement on the WRAT (Shurtleff, Fay, Abbott, & Berninger, 1988). In the same study, some but not all of the subtests on the verbal scale of the WISC-R were correlated with reading and spelling achievement on the WRAT.

Thus, the scientific support is questionable for the wide-scale practice of diagnosing reading disabilities on the basis of profile analysis of subtests on the Wechsler scales, especially on the basis of performance subtests. Drawing conclusions about the ability to learn sight vocabulary based on the WISC-R performance scale or about ability to learn phonics based on the WISC-R verbal scale is not justified. There is scientific support for diagnosing reading and spelling disabilities on the basis of measures of orthographic and phonological coding (see chapter 4 and Berninger & Abbott, 1992b). All methods of teaching word recognition have both orthographic and phonological requirements (table 4.1). Therefore, the individual learner's orthographic and phonological skills for each of these methods should be assessed.

Advantages and Disadvantages of Defining Reading and Writing Disabilities on the Basis of Discrepancy from IQ

Four methods have been used to define learning disabilities: *deviation from grade level, expectancy formulas, standard score difference, and the regression discrepancy model* (Evans, 1990). The *deviation from grade level* does not take into account IQ as an index of expected achievement, and thus only identifies those individuals in the lower part of the lower half of the achievement distribution. It fails to identify children with superior or better intelligence who are struggling to achieve at or near grade level. *Expectancy formulas* do take into account IQ but use grade equivalents to determine both expected and observed achievement. This approach suffers from the fact that grade equivalents are not comparable across tests. The *standard score difference approach* uses standard scores, which are comparable across tests, but does not take into account measurement error in a systematic way. The *regression discrepancy model* takes into account measurement error affecting the correlation between the ability and achievement measures, but assumes a unidirectional influence of IQ on achievement in which IQ sets the upper limit on expected level of achievement.

The last three approaches use IQ as an index of expected achievement, so a brighter child is more likely to have an ability-achievement discrepancy than is a less intelligent child and thus be identified as learning disabled. However, the criterion set for the size of discrepancy that counts as a reading or writing disability is always arbitrary and varies widely among states and among schools within states. (See Berninger & Abbott, in press, and Berninger, Hart, Karovsky, & Abbott, 1992, for further comparison of these methods and discussion of their limitations and of problems in defining learning disabilities.)

Siegel (1989) questioned the long-standing, unexamined assumption that a learning disability should be defined on the basis of a discrepancy between IQ and achievement. She also argued for the bidirectional influence between IQ and achievement; although IQ may set limits on achievement, measured IQ may drop if students are not learning to read and thus cannot increase their knowledge and reasoning ability at the same rate as their age peers can. Berninger, Hart, Abbott, and Karovsky (1992) used the Mahalanobis statistic (Stevens, 1986), which takes into account the bidirectional influence of IQ and achievement, and found that IQ did not always set an upper limit on achievement. In fact, there was somewhat more overachievement than underachievement on measures of component reading and writing skills.

Berninger and Hart (1993) showed that children with high IQs were most likely to have their reading and writing problems identified if a relative criterion based on IQ was used, but that children with average and low IQs were most likely to have their reading and writing problems identified if an absolute criterion *not* based on IQ was used. (See also Shaywitz, Fletcher, Holahan, & Shaywitz, 1992.) They concluded that we need a flexible approach in which different kinds of criteria are used to identify the learning problems of all children along the continuum of learning ability. Berninger, Hart, Abbott, and Karovsky (1992) argued for a two-tiered, developmental approach in assessing reading and writing disabilities. Time-consuming IQ tests are not necessary for pinpointing reading and writing problems in primary grade children; brief, validated measures could be used to identify those children with deficits in developmental skills related to reading and writing for the purpose of modifying the regular program to prevent more serious reading and writing disorders. Later in schooling, IQ tests could be included in the more in-depth assessment of those children who do not respond to modification of the regular program. However, IQ does not always need to be used to *define* learning disability. Siegel (1992) showed that reading-disabled children defined on the basis of low achievement and reading-disabled children defined on the basis of discrepancy from IQ may have the same processing problems. However, IQ may be useful for purposes other than defining learning disability. It can be used as an index of abstract reasoning ability to consider in a child's overall profile of skills across developmental domains in educational planning (Berninger & Abbott, in press).

Establishing Concurrent Validity of Static Measures of Developmental Skills to Explain Reading and Writing Disabilities

Static measures are given under standardized conditions in which the child responds correctly or incorrectly; there is no attempt to teach the test. The psychometric tradition that has dominated educational testing uses static measures to assess abilities or achievement.

Static measures were used in the research reported in chapters 4 to 6. However, unlike many psychometric tests, many of the measures were chosen based on theory in cognitive, developmental, and neural psychology to tap processes related to achievement rather than to tap only achievement outcome. These measures often explained more variance in component reading and writing skills of primary grade children than did IQ and also took less time to administer and score. Thus, they might be used as an alternative to IQ tests in the early identification of reading and writing disabilities during the first tier of the two-tier assessment approach discussed earlier.

To use these measures for prereferral assessment, it was necessary to consider their validity and set criteria for what constituted a disability. Given the well-established discontinuity in development, it was deemed more important to evaluate their *concurrent validity* than their predictive validity. The rationale is that early intervention takes place in the here and now, in reference to the current pattern of assessment results, and not in the future, at which time the pattern of assessment results could change.

Two kinds of evidence were considered in evaluating the validity of the measures of developmental skills that could influence the reading and writing acquisition process. The first was whether the zero-order correlation between a developmental skill and a component reading or writing skill was significant; the second was whether that developmental skill added a significant increment of variance to explaining a component reading or writing skill in the multiple regressions.

Three kinds of alternative criteria for defining a disability were considered: absolute, relative, and combined absolute and relative. In the case of absolute criteria, a distinction was made between being at risk (1 standard deviation or more below the mean) and being learning disabled (bottom 5 percent of the normal distribution) (Berninger & Fuller, 1992; Berninger, Hart, et al., 1992; Berninger & Rutberg,

1992). The relative criteria were based on verbal rather than performance or full-scale IQ because verbal IQ is a better predictor of scholastic achievement in both referred (Greenblatt et al., 1990) and unreferred (Sattler, 1988) samples.

Three measures each of orthographic and phonological coding, which require about 30 minutes to administer, had the best *concurrent validity for reading single words* in the *primary grades:* whole word, letter, and letter cluster orthographic coding; and phonetic/semantic, phonemic, and syllabic phonological coding (Berninger & Abbott, 1992b; also chapter 4). Grade norms for the orthographic and phonological tasks and procedures for administering and scoring the orthographic tasks are reported in Berninger, Yates, and Lester (1991); procedures for administering and scoring the phonological tasks are reported in Berninger, Thalberg, DeBruyn, and Smith (1987) for syllable and phoneme tasks, and in the WISC-R Manual (Wechsler, 1974) for the vocabulary subtest used as the phonetic/semantic task.

Three measures, which together require about 10 minutes to administer, had the best *concurrent validity for handwriting fluency* in the *primary grades* (tables 6.1 and 7.1): orthographic coding (whole word and letter cluster), finger succession, and orthographic-motor integration (alphabet task) (Berninger, Yates, et al., 1992). Procedures for administering and scoring these and grade norms are reported in Berninger and Rutberg (1992) for the finger succession and alphabet task, and in Berninger, Yates, and Lester (1991) for the orthographic coding tasks.

Three measures, which together require about 10 minutes to administer, had the best *concurrent validity for spelling* in the *primary grades* (tables 6.1 and 7.1): letter-sound knowledge as assessed by nonword reading (word attack subtest, Woodcock Reading Mastery Test-Revised, Woodcock, 1987), visual-motor integration (Beery Test, Beery, 1982), and orthographic-motor integration (alphabet task) (Berninger, Yates, et al., 1992). Procedures for administering and scoring these and grade/age norms are available in published test manuals for the first two measures and in Berninger and Rutberg (1992) for the last measure.

Three measures, which together require less than 10 minutes to administer, had the best *concurrent validity for compositional fluency* in the *primary grades* (tables 6.1 and 7.1): orthographic-motor integration (alphabet task), orthographic coding (letter cluster), and finger succession (Berninger, Yates, et al., 1992). Orthographic-motor integration (alphabet task), orthographic coding (letter cluster), and verbal IQ (Wechsler, 1974) had the best *concurrent validity for compositional quality* in the primary grades (tables 6.1 and 7.1).

TABLE 7.1 Combination of Measures Accounting for the Most Variance in Component Writing Skills

Developmental Skills	Component Writing Skills
Primary Grade Sample	
Orthographic coding + finger succession + orthographic-motor integration	Handwriting fluency
Visual-motor integration + orthographic-motor integration + letter-sound knowledge	Spelling
Orthographic coding + finger succession + orthographic-motor integration	Compositional fluency
Orthographic coding + orthographic-motor integration + verbal IQ	Compositional quality
Intermediate Grade Sample[a]	
Speeded orthographic coding + expressive orthographic coding + orthographic-motor integration	Handwriting fluency
Orthographic image measures and expressive orthographic coding tasks in table 6.1 + phonemic articulation + verbal IQ	Spelling
Speeded orthographic coding + finger succession + orthographic-motor integration + verbal working memory-sentence span	Compositional fluency
Speeded orthographic coding + orthographic-motor integration + verbal working memory-sentence span + verbal IQ	Compositional quality
Junior High Sample[a]	
Compositional fluency (number of words on first draft) + revision (developmental maturity of second draft at text level)	Compositional quality

[a]See table 6.1 for measures.

Considering that some of the measures contribute to more than one component writing skill, the primary grade battery for writing requires about 15 minutes of individual testing for the writing-related developmental skills and about 20 minutes of group testing for the handwriting, spelling, and composition skills. Considering that some of the measures contribute to both reading and writing skills, the entire primary grade battery for reading and writing requires about 45 minutes, or about the time required to administer an IQ test.

The concurrent validity of measures of developmental skills for explaining reading and writing achievement in the intermediate grades was also examined. (See Berninger, Cartwright, et al., 1993, for procedures for administering and scoring these and grade norms.) Three measures of orthographic coding, three measures of phonological coding, and verbal IQ had the best concurrent validity for *reading real words*. (These were not the same three orthographic and phonological skills as those in the primary grade battery.) The same measures, except for a measure of orthographic images with semantic address and verbal IQ, had the best concurrent validity for *reading nonwords*. Measures of orthographic and phonological coding, semantic processing, and verbal IQ had the best concurrent validity for *reading comprehension*. Speeded orthographic coding, orthographic-motor integration (alphabet task), and expressive orthographic coding had the best concurrent validity for *handwriting fluency*. The orthographic image measures, the expressive orthographic coding measures, one phonological measure, and verbal IQ had the best concurrent validity for *spelling*. Speeded orthographic coding, finger succession, orthographic-motor integration (alphabet task), and verbal working memory span had the best concurrent validity for *compositional fluency*. Verbal IQ and the same measures as for compositional fluency (except finger succession) had the best concurrent validity for *compositional quality*.

Two measures, which together require about 20 minutes to administer, had the best *concurrent validity for compositional quality* in the junior high grades (table 7.1): compositional fluency of the first draft and quality of text of the second draft.

In keeping with the two-tier approach to assessment, the intermediate grade and junior high batteries can be used as part of a more complete psychoeducational assessment for children whose problems persist in middle childhood or early adolescence. The validated developmental measures can be used to explain why there is a discrepancy between verbal IQ and reading or writing achievement or to provide clues for intervention. Individual measures in the battery can also be used for screening purposes without IQ measures during the intermediate or junior high grades.

The measures in these batteries were validated for assessing developmental skills related to *component reading and writing skills,* whereas IQ tests have not been validated in this way. IQ tests (full scale or verbal scale scores but not subtest scores) have been validated for academic achievement in general or reading achievement in general (Sattler, 1988) but not for diagnosing component reading and writing skills. Thus, it is of concern that global IQ scores are used by many schools as the *sole determinant* of a child's predicted level of achievement in defining learning disabilities.

Considering Alternative Criteria for Learning Disabilities

Who is identified as learning disabled depends on whether an absolute criterion is used (as in the grade-discrepancy method) or a relative criterion is used (as in the expectancy formula, standard score, or regression methods). Berninger, Hart, Abbott, and Karovsky (1992) compared an absolute criterion (bottom 5 percent of the normal distribution), a relative criterion (discrepant from verbal IQ, based on the Mahalanobis statistic), and combined absolute and relative criteria (low functioning and discrepant from verbal IQ) for defining learning disabilities in the unreferred primary grade sample. Of those who qualified based on the absolute criterion, only 44 percent were also discrepant from their verbal IQ. Of those who qualified based on the relative criterion, only 36 percent also met the absolute criterion. This finding is of concern because schools vary greatly in whether they use discrepancy from IQ (a relative criterion) or low functioning (an absolute criterion) in defining learning disabilities. Whether a child is or is not diagnosed as learning disabled depends on the state and local criteria where a child lives or on the personal philosophy of an independent examiner who assesses the child.

Recognizing Alternative Constraints for the Same Disability

Regardless of whether absolute, relative, or combined absolute and relative criteria were used to define learning disability, *alternative constraints* were associated with the same reading or writing disorder in the primary grade sample (Berninger & Hart, 1993). For example, based on an absolute criterion, never more than 35 percent of the individuals who had a disability in reading single words also had a disability in phonological coding (syllable and/or phoneme segmentation). Based on a relative criterion, never more than 50 percent of the individuals who were underachieving in reading single words were also underachieving in phonological coding (syllable and/or phonemic segmentation). Based on combined absolute and relative criteria, never more than 40 percent of the individuals who were disabled in reading single words were also disabled in phonological coding (syllable and/or phonemic segmentation). Those who did not have a phonological coding problem were likely to have an orthographic coding problem; in some cases they had both a phonological and an orthographic coding problem. Moreover, individuals did not have the same pattern of deficits across the three measures of orthographic and the three measures of phonological coding. Clearly, there are alternative constraints associated with deficits in reading single words. (See Berninger & Hart, 1993, for further discussion of this issue.)

Dynamic Assessment to Differentiate Functional and Structural Constraints

In contrast to static assessment, which evaluates past knowledge, dynamic assessment evaluates response to instruction or ability to learn (Brown & Campione, 1986). Learning disabilities currently are defined on the basis of static assessment, that is, as a discrepancy between achievement and IQ. Berninger and Abbott (in press) have argued that learning disabilities should be redefined on the basis of dynamic assessment, that is, as failure to respond to validated treatment protocols. The rationale is that static measures do not take into account opportunity to learn. Given the numerous educational constraints on learning to read and write discussed in chapter 3, including inadequate teacher preparation and minimal academic engaged time or practice of skills, simply sitting in a classroom where other children learn does not constitute opportunity to learn. The instructional program may be well matched to the characteristics and needs of most but not all learners.

One advantage of dynamic assessment of learning disabilities is that it provides clues to which strategies work and do not work for an individual. In contrast, static assessment shows current level of functioning but does not indicate how an individual may respond to intervention. Not all learning-disabled children respond the same way to the same teaching strategy (Lyon, 1985a, 1985b).

Another potential advantage of dynamic assessment is that it may distinguish between functional and structural constraints on learning (table 1.1). Children who respond favorably to instruction may simply have had functional constraints that can be remediated with appropriate intervention. Children who do not respond favorably to instruction may have structural constraints that can be remediated only minimally or not at all, despite appropriate intervention. Unless one is certain that instruction is well matched to the child's profile of abilities and disabilities, is balanced in that it teaches to all levels of oral and written language, and provides ample opportunity for practice, one cannot be certain that learning problems are constitutionally based. (See Berninger & Abbott, in press, and Berninger & Thalberg, 1988, for further discussion of these issues.)

Rethinking Causality in Linking Assessment to Intervention

In chapter 1 the limitations of linear, unidirectional deterministic models of causality were discussed. The importance of taking into account constraints that limit degrees of freedom operating at many levels on functional systems was emphasized. Functional systems for reading and writing are influenced by the net effect of the multiple constraints operating both in the nervous system and in the environment. Thus, the goal of the research summarized in chapters 4 to 6 was to try to identify some of these functional constraints at different levels of analysis.

To accomplish the goal of studying constraints rather than causal mechanisms, multivariate techniques such as multiple regression, canonical correlations, and structural equation modeling were used to establish which measures of developmental skills were strong predictors of learning outcomes. The next step in understanding the learning process might be to design experiments to discover how these developmental skills cause learning to read and write. Such an approach is based on a linear, unidirectional view of causality, in which antecedents cause a subsequent behavior. It assumes that if we remediate a deficient developmental skill, then learning will proceed normally. Such an approach fails to take into account the complexities of all the systems supporting reading and writing development and the need for direct instruction (Shapiro, 1989) to develop academic skills.

We need to rethink causality if we are to link assessment findings with intervention strategies. Bronfenbrenner (1979) made the point that identifying etiology does not mean that one understands a process. *To really understand a process, one must be able to show that one can change that process.* According to the multidimensional, bidirectional view of causality underlying the developmental neuropsychological perspective, etiology provides one source of constraint in changing that process, but knowledge of the normal development of that process is also essential. For example, although there is strong, widely replicated evidence that phonological skills are related to reading acquisition, and reading researchers argue endlessly about whether a causal mechanism exists between phonology and reading, it is unlikely that children will learn to read simply with remediation of phonological skills without systematic and comprehensive instruction in reading (e.g., Williams, 1980). Thus, there are links between assessment and intervention in that assessment provides clues as to how instruction might need to be modified for individual learners' characteristics; but intervention strategies must also be based on exemplary teaching practice, knowledge of the scope and sequence of reading and writing curriculum, and knowledge of the multiple developmental processes contributing to reading and writing acquisition.

Prevention Issues

Early Identification

It is well established that phonological skills play an important role in reading acquisition (e.g., Brady & Shankweiler, 1991; Wagner & Torgesen, 1987). Unfortunately, this widely replicated fact has not been widely disseminated to educators. Berninger, Thalberg, et al. (1987) recommended that school psychologists screen kindergarten and monitor first graders for development of phonemic skills, which are needed for learning phonics rules of letter-phoneme correspondence, and reviewed the test instruments available for that purpose. Since then, Torgesen, Bryant, Wagner, and Pearson (in press) have developed a nationally normed, group-administered test of phonological awareness that can be administered to kindergartners. Fortunately, research has validated effective intervention strategies for improving phonemic skills if deficits are found (e.g., Alexander, Andersen, Heilman, Voller, & Torgesen, 1991; Ball & Blachman, 1991; Bradley & Bryant, 1983; Cunningham, 1990; Lindamood & Lindamood, 1969; Lundberg, Frost, & Petersen, 1988).

Although orthographic skills also play a role in reading acquisition (see Berninger, 1990, for a review; also, Berninger & Abbott, 1992b; Berninger, Yates, & Lester, 1991), few screening measures for orthographic skills exist. Measures developed by Berninger (1987) for kindergartners and first graders or by Berninger, Yates, & Lester (1991) for first, second, and third graders could be used; but more research is needed to develop time-efficient measures for this purpose.

If measures of corresponding orthographic and phonological codes are given, one can diagnose which orthographic-phonological code connections are functional or dysfunctional and adapt instructional techniques for word recognition accordingly (table 4.1). For example, one child evaluated in the Clinical Training Laboratory at the University of Washington was grade-appropriate in whole word coding and phonetic/semantic coding, indicating that he had the code connection needed to learn sight vocabulary. He was severely delayed in letter coding and phoneme coding, indicating that he did not have the code connection needed to learn phonics, the primary approach used at his school. Another measure also showed he was grade-appropriate in processing whole strings of visual symbols, but severely delayed in letter processing. It was recommended that his instructional program change to a sight-word approach but provide training in letter and phoneme coding until those skills were sufficiently developed for him to benefit from phonics instruction.

The other measures discussed in chapters 5 and 6 might also be used for early identification of deficits in neurodevelopmental, linguistic, and cognitive skills related to reading and writing acquisition. However, much more research is needed to determine how these deficits, once identified, are most effectively remediated.

Early Intervention

Berninger and Traweek (1991) identified children at risk for reading disabilities at the beginning of second grade for a two-phase intervention program delivered to small groups of five children each. In Phase I (18 sessions), orthographic and phonological coding skills were trained, but no explicit reading instruction was provided. In Phase II (17 sessions), explicit reading instruction was provided that emphasized three of the code connections in the multiple connections model: whole word-phonetic/semantic, letter-phoneme, and letter cluster-syllable/subsyllable.

Twenty children, who were at least six months delayed in reading single words and who had no more than one functional orthographic-phonological code connection, participated in an average of 28.7 sessions spread throughout the school year. At the beginning of the intervention the children were on the average more than a standard deviation below the mean in reading real words and reading nonwords. Five of the children had one functional orthographic-phonological code connection; 15 had no functional orthographic-phonological code connections, defined with the same criteria used by Berninger, Chen, and Abbott (1988).

In keeping with the emphasis of the developmental neuropsychological perspective on the individual, each child served as his or her own control. Because the test used as the pretest, midtest (end of Phase I), and posttest (end of Phase II) yields standard scores for grade, changes in relative standing among grade-equivalent peers could be evaluated over the year. Effects due to maturation were controlled in that changes are expected in absolute scores on these measures but not in relative standing among grade peers across the year. The critical question was whether the intervention resulted in significantly higher relative standing than expected based on measurement error.

As a group, children improved significantly in relative standing from pretest to midtest and from midtest to posttest. However, the relative amount of improvement was greater for Phase I than for Phase II—almost twice as great for reading real words and almost three times as great for reading nonwords. This latter result supports Lovett's (1991) prediction that prior training in phonological awareness may be necessary to achieve transfer of knowledge of letter-sound correspondence to unknown words. Overall, from the beginning to the end of the intervention, children improved approximately 1 standard deviation in reading real words and 1 standard deviation in reading nonwords. Regression to the mean was ruled out as an explanation for the results. The number of sessions in which a child participated was not correlated with gain scores, showing that practice alone did not account for the results.

Results were also analyzed for individuals. Based on the standard error of measurement for this test, there was a 95 percent probability that a gain of 8 standard score points or more represents a true gain in relative standing. In Phase I, 55 percent showed significant gains in reading real words, and 80 percent showed significant gains in reading nonwords. In Phase II, 45 percent showed significant gains in reading real words, and 30 percent showed significant gains in reading nonwords. From beginning of Phase I to end of Phase II, 70 percent showed significant gains in reading real words, and 90 percent showed significant gains in reading nonwords.

By the end of the intervention, 45 percent had all three, 25 percent had two, 20 percent had one, and 10 percent had zero functional orthographic-phonological code connections. Overall, 80 percent had the whole word-phonetic/semantic code connection, 55 percent had the letter-phoneme code connection, and 70 percent had the letter cluster-syllable code connection. At pretest, midtest, and posttest, the number of functional orthographic-phonological code connections was correlated with achievement level in reading real words and reading nonwords.

These results, along with those reported in chapter 3 for Success for All and Reading Recovery, show that early intervention can be successful. However, it is important to monitor at-risk children throughout their schooling because early gains may not be maintained (Levy & Stewart, 1991). Individually tailored teaching, without labeling the child learning disabled, and close monitoring throughout schooling hold great promise for preventing severe learning problems.

There probably is more than one way to learn to read, and some children may learn regardless of the method used. However, other children may be at risk for reading failure unless the method is tailored to their unique profile of reading-related skills. Traweek, Cartwright, and Berninger (1992) tested and confirmed the hypothesis that individual differences in phonological and orthographic skills predicted reading achievement outcome in first graders, whereas method of reading instruction—whole language or direct instruction in phonics—did not.

The rationale for the hypothesis was that many children learn to read reasonably well regardless of the nature of the instructional program, whereas some children struggle to learn to read when given an instructional program that was successful for other children. Individual differences in orthographic and phonological skills interact with instructional methods in predictable ways. Children who have good orthographic and phonological coding skills can learn to read in a whole language program by abstracting inductively orthographic-phonological covariances from case experience with specific words, as proposed by the connectionists (see chapter 4). Alternatively, if they are in code-oriented programs, they have the necessary skills to learn to read by applying deductively the explicitly taught phonics rules of orthographic-phonological correspondence.

Children without good orthographic and phonological coding skills are in trouble in either program. If they are in a whole language program, their brain machinery is not equipped to abstract the orthographic-phonological covariances of varying unit size. If they are in a code-oriented program, their brain machinery will not allow them to benefit from explicit instruction in phonics rules. (See Berninger, Thalberg, et al., 1987, for further discussion of this issue.)

Thus, in keeping with the developmental neuropsychological perspective, we do not need more research comparing meaning- and code-oriented instruction. Rather, we need large-scale efforts to identify children with deficits in orthographic and phonological coding early in their schooling; and we need to assist teachers, regardless of their teaching philosophy, in training these coding skills, as Berninger and Traweek (1991) did, so that children can benefit from the instructional program offered.

One of the current concerns of teachers is that children enter kindergarten and first grade with wide-ranging differences in preliteracy experiences in the home. Teachers wonder how they can provide what was missed earlier in development for those children who were not read to on a regular basis. The developmental neuropsychological perspective offers an optimistic view on this issue. Although preliteracy experiences in the home are beneficial, schools do come into contact children well within the critical developmental period, when brain structures are sufficiently mature to support the production systems involved in sustained oral reading and written composition *if instructional experiences are appropriate.* Instead of engaging in external attributions—for example, blaming parents (see chapter 3)—teachers should engage in internal attributions and explore what they can do to optimize the literacy achievement of these children.

One of the teachers with whom our research team collaborates, Jenifer Katahira, has provided an existence-as-proof demonstration that schools with limited resources can make a big impact on literacy acquisition despite what may or may not have happened in the home environment. For several years she has provided an integrated reading-writing program modeled after Clay (1985) for kindergartners in a school serving low-income, culturally diverse, and high-risk children. Most of her children have not had the kinds of preliteracy experiences that middle-class parents provide (Adams, 1990). She reads to the children daily from big books (six to eight times the size of normal books with large print) while they follow along in their little book versions, and thus simulates in a group setting the lap method of reading and rereading to children familiar books. She tells the children stories and has them write their own stories using Sunshine Cards, which display each alphabet letter with a picture of a word that begins with the sound that goes with that letter. She tells the children that what you think, you can write, if you sound out your thoughts and find the letters to write them down. By the end of kindergarten these children are reading, writing daily in journals, and "publishing" books (complete stories with illustrations that have been revised many times and are displayed at a book fair and made available for other children to read).

Such immersion in literacy experiences during a critical developmental stage has great potential for learning written language naturally in functional communicative contexts. It is most likely to be successful if followed in subsequent grades by explicit instruction in letter-sound correspondence (e.g., Brown & Felton, 1990; Foorman et al., 1991) and by continued reading of high-quality literature and daily, purposeful writing experiences.

A field study based on an entire school district (grades 1 to 6) provides additional evidence that dyslexia can be prevented if the instructional program is aimed at multiple levels of oral and written language (Botel, 1968). In this school system almost every child was reading at a level commensurate with his or her intellectual ability, and the instructional program was noted for including the following components. First, children were continually assessed for oral reading fluency and silent reading comprehension; needed adjustments in instructional placement were frequently made to avoid frustration from material being too easy or too difficult. Second, explicit instruction was provided in word-attack skills, vocabulary, oral reading, and silent reading. Third, children were encouraged to read widely for pleasure in books of their own choosing at their independent reading level.

Fourth, reading and writing instruction were tied to experiences in developing oral language skills at the subword, word, and sentence levels. Fifth, phonics rules (letter-phoneme connection) and word patterns (letter cluster-rime connection) were explicitly taught, and whole word units were analyzed visually, read orally, and written from memory (whole word-phonetic/semantic connection). Children were also taught structural analysis skills for modifying root words based on suffixes. Sixth, children were taught the sentence patterns of the language—basic structures and their variations—and were given frequent opportunities to translate their oral sentences into written sentences and then to recode these sentences orally. Seventh, children who needed it were given extra help in fine motor skills or speech discrimination.

Remediation Issues

Examination of Instructional Implications

The developmental neuropsychological perspective, which takes a systems approach, has several instructional implications. First, it is a mistake to focus on a single skill to the exclusion of all the components in the functional reading or writing systems. For example, a child evaluated in the middle of third grade was found to be severely delayed in phonological awareness and all component reading skills. Systematic training in phonological awareness was recommended along with other components of a developmental reading program.

The school implemented the phonological training program, but not a balanced reading program. At the beginning of fifth grade, the child was grade-appropriate in phonological skills and in word attack (reading nonwords), but was delayed two years in reading real words and three years in reading comprehension. It cannot be assumed that gains in word attack will necessarily generalize to all components of reading (Jenkins, Stein, & Osborn, 1981).

Second, instructional intervention should be balanced and flexible and should teach multiple strategies. It is pointless to argue whether a meaning-oriented sight-word approach or a code-oriented phonics approach is better, when children benefit from both (Lovett, Warren-Chaplin, Ransby, & Borden, 1990; Vellutino & Scanlon, 1987). We need to apply both/and logic instead of either/or logic to instructional practice and to research designs to identify which combination of instructional components is the most effective.

Third, instructional intervention should take into account individual differences both prior to intervention and in response to intervention. For example, Lyon (1985a) investigated how six subtypes of learning-disabled children responded to the same intervention; he found that reading disabled children with auditory processing deficits made fewer gains than did reading disabled children without auditory processing deficits in response to synthetic phonics instruction. Lyon (1985b) investigated how children with the same kind of reading disability responded to different interventions; he found that children with auditory processing deficits benefited more from whole word techniques and analytic phonics (teaching letter-sound correspondence in the context of known sight words) than from synthetic phonics (teaching letter-sound correspondences and then blending to produce the whole word).

Fourth, a simple match between individual differences prior to intervention and in response to intervention is unlikely (Lyon et al., 1988). This lack of perfect correspondence is probably due to the constructive processes of the learning-disabled students, who, like learning-abled students, use instructional cues in varying ways (see chapter 1).

Challenges in Measuring Change

One of the reasons more research on remediation of reading and writing problems has not been conducted is that learning involves change, which is difficult to measure reliably and validly (e.g., Harris, 1963; Linn & Slinde, 1977). For example, the prevailing position in the literature for many years was that even though formulas for the reliability of difference scores (e.g., Crocker & Algina, 1986) existed, difference or gain scores from pretest to posttest were unreliable (Bereiter, 1963; Lord, 1956). Cronbach and Furby (1970) recommended that investigators reframe questions about individual learning in terms of educational *status* at a single point in time rather than growth over time, as Berninger and Traweek (1991) did.

Recently statisticians have shown that these perceived problems are more apparent than real. Reliable change is not a paradox if change across time is viewed as a separate dimension from stability of measures at one point in time (e.g., Willet, 1988). An emerging perspective for measuring change, which is completely consistent with the developmental neuropsychological perspective (see chapter 1), is that data should first be analyzed at the individual level before it is analyzed for multiple individuals (e.g., Bryk & Raudenbush, 1987; Francis, Fletcher, Stuebing, Davidson, & Thompson, 1991; Willet, 1988). Willet advocates combining within-individual and between-individual analyses for a thorough analysis of learning. In the first phase, individual growth curves over multiple data points are plotted and inspected according to a mathematical model, and the within-individual plots are summarized. In the second phase, between-subject analysis is used to identify individual differences in growth processes in relation to the treatment(s) being studied.

Berninger and Abbott (in press, table 2) proposed a general model for evaluating response to treatment that takes into account the recent changes in points of view about measuring change reliably and validly. Briefly, it involves selecting children on the basis of absolute criteria for at-risk status in component reading or writing skills, randomly assigning them to treatment groups (different combinations of instructional components) that continue for at least 10 sessions, and obtaining multiple indicators of constructs used to evaluate treatment effectiveness at each point in time. Growth curves are first analyzed for the individual; parameters of these individual growth curves are then used to evaluate effectiveness of treatments between groups. The model permits consideration of individual differences in developmental skills related to reading and writing prior to treatment and individual differences in response to treatment. Berninger and Abbott argued that the parameters of the growth curves for the treatment protocols that are validated can be used in dynamic assessment of learning disabilities to determine if an individual child is a treatment responder or a treatment nonresponder.

Theory-Based Reading Remediation

Theory-based instruction is dependent on conceptual understanding of learners' characteristics, task requirements, and setting variables (Lyon & Moats, 1988). Four concepts are fundamental to a theory-based approach to remedial reading instruction from a developmental neuropsychological perspective. First, reading disabilities can be re-mediated, at least to some degree, even though there are underlying biological constraints (Alexander et al., 1991; Lovett et al., 1989). Second, remediation of reading disabilities requires direct instruction in reading skills and not just remediation of the developmental skills contributing to the reading disability (e.g., Berninger & Traweek, 1991; Lyon & Moats, 1988; Williams, 1980).

Third, remediation of reading disabilities also benefits from re-mediating developmental skills such as phonemic coding contributing to the reading disability (Berninger, Lester, Sohlberg, & Mateer, 1991, Study 2; Berninger & Traweek, 1991) or taking into account the functional orthographic-phonological code connections (Ber-ninger, Lester, Sohlberg, & Mateer, 1991). For example, selective reminding or only presenting the words missed on previous learning trials (Buschke, 1977) was more effective than a multisensory tech-nique in teaching sight vocabulary to children deficient in the whole word-phonetic/semantic code connection.

Fourth, classroom reading instruction must be directed to all levels of language (see chapter 5) in order to stimulate optimally all the relevant brain systems that support the functional reading system. Specifically, instruction in the early grades should not be directed just to word recognition (code approach) or just to comprehension (whole language approach). Moreover, comprehension instruction needs to be as explicit as word recognition instruction; there is evidence that explicit instruction in comprehension may account for less than 1 per-cent of instructional time (Jenkins et al., 1981).

Instruction can be directed to all levels of language within the directed reading activity (DRA). The DRA is an existing conceptual model for reading instruction that can be modified to reflect the de-velopmental neuropsychological perspective (table 7.2). During the *readiness phase,* the teacher introduces new words, pointing out how they can be decoded based on phonics rules (letter-phoneme or letter cluster-phoneme correspondence), analogies or word patterns (let-ter cluster-rime correspondence), and structural analysis (segment-ing words into syllables, adding accent patterns, and modifying root stems on the basis of suffixes or prefixes). The teacher also

TABLE 7.2 Steps of Theory-Based Directed Reading Activity (DRA) Aimed at All Levels of Language[a]

I. Readiness phase
   A. Introduce new words and teach them using multiple orthographic-phonological code connections at the word and subword levels (see table 4.1)
   B. Discuss background knowledge that will enhance understanding of the passage (discourse level)
   C. Ask purpose-setting questions to guide silent reading (spark interest and motivation; promote self-regulation)
II. Silent reading for meaning phase (child may reread as frequently as desired) (discourse level)
III. Explicit comprehension instruction phase (word, sentence, and discourse levels)
   A. Answer purpose-setting questions
   B. Answer questions designed to help reader grasp the main ideas, locate supporting details, recall factual information, engage in inferential thinking, develop vocabulary understanding, and interpret text structures and cohesive devices
   C. Discuss personal reaction to text (affective response)
   D. Retell passage orally or in writing
IV. Oral reading phase (subword, word, and transword levels)
   A. Read portions of text that support answers to questions during explicit comprehension instruction
   B. Oral reading of entire passage
      1. To develop fluency (only if child needs practice to automatize word recognition)
      2. To develop literary appreciation (e.g., poetry or plays)
V. Skill development phase (didactic instruction in specific skills aimed at different levels of language depending on the group's or individual child's needs—e.g., phonological awareness, phonics, structural analysis, sentence grammar, story grammar)
VI. Skill practice phase (can be individualized for different children in the group)
   A. Review old words (written on 3 × 5 cards in file) using explicit strategies (e.g., say word, copy word, turn card over, write word from memory, use word in sentence to show meaning) (word and sentence levels)
   B. Reading for pleasure—read material at independent reading level using material not used in the reading lesson (discourse level)
   C. Writing for pleasure

---

[a]It is not necessary to read an entire passage during an instructional session, but it is necessary to cover steps I–IV in the DRA with the selected portion read during an instructional session.

176

pronounces the new words as whole units and discusses their meaning. Next, the teacher discusses the background knowledge needed to understand the story and sets the purpose for reading by asking questions to guide the silent reading. During the *silent reading for meaning phase* the child reads the designated passage.

During the *explicit instruction in comprehension phase,* the child (a) answers the purpose-setting questions and other questions about the story tapping main ideas, factual recall, inferential thinking, vocabulary meaning, and sequential organization or text structure, (b) discusses the content and personal reaction to the passage, and (c) synthesizes the passage by retelling it orally or in writing. During the *oral reading phase,* if already fluent in accuracy and rate of oral reading, the child reads aloud to answer purpose-setting questions; if not already fluent, the child reads the entire passage aloud to the teacher, a peer, or an older child-tutor, or along with a tape-recorded version of the passage.

During the *skill development phase,* the teacher provides didactic instruction in specific skills depending on the needs of the group or individual children (e.g., phonological awareness, phonics, structural analysis). During the *independent skill practice phase,* the child reads books or magazines for pleasure to practice skills, and reviews old words. The child may also compose stories, plays, or poems or write in a journal at this time. If executed carefully, the DRA teaches to all levels of language—especially sublexical and lexical during the readiness phase, lexical and translexical during the silent reading and oral reading phases, and sublexical, lexical, and translexical during the skill development and practice phase. In the spirit of the whole language movement, no step of the DRA requires workbooks or worksheets. In the spirit of code approaches, orthographic and phonological coding and decoding skills are explicitly taught in the DRA during the readiness and skill development phases.

Theory-Based Writing Remediation

Berninger, Mizokawa, and Bragg (1991) recommended theory-based interventions for specific writing disabilities. Rutberg (work in progress) is evaluating whether direct academic instruction in component writing skills alone or combined neurodevelopmental training of deficit skills and direct academic instruction is more effective in remediating writing disabilities. The general principle to be emphasized at this time is that *low-level problems,* for example, in automaticity of letter production, will probably require not only low-level neuro-developmental training but also *high-level solutions,* that is, writing instruction geared to cognitive strategies and writing for meaningful goals (Berninger, Mizokawa, et al., in press). High-level cognitive strategy programs are reviewed in Berninger, Mizokawa, and Bragg (1991) and Harris and Graham (1992).

Unanswered Questions

The developmental neuropsychological perspective has potential for teasing apart functional and structural constraints on learning to read and write. By first intervening in the regular classroom early in schooling during a critical developmental period, we can optimize achievement of all children and eliminate reading and writing problems that are due to functional constraints. By providing one-to-one tutorial intervention using validated clinical protocols for those children who do not respond to large or small group interventions, we may be able to remediate still other reading and writing problems due to functional constraints. By comparing event-related potentials, which are expected to change, before and after children learn specific skills, we may be able to describe the functional changes in the brain related to learning to read and write. By comparing magnetic resonance images of neuroanatomical structures, which are not expected to change, for children who do and do not respond to interventions, we may be able to identify the structural constraints in the brain on reading and writing acquisition. Our laboratory is now turning attention to questions such as these as we continue our investigation of reading and writing acquisition from a developmental neuropsychological perspective. In this way, basic knowledge of brain-behavior relationships can be gleaned from educational intervention studies.

Summary

Research on reading and writing acquisition from a developmental neuropsychological perspective has validated a set of measures that can be used for brief assessment of reading and writing disabilities in the primary grades and more extensive assessment of reading and writing disabilities in the intermediate grades. From a developmental neuropsychological perspective, written language can be developed naturally in a functional communicative context early in schooling, even if preliteracy experiences in the home were minimal. Early intervention has promise for prevention. Implications of the developmental neuropsychological perspective for remediating reading and writing disabilities were examined. Theory-based remediation of reading and writing disabilities was discussed. Research approaches were introduced for differentiating the *functional constraints,* which are expected to change with learning, and *structural constraints,* which are not expected to change, by comparing treatment responders and treatment nonresponders on electrophysiological and neuroimaging measures, respectively.

G L O S S A R Y

ABC method Teaching letter names first and then syllables or whole words by spelling them.

A-brain Detects world-caused stimulus events.

Accuracy disability Word recognition skills for reading are below grade level or below level expected on basis of IQ.

Agraphia Inability to learn to write or loss of ability to write.

Alphabet task Child is asked to print the alphabet in lower case letters as quickly and accurately as possible.

Alternative pathways At the structural level, different neural pathways that underlie the same behavioral outcome. At the functional level, different mechanisms or processes that lead to the same behavioral outcome.

Angular gyrus Convolution (fold) in the cortex in the parietal lobe near the junction of the association areas of the parietal, occipital, and temporal lobes. Thought to be important in language functioning, including cross-modal integration in reading.

Anomaly Abnormal, but not diseased or injured, brain structure.

Arousal unit Subcortical unit with connections to the frontal lobe that regulates arousal and responsiveness to the environment. Luria's first functional unit.

Association areas Cortical regions that are not specialized for sensory or motor functions and do not have any direct connections to the external world as do the primary sensory and motor areas of the brain.

Asymmetry Corresponding structures in the left and right brain are not the same size, or they differ in function.

Attention deficit disorder (ADD) Difficulty in selectively attending to relevant stimuli, maintaining attention to task, and/or switching attention between tasks. ADD may occur with or without hyperactivity (excessive and inappropriate activity).

Auditory level Level of processing at which preliminary analysis of the frequency and intensity of incoming acoustic signal takes place.

Automaticity A process is executed effortlessly, without making demands on limited attentional resources.

Axon A digital (off/on) neuronal process that transmits action potentials away from one cell body to other neurons, glands, or muscles.

B-brain Detects brain-created simulus events and supervises the A-brain, which detects world-caused events. B-brains may in turn be supervised by C-brains and so on.

Behavioral pathway Neural structures underlying learning of direct stimulus-response associations.

Bilateral Occurring in both the left and right sides of the brain.

Broca's area A region in the left frontal lobe, near the motor strip, that is involved in speech production and expressive language.

Canonical correlation An analysis of the relationship between two sets of variables, when each set consists of multiple measurements.

Caudate nucleus Part of the basal ganglia in the forebrain that has extensive connections with the cortex and is involved in motor functions, especially motor inhibition.

Cerebral cortex Outer layer of gray matter on the surface of the cerebral hemispheres, each of which has four lobes (occipital, parietal, temporal, and frontal).

Cerebral palsy Nonprogressive damage during gestation or the first postnatal year to portions of the cortex that control motor function. In contrast, muscular dystrophy is a progressive disease that destroys muscle function later in development.

Clinicopathological studies Behavioral deficits prior to death are correlated with lesions in the brain found in autopsies.

Cognitive pathway Neural structures underlying schema or conceptual learning.

Cohesive devices Linguistic ties for connecting text, such as pronouns,

organization signals (e.g., "first," "second"), words that refer to preceding (e.g., "this") or subsequent (e.g., "the following") text.

Compositional fluency Number of words produced within time limits. Affected by both transcription and text-generation abilities.

Compositional quality Holistic ratings of content and text organization by two independent raters.

Computed axial tomography (CT) Referred to as a "CAT scan," this radiologic procedure uses a computer to develop a three-dimensional representation of the brain. Two-dimensional slices can be examined for evidence of bleeds in the ventricles, disease, or injury.

Concordance rate Percent of twins in which both members of the pair (co-twins) have the same disorder.

Connectionism Model of brain functioning in which specific functions emerge from the connections between a large number of simple processing units in massively parallel distributed systems.

Consonant blend Two or more consonants in which each represents its conventional sound (e.g., "bl," "str").

Consonant diphthong Two consonants that together represent a different sound from that of either alone (e.g., "th," "ng").

Constraints Influencing development and behavior by limiting degrees of freedom. A variable at one level of analysis cannot determine behavior independent of variables at other levels of analysis.

Constructive processes Using instructional cues in varying ways to create mental representations and operations.

Contralateral principle One side of the brain controls the opposite side of the body.

Convolutions Folds in the cerebral cortex ("outer bark") of the forebrain.

Corpus callosum Neural fibers that connect the left and right hemispheres of the cerebral cortex.

Cortex The newest or outermost layer of the brain that has four to six layers of cells that are also organized into columns. The cortex folds over on itself and appears to be convoluted. It consists of neurons and their synaptic connections.

Covariance structures The set of empirical relationships among multiple measurements as indexed by the covariance (the average degree to which the deviations from the mean are consistent on the two measurements).

Covariant learning hypothesis Orthographic-phonological mappings are learned through crosstalk between letters and sounds of varying unit size during repeated exposure to a set of words.

Critical developmental period Window of development within which a skill is most easily acquired and after which skill acquisition is less probable but not impossible.

Cross-exclusion principle Neurons are wired to send inhibitory signals to other neurons in a system to prevent uncontrollable spreading activation.

Cytoarchitectonic studies Mapping the organization, structure, and distribution of cells in the cerebral cortex.

Decoding Applying word attack skills for figuring out how to pronounce unfamiliar words.

Deductive Going from the rule to the application. (See *Inductive*)

Dendrite Analog (continuous), branching neuronal process that receives electrochemical signals transmitted to a neuron.

Determinism Causal mechanisms are linear, unidimensional, and unidirectional with no degrees of freedom.

Developmental deep dyslexic Can read sight words but has trouble with phonics, makes paralexic errors (confusing words in the same semantic domain), and reads better in context than in isolation. All the orthographic-phonological code connections except whole word-semantic may be dysfunctional.

Developmental direct dyslexic Pronounces words (word calling) without understanding, probably because of a dysfunction in the whole word-semantic code connection.

Developmental dissociation Different skills or component processes are not developed to comparable levels.

Developmental mismatch hypothesis Failure of corresponding codes of the same unit size to develop to comparable levels interferes with formation of orthographic-phonological code connections.

Developmental phonological dyslexic Can read sight words but has trouble with phonics rules, probably because the letter-phoneme and/or letter cluster-rime code connection is dysfunctional.

Developmental surface dyslexic Can read with phonics rules but has trouble with sight words, probably because whole word-phonetic code connection is dysfunctional.

Dichotic listening Different stimuli are presented simultaneously through ear phones to each ear. Accuracy of report for each ear is used to infer which hemisphere is superior for processing certain kinds of stimuli.

Diencephalon Region of brain including hypothalamus (regulates basic physiological functions such as appetite and thirst) and thalamus (the way station for incoming stimuli).

Digraphs Two letters together representing one sound, which is associated with one of the letters (e.g., "ie" pronounced with the short "e" sound).

Diphthongs Two letters together representing one sound, which is different from either of the sounds associated with the individual letters (e.g., "th" or "oy").

Direct route The printed word is directly associated with a semantic code without intervening phonological recoding.

Discourse level Level of language processing involving multiple utterances or sentences and often long stretches of conversation or text.

Dissociation One process is disturbed, but a related process is not.

Dizygotic (DZ) twins Fraternal twins whose genetic constitution is similar to the same degree as that of siblings.

Dual route theory Word recognition is based on a direct visual route to meaning or an indirect phonological route, in which words are phonologically recoded before meaning is accessed. The direct route is used for irregular words, the indirect route for regular words.

Dyseidetic dyslexia Boder proposed that this subtype of dyslexia, which has not been validated, was related to problems in visual perception of whole words.

Dyslexia Inability to read or loss of ability to read. The nature of the reading problems are heterogeneous, and the severity varies along a continuum.

Dysphonetic dyslexia Boder proposed that this subtype of dyslexia, which has not been validated, was related to auditory deficits and poor phonetic skills.

Dysplasias Brain tissue fails to develop normally because an excessive number of large cells distorts the normal organization of the cerebral cortex into columns and layers. Malformed cellular architecture.

Ecological fallacy Drawing conclusions about one unit of analysis (e.g., the individual) based on analyses at another unit of analysis (e.g., the group). Results may not correspond across units of analysis.

Ectopias Brain tissue fails to develop normally because neural elements occur in layer I of the cerebral cortex, which usually does not have neurons. Neurons are misplaced.

Empiricism View that experience influences development. (See *Nativism*)

Evoked potentials Recorded from the scalp, these large, slow waves are thought to reflect dendritic activity.

Expressive task Individual has to construct a response, which may require considerable expressive language and motor skill.

Extragenetic factors Any factors other than those encoded in the genome.

Factor analysis Method of identifying and quantifying dimensions that explain *common covariance* among a set of correlated measurements. (See *Principal components analysis*)

Family pedigree Taking a family history across generations to determine which family members have or do not have a certain disorder. Used in genetic studies.

Finger function Assessing neurodevelopmental status based on finger tasks.

Finger succession task A child is asked to perform timed maneuvers, touching each finger, in sequence, to the thumb, with hands held up and out of view.

Fissure Folds of the cortex produce a deep valley between two gyri.

Forebrain Includes the cerebral hemispheres, basal ganglia, thalamus, amygdala, hippocampus, and septum.

Frontal lobes All of the cortex located in front of the central fissure or sulcus.

Located in front of the head, they are associated with planning, regulating, and motor acts.

Functional system Parts of the brain, which may be located in different regions but work together to perform a task.

Genome Complete set of hereditary factors contained in the chromosomes.

Genotype An individual's genetic constitution.

Gestation Development between fertilization and birth.

Grapheme Alphabet letter.

Grapheme-phoneme correspondence Letter-sound association, as in phonics rules.

Gray matter Brain areas composed mainly of cell bodies.

Gyrus (plural, *gyri*) Folds of cortex produce a raised region above the surrounding area.

Head injury A severe blow to the head resulting in damage to the skull and brain (open-head injury), or to the brain and not the skull (closed-head injury).

Heschl's gyrus Primary auditory cortex.

Heterarchy Multidomain organization that coordinates multiple hierarchies within a working brain system.

Hidden units Located between input and output units with no direct connections with the environment, these units provide computational space where processing takes place.

Hierarchy Multilevel organization within a domain.

Hindbrain Lowest part of the brain, consisting of the cerebellum, medulla, pons, and fourth ventricle.

Hippocampus Cortical structure in the region of the temporal lobe; associated with memory function.

Hyperlexia Early superior word-recognition skills associated with comprehension and language disorders.

Implications of stated propositions Spoken or written language conveys more than is stated. What is stated implies additional ideas via world knowledge and the semantic networks underlying language.

Indirect route Visual words are recoded phonologically before the semantic lexicon is accessed.

Inductive Patterns are abstracted from case experience. (See *Deductive*)

Information processing unit Occipital, temporal, and parietal lobes, which obtain, store, and process information from the external world. Luria's second functional unit.

Insula Cortex deep in the sylvian fissure.

Interhemispheric asymmetry of the planum Temporal bank on left is larger than temporal bank on right.

Interindividual differences Differences *among individuals* within the same developmental domain or component process.

Intrahemispheric asymmetry of the planum Temporal bank is larger than the parietal bank on the same side.

Intraindividual differences Differences across developmental domains or component processes *within the same individual.*

In vivo imaging Techniques used with living people, in contrast to autopsy studies.

Irregular words Words that do not conform to the phonics rules of the language (phonologically irregular) or the permissible letter sequences of the language (orthographically irregular).

K-lines Knowledge lines that reactivate partial mental states (agents that were activated when representation was created).

Latent variables Factors underlying measures of a construct.

Laterality Related to side of brain or body that is the locus of function or dysfunction.

Lateralize Project a stimulus to only one cerebral hemisphere.

Left cortex or cerebral hemisphere Consists of a frontal, temporal, parietal, and occipital lobe. Connected to the right cortex or cerebral hemisphere by the corpus callosum.

Lesions Damage to the brain.

Letter cluster-phoneme connection Two or more letters that are associated with a single sound.

Letter cluster-rime code connection Two or more letters that are associated with a spoken subsyllabic rime.

Letter cluster-syllable code connection Two or more letters that are associated with a spoken syllable.

Letter-phoneme code connection A single letter associated with a single sound.

Level band principle A K-line only activates agents that were active in memory when a representation was first created and that are within a certain band. If too many agents are activated, the present will be confused with the past. If too few agents are activated, perception will suffer from insufficient detail.

Levels of analysis The same behavior can be analyzed at multiple levels, including the microstructure and macrostructure and microfunction and macrofunction of the nervous system.

Levels of language Sublexical (phonemes, syllables, rimes, morphemes), lexical (phonetic/name codes, semantic codes), translexical (syntactic/semantic, discourse or text).

Lexical analysis Bottom-up encoding of stimulus words on the printed page.

Lexical decision task Child must decide if a stimulus word is a real word that means something. Letter strings and pronounceable nonwords may be presented along with real words.

Lexical level Level of language processing involving the single word.

Lexical selection Top-down judgments about a word's identity based on accumulating sentence context.

Limbic structures Brain structures thought to be involved in emotional and motivational aspects of behavior.

Linkage analysis Laboratory procedure that tests the location of specific genes on specific chromosomes.

Localization of function View that specific brain functions are tied to specific brain sites.

Long-term memory Permanent storage from which representations are activated or constructed.

Look-say method Children pronounce words as whole units rather than sounding them out letter by letter.

Magnetic resonance imaging (MRI) A procedure for imaging the living brain; individual is placed inside a large magnetic coil. A computer uses the measured changes in the magnetic resonance of hydrogen atoms in the brain to create a map of the brain's neuroanatomical structures.

Magnocellular pathways Neuroanatomical structures for the fast visual processing system.

Mass action View that whole brain participates in a function, and that the amount of brain tissue involved is more important than the specific brain tissue involved.

Metacognitive knowledge Knowledge about a cognitive process.

Metalinguistic Awareness of the properties of language.

Midbrain Short segment between the hindbrain and forebrain.

Modularity Functional systems organized so that there are separate, insular subsystems or modules within the larger system.

Momentary time Nonlinear time. Each agent exists on a different time scale. Memories are only indirectly linked to linear, real time in the physical world.

Monozygotic (MZ) twins Identical twins who share the same genetic constitution.

Morphologist Specialist in neuroanatomy.

Multiple constraints Multiple sources of variables at different levels of analysis that facilitate or limit learning and development.

Multiple group structural equation modeling Structural equation modeling applied to testing whether structural models are significantly different at different ages or grades.

Multiple regression A method for identifying the weighted combination of predictors that optimally predicts a criterion.

Myelin Fatty substance that insulates some nerve fibers and improves the rate of conducting neural impulses along these fibers.

Myelination Formation of myelin on axons; thought to be an index of maturation.

N 400 Event-related potential (ERP) component occurring 400 msec after stimulus onset and associated with negative electrical discharge.

Name code Phonetic code for whole word that includes segmental sound components and suprasegmental intonational contours that mark stress patterns in the whole word.

Naming A task in which a child is asked to name a printed word (as in oral reading) or a word illustrated pictorially.

Nativism View that biological maturation, rather than the experience, influences development.

Neuron The basic building block of the nervous system. A nerve cell consisting of a cell body, an axon, and dendrites. Receives, stores, and transmits information.

Neuronal migration After fertilization, germinal cells divide and migrate to target areas in the nervous system. Following migration, excessive cells are pruned. (See *Selective cell death*)

Neuropsychology Field that attempts to relate what is known about the functioning of the brain to what is understood about human behavior and development.

Noncontingent, normal variation Variation in one developmental domain occurs independently of variation in another developmental domain.

Nonword A word that can be pronounced but has no meaning (e.g., "bafmotbem").

Normal variation Diversity not related to pathology. Does not imply that learning variables are necessarily distributed along a bell-shaped curve.

Occipital lobes Area of cortex lying in the back part of the head behind the parietal and temporal lobes. Associated with visual functions.

On-line dissociation Component processes operate at substantially different levels of performance during on-line processing.

Onset Initial phoneme(s) in a syllable.

Operations Processes that act upon representations.

Orthographic Refers to visual representations specific to written words and not to visual-spatial processing that does not involve written words.

Orthographic coding Representing a printed word in memory and accessing the whole word unit, a component letter, or a letter cluster unit.

Orthographic image Representation of a specific written word in memory.

Orthographic-motor integration Synchronizing orthographic and motor skills, as in producing alphabet letters.

Orthographic-phonological code connection Link between corresponding orthographic-phonological codes at the same unit size.

Orthographically regular word Written word that conforms to the permissible letter sequences of the language.

P 300 Event-related potential (ERP) component occurring at 300 msec after stimulus onset and associated with positive electrical discharge.

Parietal lobes Behind the frontal lobes, above the temporal lobes, and in front of the occipital lobes. Associated with sensory functions.

Partial state of mind Specifies only the agents that are active at a particular moment of time and not those that are quiet.

Parvocellular pathways Neuroanatomical structures associated with the slow visual processing system.

Phenotype An individual's characteristics resulting from genetic and environmental influences.

Phoneme The smallest unit of sound that makes a difference in meaning without having a meaning of its own. Abstract category for relating sound and meaning.

Phoneme deletion task Child is asked to repeat a word and then to say it again without a designated phoneme.

Phoneme-grapheme correspondence Phonics rules.

Phonemic invariance Recognizing the same phoneme across different word contexts.

Phones Segmental sound units in speech. Not the same as phonemes, which are perceptual rather than production units.

Phonetic code Name code for the whole word, which contains the segmental phones and suprasegmental intonational contours.

Phonetic level The level of language processing at which the first linguistic coding of sound information occurs; also the level at which the whole word is processed.

Phonically irregular real word Not every letter of a word conforms to conventional phonics rules.

Phonically regular real word Every letter of the word conforms to conventional phonics rules.

Phonic method (See *Phonics*)

Phonics Rules of grapheme-phoneme correspondence. Synthetic phonics teaches blending of constituent sounds. Analytic phonics teaches sound segmentation within the context of a word.

Phonogram Letter cluster that corresponds to a spoken rime unit.

Phonological coding Representing a spoken word in memory and analyzing it at the whole word or subword level (phonemes, rimes, or syllables).

Phonological decoding or recoding Translating written words into spoken words using letter-sound associations at the subword level.

Phonological level Level of language processing that involves more abstract linguistic processing than does the phonetic level; words are analyzed into phonemes.

Planum temporale Cortical area located in the temporal lobe behind Heschl's gyrus (auditory cortex) within the sylvian fissure. Thought to be associated with phonological processing.

Plasticity Whether nervous system recovers function following injury.

Polymicrogyria Many small gyria that are structurally anomalous. Excessive folding that results in the absence of columnar organization.

Positron emission tomography (PET) Technique for imaging the living brain. A computer constructs a map of the brain based on its metabolic activity, which is traced through a radioactively labeled compound while the person performs a task.

Postmigration period After neurons have migrated to their positions in neural architecture.

Pragmatic Pertains to communicative acts—the functions performed by language.

Presuppositions Unstated assumptions of stated language that contribute to our understanding of language.

Primary projection areas or cortical zones Receive impulses from and send impulses to the external world. Modality-specific but do not obey the contralateral principle.

Principal components analysis Method of identifying and quantifying dimensions that explain the *common covariance and variance* in a set of correlated measurements. (See *Factor analysis*)

Proband The index case in each twin pair. To determine heritability, each proband's co-twin is entered into the regression analyses.

Profile analysis Comparison of relative strengths and weaknesses across different developmental domains or component processes.

Programming/regulating unit Areas of frontal lobes involved in making and carrying out plans and monitoring and regulating activity. Luria's third functional unit.

Proposition Idea units in the language.

Prosody Suprasegmental intonational contour that marks stress patterns.

Rate disability Word recognition is at grade level or expected level based on IQ, but reading rate is below grade level or expected level based on IQ.

Receptive task Processing task in which the child can select rather than construct a response. Minimal motor requirements.

Recursive view of writing Planning, translating, and revising processes interact with one another on line during the composing process.

Redundancy The same information is represented more than once (copied) in alternative ways as a safeguard against dysfunction or loss of information.

Referred sample Individuals are referred for clinical assessment of developmental, learning, or psychological problems. May be affected by referral bias (a preponderance of a certain problem).

Regular words Conform to phonics rules of the language or the permissible letter sequences of the language.

Representations Data structures for representing stimuli, or simuli in memory. Operations, which are in turn represented in memory, act upon these data structures.

Reticular activating system Nerve centers or nuclei found in the medulla that regulate life-sustaining functions and are involved in cortical arousal.

Right cortex or cerebral hemisphere Consists of a frontal, temporal, parietal, and occipital lobe. Connected to the left cortex or cerebral hemisphere by the corpus callosum.

Rime Part of syllable remaining when onset phoneme(s) is (are) deleted.

Rule-governed mechanism Used to decode unknown words. Phonics is an example of a rule-governed mechanism.

Secondary association areas or cortical zones Where information from the primary zones is synthesized. Retain some modality-specificity and show some signs of the contralateral principle.

Segmental orthographic coding Printed words can be coded at the whole word or subword level (letter or letter cluster).

Segmental phonological coding Spoken words can be coded at the whole word or subword (phoneme, rime, or syllable) level.

Segregation analysis Separation of different elements of a population to test genetic hypotheses about how a trait is transmitted in families.

Seizure disorder Abnormal electrical discharges in the brain.

Selective cell death After cells migrate to their positions in the architecture of the nervous system, excess cells are selectively pruned. Failure to eliminate excessive cells may result in developmental disorders.

Semantic Refers to meaning of single words (semantic codes) and of interrelationships among words in context.

Sentence method A method of teaching reading in which words are always presented in context and never in isolation.

Sequelae Consequences that result from a neurological anomaly or lesion or from medical treatment.

Sequential view of writing Outmoded view that prewriting always precedes drafting, which always precedes revision. There is no interaction among planning, translating, and revising.

Sex-dependent penetrance Determined by a gene located on a sex chromosome.

Short-term memory Brief, passive storage.

Sight vocabulary Words that are recognized automatically without decoding them letter by letter.

Simulus Brain-created event. Internal representation in the brain that did not originate in the external world.

Spina bifida A defect that occurs in the closure of the neural tube early in gestation.

Spinal cord injury Nature of paralysis depends on where the cord is severed. Can occur during birth but more likely to occur as a result of an accident later in life.

Splenium Rear portion of the corpus callosum.

Split brain preparation The two cerebral hemispheres are disconnected by surgically severing the corpus callosum to control intractable epilepsy.

Stimulus A world-caused event. External information represented in the brain.

Stochastic developmental mechanism Development is not caused solely by genetic programs. Knowing genetic characteristics, one can predict development with some degree of probability, but not with complete certainty.

Striatum Named for the visible striations formed by weaving of white matter through gray matter. Begins at the base of each hemisphere and enlarges into caudate nucleus.

Structural anomalies Brain structures differ from the normal developmental pattern. (See also *Anomaly*)

Structural equation modeling A method for analyzing and comparing the *correspondence* between different sets of *theoretical predictions* about the relationships among constructs and the set of *empirical relationships* among the measures of the constructs observed in the data.

Subcortical Parts of brain below the cerebral cortex. Although it was once thought that only the cortex was involved in higher order processes, it is now recognized that subcortical structures also play a role in higher functions.

Sublexical level Subword level of language processing, such as phonemic or syllabic segmentation.

Subsymbolic Pertains to processing system based on connection weights (rather than symbols and rules) that learns to perform in a manner that appears rulelike.

Subword level (See *Sublexical level*)

Subword mechanism Phonics (letter-phoneme or letter cluster-phoneme) or analogies (letter cluster-rime) used to decode unknown words.

Sulcus (plural, *sulci*) Like a fissure, but less pronounced. (See *Fissure*)

Supramarginal gyrus Gyrus in parietal lobe near the angular gyrus.

Sustained visual system Sensitive to high spatial frequencies, low temporal frequencies, and slow transmission times. Adult dyslexics may have deficits in this system.

Sylvian fissure Separates the temporal and parietal lobes.

Symmetry Corresponding structures in the left and right brain are the same size.

Synapse Structural gap between two nerve cells (e.g., between an axon terminal and another cell) that is functionally connected when the nerve impulse crosses it.

Synaptic connections Transmission of the neural impulse across the synapse.

Syntactic Pertains to grammatical structures in oral utterances or written sentences.

Tachistoscopic studies Use a special apparatus to present visual stimuli to selected portions of the visual field, which are then projected to selected hemispheres.

Temporal lobes The cortex below the lateral or sylvian fissure on the side of the head. Associated with auditory, language, and meaning functions.

Tertiary association areas or cortical zones Where input from secondary zones is integrated. Abstract, not modality-specific; reflects the contralateral principle.

Text level (See *Discourse level*)

Thalamus Waystation for incoming sensory information.

Time blinking A mechanism proposed by Minsky for synchronizing the brain's activity. Finding the difference between two mental states by activating them in rapid succession and noticing which agents change their states. May give rise to brain waves.

Total state of mind Specifies all agents—both active and quiet—at a particular moment.

Transient visual system Sensitive to low spatial frequencies, high temporal frequencies, and fast transmission times. Developmental dyslexics may have deficits in this system.

Translexical level Level of language processing beyond the single word.

Transword level (See *Translexical level*)

Unit of analysis Level at which data are analyzed (e.g., for a group or an individual).

Unreferred sample Individuals who have not been referred for clinical assessment of a developmental, learning, or psychological problem. Does not mean they do not have these problems, but the sample is unlikely to be affected by referral bias (preponderance of a particular disorder).

Vascular malformation Interferes with normal blood flow.

Ventricle Spaces within the brain that contain cerebrospinal fluid.

Vowel digraph Two vowels, only one of which is sounded (e.g., the "e" in the "ie" in "friend").

Vowel diphthong Two vowels that together form a different sound from that of either of them alone (e.g., the "oy" in "joy").

Wernicke's area Located in the left temporal lobe; associated with receptive speech and language comprehension.

White matter Areas rich in axons covered by supportive glial cells.

Whole word-lexical code connection Either the whole word-phonetic code connection or whole word-semantic code connection.

Whole word mechanism Involves orthographic and phonological codes at the lexical level.

Whole word method A method of teaching word recognition that emphasizes the whole word unit, that is, sight vocabulary rather than subword mechanisms.

Whole word-phonetic code connection Lexical code connections used in oral reading.

Whole word-semantic code connection Lexical code connections used in silent reading.

Word analogies Using the rime in a known word (e.g., "save") to recognize an unknown word with the same rime (e.g., "gave" or "mave").

Word attack Applying phonics rules or analogies to known words to decode and pronounce unfamiliar words not in the automatic sight vocabulary.

Word families Words that have a common phonogram. (See *Phonogram*)

Word level Level of language processing involving a single lexical item.

Word recognition Includes word-specific mechanisms or sight words, and rule-governed mechanisms or phonics.

Word-specific mechanism Item or exemplar learning (e.g., sight words).

Working memory Transient storage where representations are held while operations are executed.

Written reproduction task A task in which a stimulus word, pronounceable nonword, or letter string is presented briefly, and the child must reproduce it from memory in writing.

Zebra syndrome Viewing instructional issues (or other issues) as black *or* white when they are black *and* white.

REFERENCES

Aaron, P. G., & Joshi, R. M. (1992). *Reading problems. Consultation and remediation.* New York: Guilford.

Abbott, R., & Berninger, V. (1993). Structural equation modeling of relationships among developmental skills and writing skills in primary and intermediate grade students. *Journal of Educational Psychology, 85(3),* 478–508.

Adams, M. (1990). *Beginning to read: Thinking and learning about print.* Cambridge, MA: MIT Press.

Aldhous, P. (1992). The promise and pitfalls of molecular genetics. *Science, 257,* 164–165.

Alexander, A., Andersen, H., Heilman, P., Voeller, K., & Torgesen, J. (1991). Phonological awareness training and remediation of analytic decoding deficits in a group of severe dyslexics. *Annals of the Orton Society, 41,* 193–206.

Allington, R. (1984). Content coverage and contextual reading in reading groups. *Journal of Reading Behavior, 16,* 85–96.

Andrews, D. (1985, June). *Contemporary approaches to the study of learning.* Paper presented to Center for the Study of Learning Conference, Columbus, OH.

Arter, J., & Jenkins, J. (1979). Differential diagnostic prescriptive teaching: A critical appraisal. *Review of Educational Research, 49,* 517–555.

Assink, E., & Kattenberg, G. (1991, April). *The use of orthographic structure in normal and poor readers.* American Educational Research Association, Chicago.

Ball, E., & Blachman, B. (1991). Does phoneme awareness training in kindergarten make a difference in early word recognition and developmental spelling? *Reading Research Quarterly, 26,* 49–66.

Barinaga, M. (1992). Knockouts shed light on learning. *Science, 257,* 162–163.

193

Barnes, D. (1986). Brain architecture: Beyond genes. *Science, 233,* 155–156.

Barron, R. (1986). Word recognition in early reading: A review of the direct and indirect access hypothesis. *Cognition, 24,* 93–119.

Barron, R., & Baron, J. (1977). How children get meaning from printed words. *Child Development, 48,* 586–594.

Bartlett, F. (1932). *Remembering.* London: Cambridge University Press.

Beal, C. (1989). Children's communication skills: Implications for the development of writing strategies. In C. B. McCormick, G. Miller, & M. Pressley (Eds.), *Cognitive strategy research: From basic research to educational applications* (pp. 191–214). New York: Springer-Verlag.

Beckman, L. (1970). Effects of students' performance on teachers' and observers' attributions of causality. *Journal of Educational Psychology, 61,* 76–82.

Beery, K. (1982). *Revised administration, scoring, and teaching manual for the Developmental Test of Visual-Motor Integration.* Cleveland, OH: Modern Curriculum Press.

Beery, M., & Spector, R. (1986). The nerve cell. *Developmental Medicine and Child Neurology, 28* (Suppl. 51), 1.

Bentler, P. (1991). *Theory and implementation of EQS: A structural equations program.* University of California, Los Angeles.

Bereiter, C. (1963). Some persisting dilemmas in the measurement of change. In C. Harris (Ed.), *Problems in measuring change* (pp. 3–20). Madison, WI: University of Wisconsin Press.

Bereiter, C., Burtis, P., & Scardamalia, M. (1988). Cognitive operations in constructing main points in written composition. *Journal of Memory and Language, 27,* 261–278.

Berninger, V. (1986). Normal variation in reading acquisition. *Perceptual and Motor Skills, 62,* 691–716.

Berninger, V. (1987). Global, component, and serial procedures for printed words in beginning reading. *Journal of Experimental Child Psychology, 43,* 387–418.

Berninger, V. (1988a). Acquisition of linguistic procedures for printed words: Neuropsychological implications for learning. *International Journal of Neuroscience, 42,* 267–281.

Berninger, V. (1988b). Development of operational thought without a normal sensorimotor stage. *Intelligence, 12,* 219–230.

Berninger, V. (1989). Orchestration of multiple codes in developing readers: An alternative model of lexical access. *International Journal of Neuroscience, 48,* 85–104.

Berninger, V. (1990). Multiple orthographic codes: Key to alternative instructional methodologies for developing the orthographic-phonological connections underlying word identification. *School Psychology Review, 19,* 518–533.

Berninger, V. (1991). Overview of "Bridging the gap between developmental, cognitive, and neuropsychological approaches to reading." *Learning and Individual Differences, 3,* 163–179.

Berninger, V. (1993). *Intraindividual differences in levels of written language in developing sentence comprehension.* Submitted for publication.

Berninger, V. (in press). Codes, connections, context, and constructive processes: Integrating the Vygotskian and Lurian perspectives. In E. Assink (Ed.), *Literacy acquisition and social context.* Hertfordshire, United Kingdom: Harvester Wheatsheaf.

Berninger, V., & Abbott, R. (1992a). The unit of analysis and constructive processes of the learner: Key concepts for educational neuropsychology. *Educational Psychologist, 27,* 223–242.

Berninger, V., & Abbott, R. (1992b, April). *Multiple orthographic and phonological codes and code connections in reading and spelling single words.* American Educational Research Association, San Francisco. Also submitted for publication.

Berninger, V., & Abbott, R. (in press). Redefining learning disabilities: Moving beyond IQ-achievement discrepancies to failure to respond to validated treatment protocols. In G. R. Lyon (Ed.), *Frames of reference for the assessment of learning disabilities: New views on measurement issues.* Baltimore, MD: Paul H. Brookes.

Berninger, V., Abbott, R., & Shurtleff, H. (1990). Developmental changes in interrelationships among visible language codes and oral language codes and reading and spelling. *Learning and Individual Differences, 2,* 45–67.

Berninger, V., & Alsdorf, B. (1989). Are there errors in error analysis? *Journal of Psychoeducational Assessment, 7,* 209–222.

Berninger, V., Cartwright, A., Yates, C., Swanson, H. L., & Abbott, R. (1993, March). *Developmental skills related to writing and reading acquisition in the intermediate grades: Shared and unique functional systems.* Paper presented at biennial meeting of Society for Research on Child Development, New Orleans. Submitted for publication.

Berninger, V., Chen, A., & Abbott, R. (1988). A test of the multiple connections model of reading acquisition. *International Journal of Neuroscience, 42,* 283–295.

Berninger, V., & Colwell, S. (1985). Relationships between neurodevelopmental and educational findings. *Pediatrics, 75,* 697–702.

Berninger, V., & Fuller, F. (1992). Gender differences in orthographic, verbal, and compositional fluency: Implications for diagnosis of writing disabilities in primary grade children. *Journal of School Psychology, 30,* 363–382.

Berninger, V., & Gans, B. (1986). Language profiles in nonspeaking individuals of normal intelligence with severe cerebral palsy. *Augmentative and Alternative Communication, 2,* 45–50.

Berninger, V., Gans, B., St. James, P., & Connors, T. (1988). Modified WAIS-R for patients with speech and/or hand dysfunction. *Archives for Physical Medicine and Rehabilitation, 69,* 250–255.

Berninger, V., & Garvey, C. (1981). Complementary balance in the use of the interrogative form in child discourse. *Journal of Child Language, 8,* 297–311.

Berninger, V., & Hart, T. (1992). A developmental neuropsychological perspective for reading and writing acquisition. *Educational Psychologist, 27,* 415–434.

Berninger, V., & Hart, T. (1993). From research to clinical assessment of reading and writing disorders: The unit of analysis problem. In R. M. Joshi & C. K. Leong (Eds.), *Reading disabilities: Diagnosis and component processes* (33–61). The Netherlands: Kluwer Academic Publishers.

Berninger, V., Hart, T., Abbott, R., & Karovsky, P. (1992). Diagnosing reading and writing disabilities with and without IQ: A flexible, developmental approach. *Learning Disabilities Quarterly, 15,* 103–118.

Berninger, V., Lester, K., Sohlberg, M., & Mateer, C. (1991). Intervention based on the multiple connections model for developmental dyslexia and acquired deep dyslexia. *Archives of Clinical Neuropsychology, 6,* 375–391.

Berninger, V., Mizokawa, D., & Bragg, R. (1991). Theory-based diagnosis and remediation of writing disabilities. *Journal of School Psychology, 29,* 57–79.

Berninger, V., Mizokawa, D., Bragg, R., Cartwright, A., & Yates, C. (in press). Intraindividual differences in levels of written language. *Reading and Writing Quarterly.*

Berninger, V., Proctor, A., DeBruyn, I., & Smith, R. (1988). Relationship between levels of oral and written language in beginning readers. *Journal of School Psychology, 26,* 341–357.

Berninger, V., & Rutberg, J. (1992). Relationship of finger function to beginning writing: Application to diagnosis of writing disabilities. *Developmental Medicine & Child Neurology, 34,* 155–172.

Berninger, V., & Swanson, H. L. (in press). Modifying Flower and Hayes model of skilled writing to explain beginning and developing writing. In E. Butterfield (Ed.), *Children's writing: Toward a process theory of development of skilled writing.* Greenwich, CT: JAI Press.

Berninger, V., & Thalberg, S. (1988). Levels of analysis in interdisciplinary child assessment. *Journal of Psychoeducational Assessment, 6,* 3–13.

Berninger, V., Thalberg, S., DeBruyn, I., & Smith, R. (1987). Preventing reading difficulties by assessing and remediating phonemic skills. *School Psychology Review, 16,* 554–555.

Berninger, V., & Traweek, D. (1991). Effects of two-phase intervention on three orthographic-phonological code connections. *Learning and Individual Differences, 3,* 323–338.

Berninger, V., Whitaker, D., Feng, Y., & Swanson, L. (1993). *Process assessment of writing in junior high students.* Submitted for publication.

Berninger, V., Yates, C., Cartwright, A., Rutberg, J., Remy, E., & Abbott, R. (1992). Lower-level developmental skills in beginning writing. *Reading and Writing: An Interdisciplinary Journal, 4,* 257–280.

Berninger, V., Yates, C., & Lester, K. (1991). Multiple orthographic codes in reading and writing acquisition. *Reading and Writing: An Interdisciplinary Journal, 3,* 115–149.

Besner, D., Twilley, L., McCann, R., & Seergobin, K. (1990). On the association between connectionism and data: Are a few words necessary? *Psychological Review, 97,* 432–446.

Biddle, B., & Marlin, M. (1987). Causality, confirmation, credulity, and structural equation modeling. *Child Development, 58,* 4–17.

Biemiller, A. (1977–1978). Relationship between oral reading rate for letters, words, and simple text in the development of reading achievement. *Reading Research Quarterly, 13,* 223–253.

Black, M., & Byng, S. (1986). Prosodic constraints on lexical access in reading. *Cognitive Neuropsychology, 3,* 369–409.

Boder, E. (1973). Developmental dyslexia: A diagnostic approach based on three atypical reading-spelling patterns. *Developmental Medicine and Child Neurology, 15,* 663–687.

Botel, M. (1968). Therapy and therapeutic advice. In A. Keeney & V. Keeney (Eds.), *Dyslexia. Diagnosis and treatment of reading disorders* (pp. 120–130). St. Louis: Mosby Co.

Bouchard, T., Lykken, D., McGue, M., Segal, N., & Tellegen, A. (1990). Sources of human psychological difference: The Minnesota study of twins reared apart. *Science, 250,* 223–228.

Bowers, P., & Swanson, L. (1991). Naming speed deficits in reading disability: Multiple measures of a singular process. *Journal of Experimental Child Psychology, 51,* 195–219.

Bowers, P., & Wolf, M. (1993, March). *A double-deficit hypothesis for developmental reading disorders.* New Orleans: Society for Research in Child Development.

Bradley, L., & Bryant, P. (1983). Categorizing sounds and learning to read—A causal connection. *Nature, 301(3),* 419–421.

Brady, S., & Shankweiler, D. (1991). *Phonological processes in literacy. A tribute to Isabelle Y. Liberman.* Hillsdale, NJ: Erlbaum.

Bronfenbrenner, U. (1979). *The ecology of human development.* Cambridge, MA: Harvard University Press.

Brown, A., & Campione, J. (1986). Psychological theory and the study of learning disabilities. *American Psychologist, 41,* 1059–1068.

Brown, I., & Felton, R. (1990). Effects of instruction on beginning reading skills in children at risk for reading disability. *Reading and Writing: An Interdisciplinary Journal, 2,* 223–241.

Bruck, M. (1988). The word recognition and spelling of dyslexic children. *Reading Research Quarterly, 23,* 51–69.

Bryk, A., & Raudenbush, S. (1987). Application of hierarchical linear models to assessing change. *Psychological Bulletin, 101,* 147–158.

Burstein, L. (1980). The analysis of multilevel data in educational research and evaluation. In D. C. Berliner (Ed.), *Review of research in education* (pp. 158–223). Washington, DC: American Educational Research Association.

Buschke, H. (1977). Retrieval in the development of learning. In N. Castellan, D. Pisoni, & G. Potts (Eds.), *Cognitive theory,* Vol. 2 (pp. 239–267). Hillsdale, NJ: Erlbaum.

Byring, R., & Jarvilehto, T. (1985). Auditory and visual evoked potentials of schoolboys with spelling disabilities. *Developmental Medicine & Child Neurology, 27,* 141–148.

Byrne, B., & Fielding-Barnsley, R. (1990). Acquiring the alphabet principle: A case for teaching recognition of phoneme identity. *Journal of Educational Psychology, 82,* 805–812.

Byrne, B., Freebody, P., & Gates, A. (1992). Relationships between word-reading strategies and comprehension, reading time, and phonemic awareness: Longitudinal data. *Reading Research Quarterly, 27,* 140–151.

Byrnes, D., & Yamamoto, K. (1984). *Grade repetition: Views of parents, teachers, and principals.* Logan: Utah State University, School of Education.

Cacioppo, J., & Bernston, G. (1992). Social psychological contributions to the decade of the brain. *American Psychologist, 47,* 1019–1028.

Carr, T., Brown, T., & Vavrus, L. (1985). Using component skills analysis to integrate findings on reading development. In T. Carr (Ed.), *The development of reading skills* (pp. 95–107, 1–4). San Francisco: Jossey-Bass.

Carr, T., & Pollatsek, A. (1985). Recognizing printed words: A look at current models. In *Reading Research: Advances in Theory and Practice,* Vol. 5 (pp. 1–82). New York: Academic Press.

Carstens, A. (1985). Retention and social promotion for the exceptional child. *School Psychology Review, 14,* 48–63.

Chall, J. (1965). *Learning to read: The great debate,* Vol. 2. *Final report of the City College.* Carnegie Reading Study.

Chall, J. (1979). The great debate: Ten years later, with a modest proposal for research stages. In L. Resnick & P. Weaver (Eds.), *Theory and practice of early reading,* Vol. 1 (pp. 29–55). Hillsdale, NJ: Erlbaum.

Chall, J., & Feldman, S. (1966). *A study in depth of first grade reading: An analysis of the interactions of professed methods, teacher implementation, and child background.* Cooperative Research Project No. 2728.

Childs, B., Finucci, J., & Preston, M. (1978). A medical genetics approach to the study of reading disability. In A. Benton & D. Pearl (Eds.), *Dyslexia. An appraisal of current knowledge* (pp. 301–309). New York: Oxford University Press.

Chomsky, C. (1979). Reading, writing, and phonology. *Harvard Educational Review, 40,* 287–309.

Churchland, P. (1986). *Neurophilosophy. Toward a unified science of the mind/brain.* Cambridge, MA: MIT Press.

Clay, M. (1985). *The early detection of reading difficulties.* Portsmouth, NH: Heinemann.

Clay, M. (1987). Learning to be learning disabled. *New Zealand Journal of Educational Studies, 22,* 155–171.

Coltheart, M. (1978). Lexical access in simple reading tasks. In G. Underwood (Ed.), *Strategies of information processing* (pp. 151–216). London: Academic Press.

Conners, C. K. (1971). Cortical visual evoked response in children with learning disorders. *Psychophysiology, 7,* 418–428.

Corno, L., & Snow, R. (1986). Adapting teaching to individual differences among learners. In M. C. Wittrock (Ed.), *Handbook of research on teaching* (3rd ed., pp. 605–629). New York: Macmillan.

Craik, F., & Lockhart, R. (1972). Levels of processing: A framework for memory research. *Journal of Verbal Learning and Verbal Behavior, 11,* 671–684.

Crocker, L., & Algina, J. (1986). *Introduction to classical and modern test theory.* New York: Holt, Rinehart, & Winston.

Cronbach, L., & Furby, L. (1970). How we should measure "change"—Or should we? *Psychological Bulletin, 74,* 68–80.

Cunningham, A. (1990). Explicit versus implicit instruction in phonemic awareness. *Journal of Experimental Child Psychology, 50,* 429–444.

Decker, S., & DeFries, J. (1981). Cognitive ability profiles in families of reading-disabled children. *Developmental Medicine and Child Neurology, 23,* 217–227.

DeFries, J., Fulker, D., & LaBuda, M. (1987). Evidence for a genetic aetiology in reading disability of twins. *Nature, 329,* 537–539.

DeFries, J., Olson, R., Pennington, B., & Smith, S. (1991). Colorado reading project. An update. In D. Duane & D. Gray (Eds.), *The reading brain. The biological basis of dyslexia* (pp. 53–87). Parkton, MD: York Press.

Denckla, M., & Rudel, R. (1976). Rapid 'automatized' naming (R.A.N.): Dyslexia differentiated from other learning disabilities. *Neuropsychologia, 14,* 471–479.

Dennett, D. (1991). *Consciousness explained.* Boston: Little, Brown.

Diamond, M., Scheibel, A., & Elson, L. (1985). *The human brain coloring book.* Oaksville, CA: Coloring Concepts.

Doctor, E., & Coltheart, M. (1980). Children's use of phonological encoding when reading for meaning. *Memory & Cognition, 8,* 195–209.

Drake, W. (1968). Clinical and pathological findings in a child with a developmental learning disability. *Journal of Learning Disability, 1,* 486–502.

Duane, D. (1991). Dyslexia: Neurobiological and behavioral correlates. *Psychiatric Annals, 21,* 703–708.

Duffy, F. (1981). Brain electrical activity mapping (BEAM): Computerized access to complex brain function. *International Journal of Neuroscience, 13,* 55–65.

Dunn, B., Van Dyke, P., & Hill, R. (1991, April). *Changes in the brain's electrical activity pattern as a function of learning.* Chicago: American Educational Research Association.

Dykman, R., & Ackerman, P. (1991). Attention deficit disorder and specific reading disability: Separate but often overlapping disorders. *Journal of Learning Disabilities, 24,* 96–103.

Ehri, L. (1980). The development of orthographic images. In U. Frith (Ed.), *Cognitive processes in spelling* (pp. 311–338). London: Academic Press.

Ehri, L., & Roberts, K. (1979). Do beginners learn printed words better in contexts or isolation? *Child Development, 50,* 675–685.

Ellis, A. (1985). The cognitive neuropsychology of developmental (and acquired) dyslexia: A critical survey. *Cognitive Neuropsychology, 2,* 169–205.

Ellis, A. (1987). Review of problems in developing cognitively transmitted cognitive modules. *Mind & Language, 2,* 242–251.

Engel, B. (1960). Stimulus-response and individual-response specificity. *Archives of General Psychiatry, 2,* 305–313.

Englert, C., Raphael, T., Anderson, L., Anthony, H., & Stevens, D. (1991). Making strategies and self-talk visible: Writing instruction in regular and special education classrooms. *American Educational Research Journal, 28,* 337–372.

Englert, C., Stewart, S., & Hiebart, E. (1988). Young writer's use of text structure in expository text generation. *Journal of Educational Psychology, 80,* 143–151.

Evans, L. (1990). A conceptual overview of the regression discrepancy model for evaluating severe discrepancy between IQ and achievement scores. *Journal of Learning Disabilities, 22,* 406–412.

Felton, B., Wood, F., Brown, I., Campbell, S., & Harter, M. (1987). Separate verbal memory and naming deficits in attentional deficit disorder and reading disability. *Brain and Language, 31,* 171–184.

Felton, R., & Brown, I. (1990). Phonological processes as predictors of specific reading skills in children at risk for reading failure. *Reading and Writing. An Interdisciplinary Journal, 2,* 39–59.

Filipek, P., & Kennedy, D. (1991). Magnetic resonance imaging. Its role in the developmental disorders. In D. Duane & D. Gray (Eds.), *The reading brain. The biological basis of dyslexia* (pp. 133–160). Parkton, MD: York Press.

Finucci, J., Guthrie, J., Childs, A., Abbey, H., & Childs, B. (1976). The genetics of specific reading disability. *Annals of Human Genetics, 40,* 1–23.

Firth, I. (1972). *Components of reading disability*. Unpublished doctoral dissertation, University of New South Wales, Australia.

Fisher, R. (1951). *The design of experiments* (6th ed.). New York: Hafner Publishing Co.

Fitzgerald, J. (1987). Research on revision in writing. *Review of Educational Research, 57,* 481–506.

Flesch, R. (1979, Nov. 1). Why Johnny can't read. *Family Circle.*

Fletcher, J., & Taylor, H. G. (1984). Neuropsychological approaches to children. Towards a developmental neuropsychology. *Journal of Clinical Neuropsychology, 6,* 39–56.

Flexner, A. (1910). *Medical education in the United States and Canada. A report to the Carnegie Foundation for the Advancement of Teaching.* New York: Carnegie Foundation for the Advancement of Teaching.

Flowers, D., Wood, F., & Naylor, C. (1991). Regional cerebral blood flow correlates of language processes in reading disability. *Archives of Neurology, 48,* 637–643.

Foorman, B., Francis, D., Novy, D., & Liberman, D. (1991). How letter-sound instruction mediates progress in first-grade reading and spelling. *Journal of Educational Psychology, 83,* 456–469.

Forster, K. (1970). Visual perception of rapidly presented word sequences of varying complexity. *Perception & Psychophysics, 8,* 215–221.

Foss, D., & Blank, M. (1980). Identifying the speech codes. *Cognitive Psychology, 12,* 1–31.

Francis, D., Fletcher, J., Stuebing, K., Davidson, K., & Thompson, N. (1991). Analysis of change: Modeling individual growth. *Journal of Consulting and Clinical Psychology, 59,* 27–37.

Frederiksen, C. (1979). Discourse comprehension and early reading. In L. Resnick & P. Weaver (Eds.), *Theory and practice of early reading* (Vol. 1, pp. 155–186). Hillsdale, NJ: Erlbaum.

Frederiksen, J. (1981). Sources of process interactions in reading. In A. Lesgold & C. Perfetti (Eds.), *Interactive processes in reading* (pp. 361–386). Hillsdale, NJ: Erlbaum.

Freebody, P., & Byrne, B. (1988). Word reading strategies in elementary school children: Relationships to comprehension, reading time, and phonemic awareness. *Reading Research Quarterly, 24,* 441–453.

Frith, U. (1985). Beneath the surface of developmental dyslexia. In K. Patterson, J. Marshall, & M. Coltheart (Eds.), *Surface dyslexia* (pp. 301–330). London: Erlbaum.

Galaburda, A. (1986). Developmental dyslexia: A review of biological interactions. *Annals of dyslexia, 35,* 21–33.

Galaburda, A. (1988). The pathogenesis of childhood dyslexia. *Association for Research in Nervous & Mental Disease Series, 66,* 127–137.

Galaburda, A. (1991). Anatomy of dyslexia. Argument against phrenology. In D. Duane & D. Gray (Eds.), *The reading brain. The biological bases of dyslexia* (pp. 119–131; discussion, pp. 161–178). Parton, MD: York Press.

Galaburda, A., Sherman, G., Rosen, G., Aboitz, F., & Geschwind, N. (1985). Developmental dyslexia: Four consecutive patients with cortical anomalies. *Annals of Neurology, 18,* 222–233.

Garner, W., Hake, H., & Eriksen, C. (1956). Operationism and the concept of perception. *Psychological Review, 63,* 149–159.

Geschwind, N. (1985). The biology of dyslexia. In D. Gray & J. Kavanaugh (Eds.), *Behavioral measures of dyslexia* (pp. 1–24). Parkton, MD: York Press.

Gesell, A. (1925). *The mental growth of the preschool child.* New York: Macmillan.

Gesell, A. (1928). *Infancy and human growth.* New York: Macmillan.

Gleitman, L., & Rozin, P. (1977). The structure and acquisition of reading I: Relations between orthographies and the structure of language. In A. Reber & D. Scarborough (Eds.), *Toward a psychology of reading* (pp. 1–53). Hillsdale, NJ: Erlbaum.

Glushko, R. (1979). The organization and activation of orthographic knowledge in reading aloud. *Journal of Experimental Psychology: Human Perception and Performance, 5,* 674–691.

Goodlad, J. (1990). *Teachers for our nation's schools.* San Francisco: Jossey-Bass Publishers.

Goodman, K. (1976). Reading: A psycholinguistic guessing game. In H. Slinger & R. Ruddell (Eds.), *Theoretical models and processes of reading* (pp. 497–508). Newark, DE: International Reading Association.

Goswami, U. (1988). Orthographic analogies and reading development. *Quarterly Journal of Experimental Psychology, 40A,* 239–268.

Goswami, U. (1989, March). *Orthographic units and transfer in reading.* San Francisco: American Educational Research Association.

Gough, P., & Hillinger, M. (1980). Learning to read: An unnatural act. *Bulletin of the Orton Society, 30,* 180–196.

Graden, J., Thurlow, M., & Ysseldyke, J. (1983). Instructional ecology and academic responding time for students at three levels of teacher-perceived behavioral competence. *Journal of Experimental Child Psychology, 36,* 241–256.

Graham, S. (1990). The role of production factors in learning disabled students' compositions. *Journal of Educational Psychology, 82,* 781–791.

Gray, D. (1991). Introduction. In D. Duane & D. Gray (Eds.), *The reading brain. The biological basis of dyslexia* (pp. vi-xvi). Parkton, MD: York Press.

Greenblatt, E., Mattis, S., & Trad, P. (1990). Nature and prevalence of learning disabilities in a child psychiatric population. *Developmental Neuropsychology, 6,* 71–83.

Hallgren, B. (1950). Specific dyslexia ("congenital word blindness"): A clinical and genetic study. *Acta Psychiatrica Neurologica Scandinavica,* Suppl. 65, 1–287.

Harris, C. (Ed.). (1963). *Problems in measuring change.* Madison: University of Wisconsin Press.

Harris, K., & Graham, S. (1992). *Helping young writers master the craft. Strategy instruction & self-regulation in the writing process.* Cambridge, MA: Brookline Books.

Harter, M. R. (1991). Event-related potential indices: Learning disabilities and visual processing. *Neuropsychological foundations of learning disabilities* (pp. 437–473). New York: Academic Press.

Hayes, J., & Flower, L. (1980). Identifying the organization of the writing process. In L. W. Gregg & E. R. Steinberg (Eds.), *Cognitive processes in writing* (pp. 3–30). Hillsdale, NJ: Erlbaum.

Haynes, M., & Jenkins, J. (1986). Reading instruction in special education resource rooms. *American Educational Research Journal, 23,* 161–190.

Hidi, S., & Hildyard, A. (1983). The comparison of oral and written productions in two discourse types. *Discourse Processes, 6,* 91–105.

Hinton, G., & Sejnowski, T. (1986). Learning and relearning in Boltzmann machines. In D. Rumelhart & J. McClelland (Eds.), *Parallel distributed processing: Explorations in the microstructure of cognition* (Vol. 1, pp. 282–314). Cambridge, MA: MIT Press.

Hoien, T., Lundberg, I., Larsen, J., & Tonnessen, F. (1989). Profiles of reading related skills in dyslexic families. *Reading and Writing. An Interdisciplinary Journal, 1,* 381–392.

Holcomb, P., Ackerman, P., & Dykman, R. (1985). Cognitive event-related brain potentials in children with attention and reading deficits. *Psychophysiology, 22,* 656–667.

Holmes, C. T., & Matthews, K. (1984). The effects of nonpromotion on elementary and junior high school pupils. *Review of Educational Research, 54,* 225–236.

Hooper, S., & Boyd, T. (1986). Neurodevelopmental learning disorders. In J. Obrzut & G. Hynd (Eds.), *Child neuropsychology. Clinical Practice* (Vol. 2, pp. 15–58). New York: Academic Press.

Huettner, M., Rosenthal, B., & Hynd, G. (1989). Regional cerebral blood flow (rCBF) in normal readers: Bilateral activation with narrative text. *Archives of Clinical Neuropsychology, 4,* 71–78.

Huey, E. (1908). *The psychology and pedagogy of reading.* New York: Macmillan.

Humphreys, G., & Evett, L. (1985). Are there independent lexical and nonlexical routes in word processing? An evaluation of the dual-route theory of reading. *The Behavioral and Brain Sciences, 8,* 689–740.

Humphreys, P., Kaufmann, W., & Galaburda, A. (1990). Developmental dyslexia in women: Neuropathological findings in three patients. *Annals of Neurology, 28,* 727–738.

Hunt, E. (1983). On the nature of intelligence. *Science, 219,* 141–146.

Hynd, C. (1986). Educational interventions in children with developmental learning disorders. In J. Obrzut & G. Hynd (Eds.), *Child Neuropsychology* (Vol. 2, pp. 265–297). New York: Academic Press.

Hynd, G., & Hynd, C. (1984). Dyslexia: Neuroanatomical/neurolinguistic perspectives. *Reading Research Quarterly, 19,* 482–498.

Hynd, G., & Semrud-Clikeman, M. (1989). Dyslexia and brain morphology. *Psychological Bulletin, 106,* 447–482.

Hynd, G., Semrud-Clikeman, M., Lorys, A., Novey, E., & Eliopulos, D. (1990). Brain morphology in developmental dyslexia and attention deficit disorder/hyperactivity. *Archives of Neurology, 47,* 919–926.

Ingvar, D. (1983). Serial aspects of language and speech related to prefrontal cortical activity. A selective review. *Human Neurobiology, 2,* 177–189.

Jackson, J. H. (1887). Remarks on evolution and dissolution of the nervous system. *Medical Press and Circular, ii,* 461, 491, 511, 586, 617. (Reprinted in James Taylor, ed., 1958, *Selected writings of John Hughlings Jackson,* Vol. 2. New York: Basic Books).

Jackson, N., & Butterfield, E. (1989). Reading-level matched designs: Myths and realities. *Journal of Reading Behavior, 21,* 387–412.

Jastak, J., Bijou, S., & Jastak, S. (1978). *Wide Range Achievement Test.* Wilmington, DE: Jastak Associates.

Jenkins, J., Pious, C., & Peterson, D. (1988). Categorical programs for remedial and handicapped students: Issues of validity. *Exceptional Children, 55,* 147–158.

Jenkins, J., Stein, M., & Osborn, J. (1981). What next after decoding? Instruction and research in reading comprehension. *Exceptional Education, 2,* 27–39.

John, E. R., Prichep, L., Fridman, J., & Easton, P. (1988). Neurometrics: Computer-assisted differential diagnosis of brain dysfunctions. *Science, 239,* 162–169.

Johnson, N. (1978). Coding processes in memory. In W. K. Estes (Ed.), *Handbook of learning and cognitive processes* (Vol. 6, pp. 87–129). Hillsdale, NJ: Erlbaum.

Johnson, N. (1986). On looking at letters within words: Do we "see" them in memory? *Journal of Memory and Language, 25,* 558–570.

Johnson, N., Turner-Lyga, M., & Pettegrew, B. (1986). Part-whole relationships in the processing of small visual patterns. *Memory & Cognition, 14,* 5–16.

Johnson, R., Feigenbaum, R., & Weiby, M. (1964). Some determinants and consequences of the teachers' perception of causality. *Journal of Educational Psychology, 55,* 237–246.

Just, M., & Carpenter, P. (1987). *The psychology of reading and language comprehension.* Boston: Allyn & Bacon.

Kantowitz, B., & Roediger, H. (1978). *Experimental psychology.* Chicago: Rand McNally.

Keeney, A., & Keeney, V. (Eds.). (1968). *Dyslexia. Diagnosis and treatment of reading disorders* (p. 92). St. Louis: Mosby Co.

Kolb, B., & Whishaw, I. (1990). *Fundamentals of human neuropsychology* (3rd ed). New York: W. H. Freeman.

Kolers, P., & Roediger, H. (1984). Procedures of mind. *Journal of Verbal Learning and Verbal Behavior, 23,* 425–449.

Kramer, A., & Donchin, E. (1987). Brain potentials as indices of orthographic and phonological interaction during word matching. *Journal of Experimental Psychology: Learning, Memory, and Cognition, 13,* 76–86.

LaBerge, D., & Samuels, J. (1974). Toward a theory of automatic information processing in reading. *Cognitive Psychology, 6,* 293–323.

Lachman, R., Lachman, J., & Butterfield, E. (1979). *Cognitive psychology and information processing. An introduction.* Hillsdale, NJ: Erlbaum.

Languis, M., & Wittrock, M. (1986). Integrating neuropsychological and cognitive research: A perspective for bridging brain-behavior relationships. In J. Obrzut & G. Hynd (Eds.), *Child neuropsychology, Theory and research* (Vol. 1, pp. 209–239). New York: Academic Press.

Larsen, J., Hoien, T., Lundberg, I., & Odegaard, H. (1990). MRI evaluation of the size and symmetry of the planum temporale in adolescents with developmental dyslexia. *Brain and Language, 39,* 289–301.

Larsen, J., Hoien, T., & Odegaard, H. (1992). Magnetic resonance imaging of the corpus callosum in developmental dyslexia. *Cognitive Neuropsychology, 9,* 123–134.

Leonard, C., Voeller, K., Lombardino, L., Alexander, A., Andersen, H., Morris, M., Garofalakis, M., Hynd, G., Honeyman, J., Mao, J., Agee, F., & Staab, E. (1993). Anomalous cerebral structure in dyslexia revealed with magnetic resonance imaging. *Archives of Neurology, 50,* 461–469.

Leong, C. K. (1986). What does accessing a morphemic script tell us about reading and reading disorders in an alphabetic script. *Annals of Dyslexia, 36,* 82–102.

Leong, C. K. (1988). A componential approach to understanding reading and its difficulties in preadolescent readers. *Annals of Dyslexia, 38,* 95–119.

Leong, C. K. (1991, October). *On being literate: Part 1. Cognitive componential modeling of reading in ten- to twelve-year-old readers.* NATO Advanced Study Institute on Differential Diagnosis and Treatment of Reading and Writing Disorders. Chateaux de Bonas, France. In *Reading and Writing: An Interdisciplinary Journal.*

Levine, M., Oberklaid, F., & Meltzer, L. (1981). Developmental output failure: A study of low productivity in school-aged children. *Pediatrics, 67,* 18–25.

Levy, R., & Stewart, L. (1991, April). *Early diagnosis and treatment of reading problems.* Seattle: Society for Research in Child Development.

Liberman, A., Cooper, F., Shankweiler, D., & Studdert-Kennedy, M. (1967). Perception of the speech code. *Psychological Review, 74,* 431–461.

Liberman, I., Shankweiler, D., Fischer, F., & Carter, B. (1974). Explicit syllable and phoneme segmentation in the young child. *Journal of Experimental Child Psychology, 18,* 201–212.

Liberman, I., Shankweiler, D., Liberman, A., Fowler, C., & Fischer, F. (1977). Phonetic segmentation and recoding in the beginning reader. In A. Reber & D. Scarborough (Eds.), *Toward a psychology of reading* (pp. 207–225). Hillsdale, NJ: Erlbaum.

Liberman, I., Shankweiler, D., Orlando, C., Harris, K., & Berti, F. (1971). Letter confusions and reversals of sequence in the beginning reader: Implications for Orton's theory of developmental dyslexia. *Cortex, 7,* 127–142.

Lindblom, B. (1989). Some remarks on the origin of the phonetic code. In C. von Euler, I. Lundberg, & G. Lennerstrand (Eds.), *Brain and reading. Structural and functional anomalies in developmental dyslexia* (pp. 27–44). New York: Stockton.

Lindamood, C. H., & Lindamood, P. C. (1969). *Auditory discrimination in depth.* Boston: Teaching Resources.

Linn, R., & Slinde, J. (1977). The determination of the significance of change between pre- and posttesting periods. *Review of Educational Research, 47,* 121–150.

Livingstone, M., Rosen, G., Drislane, F., & Galaburda, A. (1991). Physiological and anatomical evidence for a magnocellular deficit in developmental dyslexia. *Proceedings National Academy of Science, 88,* 7943–7947.

Lord, F. (1956). The measurement of growth. *Educational and Psychological Measurement, 16,* 421–437.

Lovegrove, W. (1993, March). *Visual transient system deficits in specific reading disability.* New Orleans: Society for Research in Child Development.

Lovegrove, W., Martin, F., & Slaghuis, W. (1986). A theoretical and experimental case for a visual deficit in specific reading disability. *Cognitive Neuropsychology, 3,* 225–267.

Lovett, M. (1987). A developmental approach to reading disability: Accuracy and speed criteria of normal and deficient reading skill. *Child Development, 58,* 234–260.

Lovett, M. (1991). Reading, writing, and remediation: Perspectives on the dyslexic learning disability from remedial outcome data. *Learning and Individual Differences, 3,* 295–305.

Lovett, M., Benson, N., & Olds, J. (1990). Individual difference predictors of treatment outcome in the remediation of developmental dyslexia. *Learning and Individual Differences, 2,* 287–314.

Lovett, M., Ransby, M., & Barron, R. (1988). Treatment, subtype, and word type effects in dyslexic children's response to remediation. *Brain and Language, 34,* 328–349.

Lovett, M., Ransby, M., Hardwick, N., Johns, M., & Donaldson, S. (1989). Can dyslexia be treated? Treatment specific and generalized treatment effects in dyslexic children's response to remediation. *Brain and Language, 37,* 90–121.

Lovett, M., Warren-Chaplin, P., Ransby, M., & Borden, S. (1990). Training the word recognition skills of reading disabled children: Treatment and transfer effects. *Journal of Educational Psychology, 82,* 769–780.

Lubs, H. (1990, September). *Dyslexia subtypes: Genetics, behavior, and brain imaging.* Paper presented at the XVI International Rodin Remediation Scientific Conference, Boulder, CO.

Lubs, H., Duara, R., Levin, B., Jallad, B., Lubs, M., Rabin, M., Kushch, A., & Gross-Glenn, K. (1991). Genetics, behavior, and brain imaging. In D. Duane & D. Gray (Ed.), *The reading brain. The biological basis of dyslexia* (pp. 89–117). Parkton, MD: York Press.

Lundberg, I., Frost, J., & Petersen, O. (1988). Effects of an extensive program for stimulating phonological awareness in preschool children. *Reading Research Quarterly, 23,* 263–284.

Lunneborg, C., & Abbott, R. (1983). *Elementary multivariate analysis for the behavioral sciences.* New York: North Holland.

Luria, A. R. (1973). *The working brain.* New York: Basic Books.

Lyon, G. R. (1985a). Educational validation studies of learning disability subtypes. In B. Rourke (Ed.), *Neuropsychology of learning disability. Essentials of subtype analysis* (pp. 228–256). New York: Guilford Press.

Lyon, G. R. (1985b). Identification and remediation of learning disability subtypes: Preliminary findings. *Learning Disabilities Focus, 1,* 21–35.

Lyon, G. R., & Moats, L. (1988). Critical issues in the instruction of the learning disabled. *Journal of Consulting and Clinical Psychology, 56,* 830–835.

Lyon, G. R., Moats, L., & Flynn, J. (1988). From assessment to treatment. Linkage to interventions with children. In M. Tramontana & S. Hooper (Eds.), *Issues in child neuropsychology: From assessment to treatment* (pp. 113–142). New York: Plenum Press.

Lyon, G. R., Vaasen, M., & Toomey, F. (1989). Teachers' perceptions of their undergraduate and graduate preparation. *Teacher Education and Special Education, 12,* 164–169.

Massaro, D., & Oden, G. (1980). Speech perception: A framework for research and theory. In N. J. Lass (Ed.), *Speech and language: Advances in basic research and practice* (Vol. 3, pp. 129–165). New York: Academic Press.

McArthur, C., Schwartz, S., & Graham, S. (1991). A model for writing instruction: Integrating word processing and strategy instruction into a process approach to writing. *Learning Disabilities Practice, 6,* 230–236.

McClearn, G. (1978). Review of 'dyslexia—genetic aspects.' In A. Benton & D. Pearl (Eds.), *Dyslexia: An appraisal of current knowledge* (pp. 287–297). New York: Oxford University Press.

McClelland, J., Rumelhart, D., & Hinton, G. (1986). The appeal of parallel distributed processing. In D. Rumelhart & J. McClelland (Eds.), *Parallel distributed processing: Explorations in the microstructure of cognition* (Vol. 1, pp. 3–44). Cambridge, MA: MIT Press.

McCutchen, D. (1986). Domain knowledge and linguistic knowledge in the development of writing ability. *Journal of Memory and Language, 25,* 431–444.

McCutchen, D. (1988). "Functional automaticity" in children's writing: A problem of metacognitive control. *Written Communication, 5,* 306–324.

McCutchen, D. (in press). The magical number three, plus or minus two: Planning, translating, and reviewing and the implications of limited working memory. In E. Butterfield (Ed.), *Children's writing: Toward a process theory of development of skilled writing.* Greenwich, CT: JAI Press.

McCutchen, D., & Perfetti, C. (1982). Coherence and connectedness in the development of discourse production. *Text, 2,* 113–139.

McManus, I., & Bryden, M. (1991). Geschwind's theory of cerebral lateralization: Developing a formal, causal model. *Psychological Bulletin, 110,* 237–253.

Mills, R. (1970). *The teaching of word recognition.* Fort Lauderdale, FL: The Mills School.

Minsky, M. (1986). *The society of mind.* New York: Simon & Schuster.

Mishkin, M., & Appenzeller, T. (1987, June). The anatomy of memory. *Scientific American,* 80–89.

Moats, L. (in press). Assessment of spelling in learning disabilities research. To appear in G. R. Lyon (Ed.), *Frames of reference for assessment of learning disabilities: New views on measurement issues.* Baltimore: Paul H. Brookes.

Molfese, D., & Molfese, V. (1985). Electrophysiological indices of auditory discrimination in newborn infants. The bases for predicting latter language development. *Infant Behavior and Development, 8,* 197–211.

Molfese, D., Morse, P., & Peters, C. (1990). Auditory evoked responses to names for different objects: Cross-modal processing as a basis for infant language acquisition. *Developmental Psychology, 26,* 780–795.

Morais, J., Carey, L., Alegria, J., & Bertelson, P. (1979). Does awareness of speech as a sequence of phonemes arise spontaneously? *Cognition, 7,* 323–331.

Morrison, F. (1991, April). *Making the cut: Early schooling and cognitive growth.* Seattle: Society for Research on Child Development.

Morrison, F., & McMahon, E. (1992). *Nature-nurture in the classroom: Entrance age, school readiness and learning in children.* Manuscript submitted for publication.

Morrison, F., Smith, L., & Dow, M. (1992). *Education and cognitive development: A natural experiment.* Manuscript submitted for publication.

Mountcastle, V. (1957). Modality and topographic properties of single neurons of cat's somaticsensory cortex. *Journal of Neurophysiology, 20,* 408–434.

Muehl, S., & Forell, E. (1973). A follow-up study of disabled readers: Variables related to high school reading performance. *Reading Research Quarterly, 9,* 110–123.

National Assessment of Educational Progress. (1980). *Writing achievement 1969–1979. Results from the third national writing assessment* (Vol. 3: 9-year-olds). Denver, CO: National Assessment of Educational Progress (ERIC Document Reproduction Service No. ED 196 044).

National Association of School Psychologists. (1988, September). NASP position statement on student retention, *Communique,* p. 1.

Neville, H., Nicol, J., Barss, A., Forster, K., & Garrett, M. (1991). Syntactically based sentence processing classes: Evidence from event-related brain potentials. *Journal of Cognitive Neuroscience, 3,* 151–165.

Newcomer, P., & Barenbaum, E. (1991). The written composing ability of children with learning disabilities. A review of the literature from 1980 to 1990. *Journal of Learning Disabilities, 24,* 578–593.

Nolen, P., McCutchen, D., & Berninger, B. (1990). Ensuring tomorrow's literacy: A shared responsibility. *Journal of Teacher Education, 41,* 63–72.

Nowakowsi, R. (1990, September). *Neurogenetics of cell proliferation and migration in mutant mice.* Paper presented at the XVI International Rodin Remediation Scientific Conference, Boulder, CO.

Obrzut, J., & Hynd, G. (1986). Child neuropsychology: An introduction to theory and research. In J. Obrzut & G. Hynd (Eds.), *Child neuropsychology. Theory and research* (Vol. 1, pp. 1–12). New York: Academic Press.

Oden, G., & Spira, J. (1983). Influence of context on the activation and selection of ambiguous word senses. *Quarterly Journal of Experimental Psychology, 35,* 51–64.

Ojemann, G. (1988). Some brain mechanisms for reading. In C. Von Euler, I. Lundberg, & G. Lennerstrand (Eds.), *Brain and reading* (pp. 47–59). New York: Macmillan.

Ojemann, G. (1991). Cortical organization of language. *The Journal of Neuroscience, 11,* 2281–2287.

Ojemann, G., Creutzfeldt, O., Lettich, E., & Haglund, M. (1988). Neuronal activity in human lateral temporal cortex related to short-term verbal memory, naming, and reading. *Brain, 111,* 1383–1403.

Olson, R. (in press). Language deficits in "specific" reading disability. In M. Gernsbacher (Ed.), *Handbook of psycholinguistics.* New York: Academic Press.

Olson, R., Davidson, B., Kliegl, R., & Davies, S. (1984). Development of phonetic memory in disabled and normal readers. *Journal of Experimental Child Psychology, 37,* 187–206.

Olson, R., Wise, B., Conners, F., Rack, J., & Fulker, D. (1989). Specific deficits in component reading and language skills: Genetic and environmental influences. *Journal of Learning Disabilities, 22,* 339–348.

Overman, M. (1986, April). Student promotion and retention. *Phi Delta Kappan,* pp. 609–613.

Owen, F. (1978). Dyslexia—genetic aspects. In A. Benton & D. Pearl (Eds.), *Dyslexia: An appraisal of current knowledge* (pp. 267–284). New York: Oxford University Press.

Pearson, L., & Barron, R. (1989, March). *Orthography influences beginning readers' auditory rhyme judgments.* San Francisco: American Educational Research Association.

Pennington, B., Gilger, J., Pauls, D., Smith, S. A., Smith, S. D., & DeFries, J. (1991). Evidence for major gene transmission of developmental dyslexia. *Journal of the American Medical Association, 266,* 1527–1534.

Pennington, B., & Smith, S. (1988). Genetic influences on learning disabilities: An update. *Journal of Consulting and Clinical Psychology, 56,* 817–823.

Perfetti, C. (1985). *Reading ability* (pp. 207–232). New York: Oxford University Press.

Perfetti, C., & Hogaboam, T. (1975). The relationship between single word decoding and reading comprehension skill. *Journal of Educational Psychology, 67,* 461–469.

Perfetti, C., & McCutchen, D. (1987). Schooled language competence: Linguistic abilities in reading and writing. *Advances in applied psycholinguistics, 2,* 105–141.

Petersen, S., Fox, P., Posner, M., Mintun, M., & Raichle, M. (1989). Positron emission tomographic studies of the processing of single words. *Journal of Cognitive Neuroscience, 1,* 153–170.

Petersen, S., Fox, P., Snyder, A., & Raichle, M. (1990). Activation of extrastriate and frontal cortical areas by visual words and word-like stimuli. *Science, 249,* 1041–1044.

Piaget, J. (1952). *The origins of intelligence in children.* New York: International Universities Press.

Pick, A. (1978). Perception in the acquisition of reading. In F. Murray, H. Sharp, & J. Pikulski (Eds.), *The acquisition of reading: Cognitive, linguistic, and perceptual prerequisites* (pp. 99–122). Baltimore: University Park Press.

Pinnell, G. (1989). Reading recovery: Helping at-risk children learn to read. *The Elementary School Journal, 90,* 161–183.

Pinnell, G., Fried, M., & Estice, R. (1990, January). Reading recovery: Learning how to make a difference. *The Reading Teacher,* pp. 282–295.

Pinnell, G., Lyons, C., DeFord, D., Bryk, A., & Seltzer, M. (1991). Educational Report 16. *Studying the effectiveness of early intervention approaches for first grade children having difficulty in reading.*

Martha L. King Language and Literacy Center, The Ohio State University, Columbus, OH.

Polich, J., & Burns, T. (1987). P300 from identical twins. *Neuropsychologia, 25,* 299–304.

Posner, M. (1979). Applying theories and theorizing about applications. In L. Resnick & P. Weaver (Eds.), *Theory and practice of early reading* (Vol. 1, pp. 331–342). Hillsdale, NJ: Erlbaum.

Posner, M., Lewis, J., & Conrad, C. (1972). Component processes in reading: A performance analysis. In J. Kavanagh & I. Mattingly (Eds.), *Language by ear and by eye: The relation between speech and reading* (pp. 159–192). Cambridge, MA: MIT Press.

Posner, M., Petersen, S., Fox, P., & Raichle, M. (1988). Localization of cognitive operations in the human brain. *Science, 240,* 1627–1631.

Potter, M., Kroll, J., & Harris, C. (1980). Comprehension and memory in rapid sequential reading. In R. Nickerson (Ed.), *Attention and performance VIII* (pp. 395–418). Hillsdale, NJ: Erlbaum.

Rayner, K. (1984). Visual selection in reading, picture perception, and visual search: A tutorial review. In H. Bouma & D. G. Bouwhuis (Eds.), *Attention and performance X* (pp. 67–96). Hillsdale, NJ: Erlbaum.

Read, C. (1981). Writing is not the inverse of reading for young children. In C. H. Frederickson & J. Dominick (Eds.), *Writing: The nature, development, and teaching of written communication* (Vol. 2, pp. 105–117). Hillsdale, NJ: Erlbaum.

Robinson, W. (1950). Ecological correlations and the behavior of individuals. *American Sociological Review, 15,* 351–356.

Roeltgen, D., & Heilman, K. (1984). Lexical agraphia. Further support for the two-system hypothesis of linguistic agraphia. *Brain, 107,* 811–827.

Rotter, J. (1966). Generalized expectancies for internal versus external control of reinforcement. *Psychological Monographs, 80,* No. 1 (Whole No. 609).

Rueckl, J., & Oden, G. (1986). The integration of contextual and featural information during word identification. *Journal of Memory and Language, 25,* 445–460.

Sandler, A., Watson, T., Footo, M., Levine, M., Coleman, W., & Hooper, S. (1992). Neurodevelopmental study of writing disorders in middle childhood. *Journal of Developmental and Behavioral Pediatrics, 13,* 17–23.

Sanquist, T., Rohrbaugh, J., Syndulko, K., & Lindsley, D. (1980). Electrocortical signs of levels of processing: Perceptual analysis and recognition memory. *Psychophysiology, 17,* 568–576.

Sattler, J. (1988). *Assessment of children* (3rd ed.). San Diego: Sattler.

Satz, P., Taylor, H. G., Friel, J., & Fletcher, J. (1978). Some developmental and predictive precursors of reading disabilities: A six year follow-up. In A. Benton & D. Pearl (Eds.), *Dyslexia: An appraisal of current knowledge* (pp. 313–347). New York: Oxford University Press.

Scarborough, H. (1989). Prediction of reading disability from familial and individual differences. *Journal of Educational Psychology, 81,* 101–108.

Scarborough, H. (1990). Very early language deficits in dyslexic children. *Child Development, 61,* 1728–1743.

Scardamalia, M., & Bereiter, C. (1986). Research on written composition. In M. C. Wittrock (Ed.), *Handbook on research on teaching* (3rd ed., pp. 778–803). New York: Macmillan.

Scardamalia, M., Bereiter, C., & Goleman, H. (1982). The role of production factors in writing ability. In M. Nystrand (Ed.), *What writers know: The language, process, and structure of written discourse* (pp. 175–210). San Diego: Academic Press.

Schneider, W., & Graham, D. (in press). Introduction to connectionist modeling in education. *Educational Psychologist.*

Sebesta, S. (1981). Why Rudolph can't read. *Language Arts, 58,* 545–548.

Segalowitz, S. (1980). Piaget's Achilles' heel: A safe soft spot? *Human Development, 23,* 137–140.

Segalowitz, S. (1986). Validity and reliability of noninvasive lateralization measures. In J. Obrzut & G. Hynd (Eds.), *Child neuropsychology. Theory and research* (Vol. 1, pp. 191–208). New York: Academic Press.

Seidenberg, M., & McClelland, J. (1989). A distributed developmental model of word recognition and naming. *Psychological Review, 96,* 523–568.

Semrud-Clikeman, M., Hynd, G., Novey, E., & Eliopulos, D. (1991). Dyslexia and brain morphology: Relationships between neuroanatomical variation and neurolinguistic tasks. *Learning and Individual Differences, 3,* 225–242.

Shallice, T., & Warrington, E. (1980). Single and multiple component central dyslexic syndromes. In M. Coltheart, K. Patterson, & J. Marshall (Eds.), *Deep dyslexia,* pp. 119–145. London: Routledge & Kegan Paul.

Shallice, T., Warrington, E., & McCarthy, R. (1983). Reading without semantics. *Quarterly Journal of Experimental Psychology, 35A,* 111–138.

Shankweiler, D., & Crain, S. (1986). Language mechanisms and reading disorder: A modular approach. *Cognition, 24,* 139–168.

Shapiro, E. (1989). *Academic skills problems. Direct assessment and intervention.* New York: Guilford Press.

Shaywitz, B., Fletcher, J., Holahan, J., & Shaywitz, S. (1992). Discrepancy compared to low achievement definitions of reading disability: Results from the Connecticut Longitudinal Study. *Journal of Learning Disabilities, 25*(10), 639–648.

Shaywitz, S., Escobar, M., Shaywitz, B., Fletcher, J., & Makuch, R. (1992). Evidence that dyslexia may represent the lower tail of a normal distribution of reading ability. *New England Journal of Medicine, 326,* 145–150.

Shaywitz, S., Shaywitz, B., Fletcher, J., & Escobar, M. (1990). Prevalence of reading disability in boys and girls. Results of the Connecticut Longitudinal Study. *Journal of the American Medical Association, 264,* 998–1002.

Shurtleff, H., Abbott, R., Townes, B., & Berninger, V. (1993). Luria's neurodevelopmental stages in relation to intelligence and academic achievement in kindergarten and first grade. *Developmental Neuropsychology, 9,* 55–75.

Shurtleff, H., Fay, G., Abbott, R., & Berninger, V. (1988). Cognitive and neuropsychological correlates of academic achievement. A levels of analysis assessment model. *Journal of Psychoeducational Assessment, 6,* 298–308.

Siegel, L. (1984). A longitudinal study of a hyperlexic child: Hyperlexia as a language disorder. *Neuropsychologia, 22,* 577–585.

Siegel, L. (1989). IQ is irrelevant to the definition of learning disabilities. *Journal of Learning Disabilities, 22,* 469–486.

Siegel, L. (1992). An evaluation of the discrepancy definition of dyslexia. *Journal of Learning Disabilities, 25*(10), 618–629.

Siegler, R. (1981). Developmental sequences within and between concepts. *Monographs of the Society for Research in Child Development, 46.*

Skinner, K. (1991, October 7). The chemistry of learning and memory. *Chemical & Engineering News,* 24–41.

Slavin, R., Madden, N., Karweit, N., Dolan, L., Wasik, B., Shaw, A., Mainzer, K. L., & Haxby, B. (1991). Neverstreaming: Prevention and early intervention as an alternative to special education. *Journal of Learning Disabilities, 24,* 373–378.

Slavin, R., Madden, N., Karweit, N., Liverman, B., & Dolan, L. (1990). Success for All: First-year outcomes of a comprehensive plan for reforming urban education. *American Educational Research Journal, 27,* 255–278.

Smith, M., & Shepard, L. (1987, October). *Phi Delta Kappan,* pp. 129–134.

Smith, M., & Shepard, L. (1988, September). What doesn't work: The practice of retention in the elementary grades. *Communique,* pp. 6–8.

Smith, S., Kimberling, W., Pennington, B., & Lubs, H. (1983). Specific reading disability: Identification of an inherited form through linkage analysis. *Science, 219,* 1345–1347.

Smith, S., Pennington, B., Fain, P., Kimberling, W., & Lubs, H. (1986). Genetic heterogeneity of specific reading disability. *American Journal of Human Genetics, 39,* A169.

Snow, C., & Ferguson, C. (1977). *Talking to children: Language input and acquisition.* Cambridge, England: Cambridge University Press.

Springer, S., & Deutsch, G. (1985). *Left brain, Right brain. Revised Edition.* New York: W. H. Freeman.

Squire, L. (1986). Mechanisms of memory. *Science, 232,* 1612–1619.

Stahl, S. (1992). Saying the ''p'' word: Nine guidelines for exemplary phonics instruction. *The Reading Teacher, 45,* 618–625.

Stanovich, K. (1984). The interactive-compensatory model of reading: A confluence of developmental, experimental, and educational psychology. *Remedial and Special Education, 5,* 11–19.

Stanovich, K. (1986). Matthew effects in reading: Some consequences of individual differences in the acquisition of literacy. *Reading Research Quarterly, 21,* 360–407.

Stanovich, K. (1990). Concepts in developmental theories of reading skill: Cognitive resources, automaticity, and modularity. *Developmental Review, 10,* 72–100.

Stanovich, K., West, R., & Cunningham, A. (1991). Beyond phonological processes: Print exposure and orthographic processing. In S. Brady & D. Shankweiler (Eds.), *Phonological processes in literacy* (pp. 219–235). Hillsdale, NJ: Erlbaum.

Steiger, J. (1980). Tests for comparing elements of a correlation matrix. *Psychological Bulletin, 87,* 245–251.

Sternbach, R. (1966). *Principles of psychophysiology.* New York: Academic Press.

Stevens, J. (1986). *Applied multivariate statistics for the sciences.* Hillsdale, NJ: Erlbaum.

Stevenson, J., Graham, P., Fredman, G., & McLoughlin, V. (1987). A twin study of genetic influences on reading and spelling ability and disability. *Journal of Child Psychology and Psychiatry, 28,* 229–247.

Studdert-Kennedy, M. (1974). The perception of speech. In T. Sebeok (Ed.), *Current trends in linguistics* (Vol. 12, pp. 2349–2385). The Hague: Mouton.

Swanson, H. L. (1992). Mental Processing Potential Test (MPPT). Manual in preparation. Austin, TX: Pro-Ed.

Swanson, H. L. (in press). The generality and modifiability of working memory among skilled and less skilled readers. *Journal of Educational Psychology.*

Swanson, H. L., & Berninger, V. (in press). Working memory as a source of individual differences in children's writing. In E. Butterfield (Ed.), *Children's writing: Toward a process theory of development of skilled writing.* Greenwich, CT: JAI Press.

Swets, J. (1964). *Signal detection and recognition by human observers.* New York: Wiley.

Swinney, D. (1979). Lexical access during sentence comprehension: Reconsideration of context effects. *Journal of Verbal Learning and Verbal Behavior, 18,* 645–659.

Tallal, P. (1980). Auditory temporal perception phonics and reading disabilities in children. *Brain and Language, 9,* 182–198.

Tallal, P., Galaburda, A., Llinás, R., & von Euler, C. (1993). *Temporal information processing in the nervous system. Special reference to dyslexia and dysphasia.* New York: The New York Academy of Sciences.

Thomas, C. J. (1905). Congenital "word blindness" and its treatment. *Ophthalmoscope, 3,* 380–385.

Thompson, G. (1916). A hierarchy without a general factor. *British Journal of Psychology, 8,* 271–281.

Thompson, L., Detterman, D., & Plomin, R. (1991). Associations between cognitive abilities and scholastic achievement: Genetic overlap but environmental differences. *Psychological Science, 2,* 158–165.

Thurlow, M., Graden, J., Ysseldyke, J., & Algozzine, R. (1984). Student reading during reading class: The lost activity in reading instruction. *Journal of Educational Research, 77,* 267–272.

Torgesen, J., Bryant, B., Wagner, R., & Pearson, N. (in press). Toward development of a kindergarten group test for phonological awareness. *Journal of Research & Development in Education.*

Traweek, D., Cartwright, A., & Berninger, V. (1992, April). *Effects of integrated reading-writing instruction versus direct instruction in phonics on achievement outcome and orthographic-phonological processes.* San Francisco: American Educational Research Association.

Trieman, R. (1985). Onsets and rimes as units of spoken syllables: Evidence from children. *Journal of Experimental Child Psychology, 39,* 161–181.

Ungerleider, L., & Mishkin, M. (1982). Two cortical visual systems. In D. Ingle, M. Goodale, & R. Mansfield (Ed.), *Analysis of visual behavior* (pp. 549–586). Cambridge, MA: MIT Press.

Van Orden, G. (1987). A ROWS is a ROSE: Spelling, sound, and reading. *Memory & Cognition, 15,* 181–198.

Van Orden, G., Pennington, B., & Stone, G. (1990). Word identification in reading and the promise of subsymbolic psycholinguistics. *Psychological Review, 97,* 1–35.

Vaughan, S., Haager, D., Hogan, A., & Kouzekanani, K. (1992). Self-concept and peer acceptance in students with learning disabilities: A four- to five-year prospective study. *Journal of Educational Psychology, 84,* 43–50.

Vellutino, F. (1979a). *Dyslexia, theory, and research.* Cambridge, MA: MIT Press.

Vellutino, F. (1979b). The validity of the perceptual deficit explanations of reading disability. A reply to Fletcher and Saby. *Journal of Learning Disabilities, 12,* 27–34.

Vellutino, F., & Scanlon, D. (1987). Phonological coding, phonological awareness, and reading ability: Evidence from a longitudinal and experimental study. *Merrill Palmer Quarterly, 33,* 321–363.

Vellutino, F., Scanlon, D., Clark, R., Small, S., Fanuele, D., & Pratt, A. (1992, April). *Gender differences in early reading, language, and arithmetic abilities in kindergarten children.* San Francisco: American Educational Research Association.

Vellutino, F., Scanlon, D., Small, S., & Tanzman, M. (1991). The linguistic basis of reading ability: Converting written to oral language. *Text, 11,* 99–133.

Vellutino, F., Scanlon, D., & Tanzman, M. (1991). Bridging the gap between cognitive and neuropsychological conceptualizations of reading disability. *Learning and Individual Differences, 3,* 181–203.

Venezky, R. (1970). *The structure of English orthography.* The Hague: Mouton.

Venezky, R. (1979). Orthographic regularities in English words. In P. Kolers, M. Wrolstad, & H. Bouma (Eds.), *Processing of visible language* (pp. 283–293). New York: Plenum Press.

Venezky, R., & Massaro, D. (1979). The role of orthographic regularity in word recognition. In L. Resnick & P. Weaver (Eds.), *Theory and practice of early reading* (Vol. 1, pp. 85–108). Hillsdale, NJ: Erlbaum.

Vogel, J. (1989, April). *Straightening out the role of reversal errors in reading disability: An historical analysis and reevaluation of the views of Samuel T. Orton.* Kansas City, MO: Society for Research on Child Development.

Wagner, R., & Torgesen, J. (1987). The nature of phonological processing and its causal role in the acquisition of reading skills. *Psychological Bulletin, 101,* 192–212.

Walberg, H., & Tsai, S. (1983). Matthew effects in education. *American Educational Research Journal, 20,* 359–373.

Wechsler, D. (1974). *Manual for the Wechsler intelligence scale for children-revised.* San Antonio: Psychological Corporation.

Weinstein, C., & Mayer, R. (1986). The teaching of learning strategies. In M. C. Wittrock (Ed.), *Handbook of research on teaching* (3rd ed., pp. 315–327). New York: Macmillan.

Whitaker, D., Berninger, V., Johnston, J., & Swanson, H. L. (in press). Intraindividual differences in levels of written language in intermediate grade writers: Implications for the translation process. *Learning and Individual Differences.*

Willet, J. (1988). Questions and answers in the measurement of change. In E. Rothkopf (Ed.), *Review of research in education* (pp. 345–422). Washington, DC: AERA.

Williams, J. (1980). Teaching decoding with an emphasis on phoneme analysis and phoneme blending. *Journal of Educational Psychology, 72,* 1–15.

Wilson, B. (1986, June). *Developmental neuropsychology.* Paper presented at the Cape Cod Institute, Wellfleet, MA.

Wise, B. (1987). Word segmentation in computerized reading instruction. *Dissertation Abstracts,* University of Colorado, Boulder.

Wise, B. (1991). Whole words and decoding for short-term learning: Comparisons on a "Talking-Computer" system. *Journal of Experimental Child Psychology, 54,* 147–167.

Wise, B., Olson, R., Anstatt, M., Andrews, L., Terjak, M., Schneider, V., Kostuch, J., & Kriho, L. (1989). Implementing a long-term computerized remedial reading program with synthetic speech feedback: Hardware, software, and real-world issues. *Behavior Research Methods, Instruments, and Computers, 21,* 173–180.

Wise, B., Olson, R., & Trieman, R. (1990). Subsyllabic units in computerized reading instruction: Onset-rime versus post-vowel segmentation. *Journal of Experimental Child Psychology, 49,* 1–19.

Wise, R., Chollet, F., Hadar, U., Friston, K., Hoffner, E., & Frackowiak, R. (1991). Distribution of cortical neural networks involved in word comprehension and word retrieval. *Brain, 114,* 1803–1817.

Witelson, S. (1982). Bumps on the brain: Right-left anatomic asymmetry as a key to functional lateralization. In S. Segalowitz (Ed.), *Language functions and brain organization* (pp. 117–144). New York: Academic Press.

Wittrock, M. (1974). Learning as a generative process. *Educational Psychologist, 11,* 87–95.

Wittrock, M. (1986). Students' thought processes. In M. C. Wittrock (Ed.), *Handbook of research on teaching* (3rd ed., pp. 297–314). New York: Macmillan.

Wittrock, M. (1990). Generative processes in comprehension. *Educational Psychologist, 24,* 345–376.

Wittrock, M. (1991). Relations among educational research and neural and cognitive sciences. *Learning and Individual Differences, 3,* 257–263.

Wittrock, M. (in press). Generative learning processes of the brain. *Educational Psychologist.*

Wolf, M., Bally, H., & Morris, R. (1986). Automaticity, retrieval processes, and reading: A longitudinal study in average and impaired reading. *Child Development, 57,* 988–1000.

Wolf, M., & Goodglass, H. (1986). Dyslexia, dysnomia, and lexical retrieval: A longitudinal investigation. *Brain and Language, 28,* 154–168.

Wolff, P. H. (1981). Normal variation in human maturation. In K. Connolly & H. Prechtl (Eds.), *Maturation and development: Biological and psychological properties* (pp. 1–18). London: Heinemann.

Wolff, P. H., Cohen, C., & Drake, C. (1984). Impaired motor timing control in specific reading retardation. *Neuropsychologia, 22,* 587–600.

Wolpaw, J., Schmidt, J., & Vaughan, T. (Eds.). (1991). *Activity-driven CNS changes in learning and development. Annals of the New York Academy of Sciences* (Vol. 627). New York: The New York Academy of Sciences.

Wood, F. (1990). Functional neuroimaging in neurobehavioral research. In A. Boulton, G. Baker, & M. Hiscock (Eds.), *Neuromethods* (Vol. 17: *Neuropsychology,* pp. 107–125). Clifton, NJ: Humana Press.

Wood, F., Felton, R., Flowers, L., & Naylor, C. (1991). Neurobehavioral definition of dyslexia. In D. Duane & D. Gray (Eds.), *The reading brain. The biological basis of dyslexia* (pp. 1–25). Parkton, MD: York Press.

Wood, F., Flowers, L., Buchsbaum, M., & Tallal, P. (1991). Investigation of abnormal left temporal functioning in dyslexia through rCBF, auditory evoked potentials, and positron emission tomography. *Reading and Writing: An Interdisciplinary Journal, 3,* 379–393.

Woodcock, R. (1987). *Woodcock Reading Mastery Test-Revised.* Circle Pines, MN: American Guidance Service.

INDEX